MY FIRST GUITAR

TALES OF TRUE LOVE
AND LOST CHORDS

JULIA CROWE

FOREWORD BY
ANDY SUMMERS

ECW PRESS

Published by ECW Press
2120 Queen Street East, Suite 200, Toronto, Ontario, Canada M4E 1E2
416-694-3348 / info@ecwpress.com

LIBRARY AND ARCHIVES CANADA CATALOGUING IN PUBLICATION

Crowe, Julia
My first guitar : tales of true love and lost chords from 70
legendary musicians / Julia Crowe.

ISBN 978-1-77041-055-8
ALSO ISSUED AS: 978-1-77090-274-9 (PDF); 978-1-77090-275-6 (EPUB)

1. Guitarists—Biography. 2. Musicians—Anecdotes.
I. Title.

ML399.C953 2012   787.87092'2   C2012-902723-5

Editor for the press: Jennifer Hale
Cover and text design: David Gee
Cover images: © Julie Marshall / iStockPhoto
Author photo: Lisa-Marie Mazzucco
Typesetting: Troy Cunningham
Printing: Thomson-Shore   5   4   3   2

PRINTED AND BOUND IN THE UNITED STATES

To Terrence & Taidgh

with all my love.

Table of Contents

Foreword

In the pages of this book you will read the stories of many guitarists who have reached the world with their guitars — those who have affected us, changed us and stirred our emotions with their passion for this most wonderful of instruments.

The character of the guitar is such that it tends to bring about a relationship that is obsessive, engaging, unrelenting in its pull back toward that magic matrix of frets and strings. Probably, for most of the players in this book, this is a fact of life. The first guitar is then, by definition, the beginning of a musical life. It is the primary instrument that ignites the germinal instinct to make music, to pluck a string. And after all the other guitars that are sought, collected, lusted after, specially built, exchanged, bought back and cried over, it is the first guitar that has a special place, no matter how cheap, battered or unplayable it might have been. This first guitar is the herald, the awakener of the impulse to play and the impulse that will become a life-long rapport.

Just after my thirteenth birthday I was handed a battered old Spanish guitar by an uncle who had no use for it anymore. When he placed it in my hands I suppose I received the call, because it felt as if my heart had stopped beating, as if I had pulled Excalibur from the stone. I could not play a note but it didn't matter because I was so thrilled to have this object in my life. Aged and beaten as it was, I absolutely loved it, like a child with a tattered rag doll that is preferred to all the shiny new toys. With this first guitar my life changed as if, in an instant, an alchemy had taken place. I transformed from a typical rowdy English schoolboy who couldn't be bothered with homework, who was late for school, who made trouble with a pack of other boys, who sneaked into the pictures without paying — into a hardcore guitar aficionado.

From here on I became a loner. Just me and the guitar, unless I was sitting and swapping chords with another aspiring guitarist. And it was on this first guitar, after I had finally got a sixth string for it, that I learned the rudimentary chords, ran my fingers up to the twelfth fret, twanged the low E string and finally learned how to tune it to the piano. This was the adventure, this was the thrill and the knowledge that had to be constantly sought after no matter how hard the battle. Later I moved to other guitars that were sleeker, faster, smoother in their response. But my first guitar, with its already lived life of a thousand songs, changes of strings and strummed chords, will always remain in my memory as the signifier, the flame that began the rest of my life.

— Andy Summers,
solo artist and guitarist for The Police,
author of *One Train Later*

Prologue

My idea for writing this book came about in late autumn 2003, when the classical guitar duo Michael Newman and Laura Oltman had invited me to attend a house concert CD release party for a save-music-in-schools compilation of guitarists. The party was hosted in a Central Park West apartment with sky-high panoramic views overlooking the park. The place conveyed the fabulous kind of ease and generous space that one only sees in movies or else real estate ads printed in the back of the *New York Times* magazine.

The head of Tower Records' classical music department muttered that the bathroom alone was bigger than his entire apartment. I darted between white-jacketed waiters bearing silver platters of hors d'oeuvres to search for Michael and Laura, and burst into a little girl's frilly fantasy of a bedroom. There sat Gary Lucas of Captain Beefheart — and songwriting collaborator of Jeff Buckley — perched on the edge of a floral-patterned bed, dressed head-to-toe in badass black as he tuned his 1930s vintage nickel steel Dobro.

He peered at me from beneath the brim of his hat and grimaced. Then he decided to get up off this bed, with its heap of ruffle-edged pillows, and extended his hand for a proper introduction. I noticed that he left behind a staggering menagerie of mashed and flattened soft animals. A small pink giraffe teetered and tumbled over the edge of the bed and bounced against the floor.

This is the image that conceived this book. I knew that, in a few years, the toys would more than likely lose favor to newer infatuations, stuffed animals exchanged for musical heroes peering down from an array of posters taped up on the walls. Odds were, in a few years, a guitar would sit tucked in the corner.

Just how does anyone become so passionate about the guitar that they cannot imagine a life without it? Where does it all begin? I wanted to know how guitarists came into owning their first guitar and what made them realize they had found their life's work.

I started aggressively pursuing whatever interviews I could with anyone who was willing. I chased down the not willing. I used my best facsimile of charm and wit. I stuck my foot into countless doors. I attended guitar festivals and, if no one assisted, I found my way through backstage labyrinths to corner rock legends, backing them up against the wall and cajoling them into telling me their stories. Sometimes, the story was tough to tell — I could personally identify with the emotional catch in Joey Santiago's voice when he recalled what his father did to his guitar out of misguided parental concern. There had been entirely unexpected connections between some of the guitarists, such as Daron Malakian's account of purchasing a guitar from his idol Tracii Guns when he was 17, long before Malakian became a rock star himself. Collecting these tales has been admittedly addictive because each story is as unique, compelling and illuminating as the performer.

The tales that emerged surprised even those in the guitarists' inner circles, who had never heard some of these details before. Artists, especially rock stars, tend to be an over-interviewed lot. In fact, a few of my guitar-obsessed friends doubted some of my unearthed details simply because they had not read them before elsewhere.

My intent was simple — to ask the artists to speak for themselves. There is beauty and music in one's own way of telling a story that is just as distinctive and unique as the tonal quality and instantly recognizable sound these artists are renowned for coaxing from the guitar.

It has been a privilege, a joy and an unforgettable experience for me to participate in such personal conversations with music legends. It is my hope that readers can see themselves within these stories and come to discover, or even rediscover, their own love for the guitar. And it is also my fervent hope that the passion in these fascinating stories encourages readers to expand their musical interests to genres that they might have not yet explored or considered.

Traveling Seven Hours for a Cup of Coffee

Many years ago, during a hiatus from college, I arrived at London's Heathrow Airport wearing my sincerity and best dress with the misguided notion that I would be taken seriously for at least not looking like a grungy backpacker. I approached the stone-faced customs officer to explain the reason for my visit: I was a writer working on my first book. I planned to visit London for three days and spend the rest of my time hanging out with sheep in Ireland. The officer scrutinized the glaringly empty contents of my brand new passport, as blank as my unwritten book. She then sized up my youth and asked the fatal question: "What's the book about?" Jet lag is its own truth serum. I told her I had no idea because I had only started writing it. Anything could happen, just like life itself. How can you accurately plot what may happen before you arrive?

I was having a brand new panic attack now, reliving this episode now that I was going to be traveling again to London. Jimmy Page had invited me to meet him for coffee. This time, I told the customs officer that I was on holiday. It wasn't a complete lie. According to my friends, I was on holiday from all common sense to be traveling eight-plus hours from New York via Charlotte, North Carolina, to London to meet a rock star with a lurid reputation, who may or may not show, all for a dubious cup of coffee.

Two months earlier, I'd received an email from a lady, stating that Mr. Page would like to meet me over said cup of coffee to discuss a new book I was writing. He was keenly interested in being part of it. I had assumed this was a prank because a few friends knew I was compiling interviews with famous guitarists for a book proposal. I refused to bite. I mean, what self-respecting Englishman drinks coffee? Weeks later, a second email arrived from the same address. It was not a joke.

When the postal clerk at Church Street Station asked my reason for a passport renewal, I hesitated then told her the truth, thinking this might possibly seem a little more real if I confessed it to a complete stranger. I was excited but uncertain about what I was getting into with all this.

"No shit! Jimmy Page" was the clerk's response. "My brother made me listen to all those Led Zeppelin albums when they first came out. Drove me crazy, always saying, 'You've got to hear this.'" She waved my passport form up into the air, turned her head and bellowed to the rest of her coworkers, "Yo! We gotta process this on the double because this lady here is gonna be meeting Mistah Jimmy Page in London, ENGLAND!" I slinked away, aware of heads straining curiously from postal booths. I could hear some joker from the back singing the guitar lick from "Kashmir" so loudly it echoed off the stately marble walls: "DUN-na-nunt. NUNNA-nunt. DUH-na-nunt Nunna-nunt. NUNNA-nunt!"

Next, I visited the local bookstore to buy Led Zeppelin CDs. Sure I'd heard their music before but, as a classical musician, I knew it best in an indirect sense. For example, I knew that Matt Haimovitz plays his own cool rendition of "Kashmir" on cello. I wanted to absorb the original albums in their proper sequential order. I listened to them on a portable CD player stuffed into my coat pocket because I could not afford an iPod. In fact, I did not even know how I was going to pay for this trip.

Besides writing for peanuts for guitar magazines, I teach guitar and spend my days criss-crossing Manhattan on foot like a doctor making musical house calls to guitar students, realigning their hand positions upon the fretboard and curing phobias about playing barre chords. I was loping up to Union Square to one of these lessons when I realized just how good a guitarist Page truly is. Most guitar magazines will insist that I spell out the exact diatonic scale, mode and key signature in both notation and tab with a comprehensive sidebar on gear, but let's just set all the piranha-jock posturing on the anatomical and technical details of the music aside for a moment and say my realization had been simply like that scene from the film *Easter Parade*, when Fred Astaire suggests to Judy Garland that she walk ahead of him and prove she has the magical ability to turn men's heads. Garland pulls this off by making a cross-eyed, blowfish face. I swung along at a good clip, thoroughly spaced out in my own mental zone, until it dawned on me that strangers were rubbernecking at me on the sidewalk. I had not been making any face but I *was* plugged into the 12-bar blues song "Rock 'n' Roll," from *Led Zeppelin IV*. Let's just say that listening to classical guitar by headphones rarely alters one's gait. Nor does it cause strangers' heads to turn when one is walking innocently down the street. After this musical epiphany, I knew I had to go to London.

Lisa Hoffman, the mother of my guitar student Alex, generously advanced me a couple months' worth of lesson fees to cover my airfare to London. On her living room wall, Lisa has a gigantic autographed "Born to Run" poster alongside a framed, coffee table photograph of her younger self gleefully embracing The Boss himself.

I informed my U.K. magazine publisher, Maurice Summerfield, that I was coming to London and asked if there might be any concert for me to review while I was there to help defray expenses. "Have you heard of the expression 'Carrying coals to Newcastle'?" he asked me. "I have twenty editors in London, which is why you're in New York. And Jimmy Page?" A hint of disdain inflected his voice. "Why not Brian May? Brian May performed for the Queen's Fiftieth Jubilee, you know."

I discovered that when it comes to Jimmy Page everyone has an opinion. Or a request.

"Didn't Page chew the head off a bat?" someone asked. "Or was that Ozzie? He did something, though. Occult stuff. I think the whole band worshipped the Devil."

"I hear Page likes young girls. And he's old now. Real old guy with real young girls. God, I wonder how old he has to be by now. I wish I was him."

"Shame on you. You call yourself a Chicagoan but then you go off to meet with the man who ripped off Willie Dixon! Shame!"

"He's the greatest. Can you have him autograph this CD for me?"

"He's overrated. Can you give him my CD?"

I had all this swirling through my jet-lagged brain as I lay exhausted upon the tiny bed inside my Bayswater hotel room, with its seasick floor and a staff left over from lost episodes of *Fawlty Towers*. I forced myself to sit upright and dial Jimmy's office. The lady who had emailed me, Sue Frankland-Haile, was very kind, asking me how I had fared on my trip.

"I'm afraid I have some rather disappointing news," she said.

Something had come up in Mr. Page's schedule and we could not be certain this meeting would happen after all. "Was it your main reason for coming out?" she asked. Lacking a swift response, I'd confessed that it was. She said she would check back with me later. I hung up and flopped over the concave mattress.

I was alone in London far away from home, with possibly nothing to show for the effort. I decided to make the best of it by visiting every possible guitar shop in London, starting with Hank's, where a line of guitars stood on floor stands like sentries guarding the tombs of more expensive guitars locked inside glass cases. I played Pujol's "El Abejorro" for an appreciative sales clerk who wore his hair like Steve McQueen and kept his tinted aviator glasses on inside the darkened shop. The kid behind the counter at Macari's had been a bit reluctant about showing me capos. A young schoolboy, still wearing his dark blue uniform jacket, played the beautiful acoustic instrumental intro to "Babe I'm Gonna Leave You" on a cedar-top classical guitar in the basement of Ivor Mairants. At the Spanish Guitar Centre on Cranbourn Street in Soho, the sales clerk, who assumed I did not know any better, commanded me to remove my coat so that the buttons would not scratch the back of the fine spruce concert guitar I had picked up. He then returned to impressing a real customer with his tale of a recent visit by Sting, who had dropped a small fortune on one of their guitars. Once the customer departed, he looked back toward me and said curiously, "We do not see many American girls here."

When I returned to my hotel room, I found the red message light blinking on the phone. It was Sue Frankland-Haile from Page's office. I called back immediately. "Where have you been?" she asked. I told her that I had scoured every guitar shop I could find in Soho. She expressed shock that I had walked all the way from Bayswater to Soho but I assured her that perambulating halfway across town was a New York thing to do.

"There is a chance we might be able to make this work," she told me. "You must appear at this coffee shop. If Jimmy cannot make it, there will be a phone message waiting for you at the counter inside." Then she added, "Now you happen to know what he looks like but he does not know at all what you look like. Please tell me something identifying about yourself so I can let him know."

I told her that I have long auburn hair and would be wearing a brown silk scarf printed with red poppies.

Unable to sleep, I woke early the next morning and stepped out for a walk, passing by schoolchildren who were neatly lined up on Moscow Street in uniforms, bright red scarves tied at the necks of very long brown tweed coats clearly purchased oversized so they'd fit the following year. In Notting Hill, I overheard a mother sound like any mother the world over as she pushed her child along with an air of resigned exasperation, "If only we'd left a few minutes earlier, we wouldn't have to rush so!"

It was the last day of November. At that time of year, the light fades quickly in London, just past mid-afternoon. I'd scouted out the neighborhood near the designated coffee shop and noted a bus stop where I could loiter with seeming purpose and not look like a complete idiot. The refuge also allowed me to sort out how I was going to approach the counterperson inside the coffee shop. I knew that if you dared to walk into a coffee shop in New York City and ask if there was a phone message waiting for you at the counter, you'd be tossed promptly to the curb with a sneer and a resounding "Geddouddaheeyah."

When I'd scraped up sufficient courage, I pushed my way through the front door and told the girl at the counter that I was about to ask her an odd question. Was there a phone message waiting for me at all? Me, Julia? She smiled, squinted strangely at me and assured me there was no such message.

I stepped outside, feeling joyously elated yet ill. I had been sick with anticipation along with the weight of knowing that at least half of the world — the half composed of diehard, lighter-waving Led Zeppelin fans — would probably tear me into bitty pieces if it meant they could trade places at this very moment. Here I was, an unworthy, uncool rock 'n' roll ignoramus of a classical guitar journalist about to meet the Wizard of All Rock Guitar. I decided in that very moment that I would shut out the swirl of preconceptions, hearsay and idle crap foisted upon me by well-meaning friends and stick to my interview questions.

Les Paul

Les Paul is legendary for creating an amplified solid-body electric guitar that could play without distortion — the renowned Gibson Les Paul guitar. He realized that if the body of the guitar was solid and did not vibrate, it meant that the sound of the plucked strings would sustain longer. Les Paul also engineered the first 8-track recorder, marketed by Ampex. He won a Grammy for a 1976 album of instrumental duets with Chet Atkins, called *Chester and Lester*, and also for an album released in 2005, *American Made, World Played*, featuring guest spots with various Gibson-playing rock stars.

My first guitar came from a Sears-Roebuck catalog. I was seven years old when I sent away for it and it had cost $3.95. At first, I was interested in playing the piano but my mother criticized it. "With a piano, you've got your back turned to the audience," she told me. "How are you going to play a piano at the beach or in the back seat of a car? It's not convenient." So I switched to playing drums and she immediately ordered that out of the house. I got an accordion and that — I agree with everybody — is one instrument that should be in the city dump. I finally whittled it down: the best thing for me to do was play the guitar, my harmonica and sing.

I still have that Sears-Roebuck guitar. Mother was in the kitchen when it arrived and she told me, "Well, you can undo the box in the dining room." I was very anxious to tear this carton open, see the guitar and play it. As I took it out of the cardboard wrapping, one of the strings got caught in that cardboard and went *ping*! My mother came rushing through that swinging door of the kitchen and said, "Lester, you sound great on that thing already!"

In 1942, I was asked who my ten favorite guitar players were. My first was Andrés Segovia, the second was Django Reinhardt, the third one was Eddie Mack and my list went on to the top ten guitar players at that time. It was hard to find more than seven guitar players that you could rave about, who were popular and well known — ones who inspired you to learn how to play. That's how rare the guitar was in those days.

I only took one music lesson, from a lady named Miss Wilson. It was a piano lesson and she pinned a note on my lapel telling my mother to save her money and not have me come back. The reason for this was whenever she sat down and played something for me, I played it right after her. She said, "Oh, you're my number one pupil! This is terrific." She couldn't believe how fast I learned. But she did not realize that by listening and watching what she was doing, I could memorize and play it instantly. Of course, she found this out when she selected a piece of strange music for me to sight-read. Because she did not play it, I did not play it. That's when she realized I was a person who played by ear, not by reading music. So I was out.

My brother thought my studying music was a boring waste of time. He didn't like music and he didn't particularly understand it. My mother *loved* music. She was very much an important part of my life for how she encouraged me. My brother would say, "He's at it again, Ma," as if to say, "Get rid of him!" Radio broadcasts always sounded like they were from a tight-sounding room. Back in those days, they used to broadcast from a hotel room. I began to practice in the bathroom, where there was tile, because it had a great echo. I figured out how to place my guitar halfway between the bedroom and the bathroom for the best sound. My brother was ready to place me in the outhouse.

From the very beginning, I was always interested in sound and music and finding out how things worked. Back then I couldn't go to Home Depot so I had to figure things out by myself. Mother wanted a piano, a Victrola, a telephone and a radio in the house and I was tempted to find out how these things worked. I'd performed a hysterectomy on the piano. Then I took the phone apart. I managed to rig the mouthpiece of Mom's phone and hook it up to the radio and heard myself talk and play the harmonica on it.

I had a lot of first gigs. The very first gig, we were on a truck — The Optimist Club, we were called. I wore a wig, blacked-out a tooth and I had my bass player — we called him Susie — dressed up like a girl. He also played the banjo. We had this truck all loaded up with all these people as Red Hot Red and the Optimists. I was about thirteen years old. This was in Springfield, Missouri, and these Chicago guys heard us. It was during the Depression era. Al Capone was at his peak of fame. We played at the WLS Barn Dance. I had my dreams and set a goal, making sure it was not so difficult I'd give up. I was reasonably certain that I could succeed if I had courage and the willingness to practice.

During the night, I was Rhubarb Red, playing hillbilly songs, and from noon on I was Les Paul. Performing allowed me to be two people, and it was the best of all worlds. For my first job, I rigged the PA system with Mom's radio. I was playing at a BBQ stand in Waukesha, Wisconsin, when a music critic pulled up to order a hamburger. He wrote me a note from his rumble seat while ordering food, "Hey, Red, I can hear your jokes and singing but I can't hear the guitar." You see, the guitar was not loud enough.

My first idea to solve this was to take Dad's radio and use that, too, but then I'd thought to use the magnetic pickups made by Bell Labs inside the telephone. I took the phonograph needle and cartridge and jammed it into my guitar. It howled with feedback. I stuffed towels and shirts and socks inside that guitar. I even filled that Sears guitar with plaster of paris. This seemed to help a little with taming the feedback.

I made another guitar from a two-by-four piece of railroad track and stretched a string across it. This was my precursor to the "log." I ran to my mother and yelled, "I've got it!" She just looked at that string stretched across a railroad track and said, "That'll be the day, when you see Gene Autry riding upon a horse holding a piece of railroad track." She shot me down so I went back to using wood. I made the same guitar but it looked like a log. When I played it at a club, people were not too impressed. I came home wondering what had gone wrong. That's when I realized people sometimes hear with their eyes instead of their ears. So I remade the log into the shape of a guitar, went back into that club and brought the house down.

When I showed this guitar to executives at Gibson, they later told me they'd laughed at me, calling my guitar a "broomstick with a pickup." This was about in 1947 or 1948. They made only four of these guitars and were hesitant to make more. The first ones looked like an ironing board with a pickup, so they had me come in and look at Stradivarius violins for their lovely shape. I wanted something nice so you could love it and hug it, so we chose to make the guitar with similar curves. When they asked me what color I wanted it to be, my answer was "gold." Why? My first car had a gold-colored finish.

It was a big leap for Gibson to go from making just hollow-body guitars to solid. Hollow bodies tend to vary in sound from instrument to instrument and we wanted to be able to repeat construction and have the same response. To this day, Gibson still makes guitars with the pickups exactly where I placed them. If the pickups are moved, they will pick up something and lose something. I picked a point of placement where the sound is most pleasing.

What I love about the guitar is everything that has happened throughout my career and all the people I have met along the way. When I play onstage, there will be a musician who comes and sits in and I'll say, "I wonder why he does what he does," or "That's strange, I've never seen that done before." At eighty-nine, I am still learning. And today, with the guitar, nobody plays alike. Everyone plays different styles, different tunes. Everybody's up for grabs and that's what makes it so wonderful. It's full of surprises. If you play the piano and hit a key right there, that note is fixed on the keyboard and never moves. But on the guitar, that note is everywhere, absolutely everywhere on that guitar. So it's quite a challenge because of the difference in the instrument that you're playing. The guitar has so much more flexibility.

I have had moments where I've thought to myself that I'll never conquer the instrument. Sometimes the other side of the fence looks better as I will admire what another person is doing. One time, Pat Martino, George Benson, Wes Montgomery and myself were standing out on the corner at eight o'clock in the morning, talking after work, and the four of us were complimenting each other on what we knew. One guitarist said, "If only I could do what you do." And another guitarist said, "Well, if only I could do what *you* do." That's when I said, "Do you realize how much talent is standing on this corner? And how different they are? One doesn't need to use a pick, the other one does. And we all admire what the other guy does — in most cases." There are a few dogs out there that we won't talk about.

The one thing I can say about a guitar is that as soon as you hit a note, it sounds sweet and nice. You can't say that about a clarinet player. If you give a kid a clarinet, you'll want to kill him for about the first five years. And a violin, without a doubt, is the worst. You hear that guy pick up a violin and go through all that — and a drummer is bad, too. But the guitar is very sweet, very apologetic, a very nice instrument.

Howard Hite on Elvis' First Guitar

Tupelo Hardware has been a family business for over eighty-five years, owned and managed by three generations of the Booth family. It is well known that ten-year-old Elvis Presley purchased his first guitar here. Current owner, manager and Elvis historian Howard Hite welcomes visitors to the shop at 114 W. Main Street in Tupelo, Mississippi. Store hours are Monday through Friday, at seven thirty a.m. to five thirty p.m. and Saturdays, seven thirty a.m. to twelve thirty p.m.

People often make their visit first to Elvis' birthplace before they come here to the Tupelo Hardware store, where Gladys bought her son his first guitar. My wife Julia's grandfather is George Booth, the original owner of Tupelo Hardware, which opened in 1926.

Today Tupelo Hardware has anywhere in the neighborhood of 12,000 to 15,000 visitors annually who come from all around the world. Our busiest season is around the time of Elvis' birthday, January 9th, which turns into something more like Elvis' month-long birthday — and then during the week of Elvis' death, in August. At any of these given times, it is not unusual for us to see two to three busloads of tourists parked outside the store.

We have an unusual mix of products here. Surrounding the original music counter is cast iron and aluminum cookware, spray paint, Briggs-Stratton engines, precision machinist tools, cabinet pulls, plumbing supplies and masonry tools. The company's present mainstay is their contractor, wholesale and industrial business, but the staff gladly serves anyone in town, including Elvis fans.

As the story is recorded in a letter dated October 2, 1979, written by Forrest Bobo, a Tupelo Hardware store employee, a young Elvis and his mother, Gladys, visited the store in January 1945 to buy him a birthday gift. According to Bobo, Elvis wanted a rifle but his mother prevailed with the guitar, which he strummed before his mother purchased it for the sum of $7.75 plus two percent sales tax.

Today we carry a small line of inexpensive imported acoustic guitars in the $79–$100 range that come in different finishes, like black, natural, starburst, red and a blue one, which I call the "Blue Suede Shoes" model. This year, Joe Perry from Aerosmith dropped by to purchase a sunburst acoustic guitar because he said he had to have a guitar from the place where Elvis first got his. Country singer Mel Tillis' daughter, Pam Tillis, also bought a guitar here recently.

Unfortunately, I don't play guitar myself but I have seen Elvis play, first in Hawaii in 1957 and then at the University of Alabama in Tuscaloosa in 1971 and later in Memphis, at the Coliseum. I love his gospel singing because he sings with a whole lot of soul.

Many people who stop by here become very emotional. Of course, Elvis' playing had that effect on people, too. When he opened a concert with something like "2001: A Space Odyssey," [Richard Strauss' *Also Sprach Zarathustra*], you're just *in* — the hair just stands up on your arms. He had this effect on nearly everybody.

In the experience I've had in working here, I have seen groups as large as fifty-five to sixty people. One group of tourists from Japan had me tell the story of Elvis' first guitar through an interpreter. A man in the group asked through the interpreter if he could play one of the guitars and I said yes. He proceeded to sing four Elvis songs that he had memorized, in perfect English.

One man from New Jersey visited with his wife and their son, who was about six or seven years old. As I was telling him the story, his son walked toward the front door and his father called out to him, "Elvis, get back over here."

I also remember a mother and her two daughters visiting from Louisville, Kentucky. They were dressed very fine, as anything I've ever seen. When I tell my story, I am often standing behind the original store counter upon the same flooring where Elvis first stood when his mother bought him the guitar. This mother and her daughters were looking around in awe. Before they left, each one of them took their shoes off and stood at the counter barefoot to be able to say they felt right where Elvis had once stood.

A man and his wife who had dropped by from Brazil — they were both courtroom judges. After I told the story, I saw tears come into this man's eyes and he asked, "You don't mind if I give you a hug?" That took me by surprise.

Scotty Moore

Scotty Moore is considered the pioneer of rock lead guitar, serving as inspiration for generations to come for his guitar work with Elvis Presley. Moore not only auditioned Elvis for Sun Studios but served as his first guitarist and manager. During this phone interview, to set the scene, Scotty's hound dog was barking vociferously in the background at a grey squirrel in the backyard of his home in Tennessee. "You've spoken to Jimmy Page?" he asked. "I'll tell you something. He and Jeff Beck — those two boys have more talent in their pinky fingers than anyone else I know."

My first guitar was a small Kalamazoo brand acoustic guitar. This was before Gibson bought out the Kalamazoo company. I was about eight years old at the time and one of my brothers, who was fourteen years older, called me up at home in Humbolt, Tennessee, to see if I'd be willing to swap my guitar for his beautiful red Gene Autry archtop. He was already married and living in Memphis. I didn't know anything about guitars. He'd said to me, "I'm fixing to go into the service. How about trading guitars?" Of course now, all these years later, I realize I got the raw end of the deal because his guitar came from a catalog. Then again, my Kalamazoo guitar had seen some rough treatment.

All three of my older brothers played music when they were home. Dad played the banjo and fiddle, and my oldest brother played mandolin and violin. Together they played at community square dances. I was about ten years old when all my brothers were getting married and leaving the house. I'd thought I completely missed out on something and wanted to play guitar, too.

My next-door neighbor, James Lewis, was four years older than me and played acoustic guitar. We played together a lot, mostly country music. One man who definitely served as inspiration to me lived about a mile away, and who had a weekend radio show in Jackson, was Oscar Tinsley. He was a fantastic guitarist. I listened mostly to the radio, to a lot of R&B music and country. I can't remember titles of songs at the moment but it was a battery-operated radio so we did not have it on all the time — we lived on a farm.

When my dad got up in years, he used to say, "Don't beat on that thing all day long, now!" I'd taught myself to play entirely by ear so learning and picking up pieces was a challenge. I could work days on a song until I was satisfied with it.

I quit school in the ninth grade and my dad told me I could work so I stayed on the farm that year. He gave me an acre of cotton, which created the bale that I sold to buy my first jumbo Gibson acoustic. I don't know what happened to that guitar. Maybe my dad sold it later.

When I was in the service, two or three other guys on our ship bought these small Japanese guitars with fret posts that wore down so quickly we joked they must have been made out of beer cans for how soft the metal was.

What I love about playing the guitar is that there is no end in sight to what can be done on the instrument. I always loved to play, even in the Navy. I played on the ship, started a little radio show and formed a trio. After the service, I came to Memphis in search of a day job and played on my own for a bit, which I did not like. I prefer playing in a group, so I formed one named the Starlite Wranglers. Later on I bought a Fender Esquire and an amp, which I had for a little while when I played gigs. Standing up with this guitar was not comfortable for me. I happened to be downtown one day when I spotted a large, gold-covered ES-295 Gibson, which looked almost like a Les Paul, and I said to myself, "I've gotta have it." I traded in the Fender and used this Gibson throughout the early Sun Studios days.

I came to work with Elvis through Sam Phillips, the man who ran Sun Records. Sam had agreed to put out a record on the Starlite Wranglers and we had also become fast friends. Every day I would drop by Sun to go have coffee with him. I haven't thought about this for years, but I guess, in the back of my mind, I'd probably been hopeful for some studio work. One day when we were out for coffee, I overheard his secretary, Marion Keisker, say, "Did you ever do anything more about that boy?"

Sam said, "No."

Later on, I asked him, "What about this boy Marion mentioned?"

He turned to her and said, "Yeah, give him a call." Sam handed me a piece of paper with a name and number on it and asked me to go ahead and audition him.

I stared at the name and said, "ELVIS? What kind of name is *that*?" I called Elvis when I got home because Sam was looking for new material. Elvis came over to my house on a Sunday, July 4, and spent a couple of hours singing just about every song in the world. I called Sam after he left and told him Elvis had a good voice. I felt he could sing anything you asked him. Sam told me, "I'll ask him to come to the studio then, and I'd like you to sit in and play a little music."

Tape was still a new means of recording back then, and it was very expensive to use. The original way was to record by wire. Now Sam had heard Elvis sing before because he had come by Sun to cut a song for his mother as a birthday present. This time, we were going to record him on tape, which would sound just like it was coming through a radio.

Elvis and I went into Sun Studios on July 5th for an audition. Sam said, "Sing me a pop song." And he'd do it. "Now sing me an R&B song." He did it. Elvis could sing anything. Now the funny thing is, Sam would put two and three of these songs on tape at the beginning of the tape when he'd cut that first record. However, because tape was expensive and could be reused, he erased many of those early recordings. It's not like nowadays, when they have absolutely every little bit of everything saved up on first recordings.

For the last Sun session, I purchased the Echosonic amplifier for $500 from the builder Ray Butts. Back then, $500 was quite a sum, but I managed to get financing from the O.K. Houck Piano Co. in Memphis, where I had purchased other equipment, including my second Gibson guitar, an L-5 natural finish archtop. The Echosonic had been used to record Elvis' "Mystery Train," and I used this amplifier on every subsequent recording and performance throughout my career with Elvis, up to the 1968 NBC-TV special.

Aaron Shearer

No American classical guitarist can escape the volumes of guitar technique known as the Aaron Shearer Method, with its practice studies and neat diagrams of finger placement upon the strings. Dr. Shearer died in 2008 at the age of eighty-nine and it can be said that his work was the first real American contribution to pedagogy for the guitar.

I traded three white geese that I had raised for a beautiful old Martin gut string guitar with ivory inlay with mother-of-pearl and ivory tuning pegs, though the neck had been a bit bowed. The guitar was hardly playable but I wouldn't have known this at the time. I did not raise the geese initially for this purpose of buying a guitar. I just wanted to sell them and make a few dollars, which would have meant so much, as we were Idaho farm people. No one knows how poor you can be as a farmer when you cannot grow your own food. We would trade some eggs for some flour.

My father learned to play a type of Spanish fandango but he hadn't touched a guitar in a good thirty years, probably. The Spanish fandango sounded a bit like the classical guitar piece Romanza. I only heard him play three or four times and I do not think he was necessarily interested in the guitar. He did not intend to be of any help because he was a very religious man who thought music was a sin to pursue as a career. Mother was different. She played piano a little and was an expert at playing a melody and filling it in improvisationally. Her talent was remarkable, now that I think about it.

I'd recognized by that point that the guitar I owned was unplayable. I had been playing it with a steel bar, which I slid across the strings. In 1929, when I was ten years old, the neighboring Ankney family invited me to come hear Bing Crosby's Kraft Music Hall radio program. Crosby announced there would be a Spanish guitarist by the name of Segovia performing that evening. Before I left their house, I told these neighbors, "This is what I want to do!" after hearing Segovia play.

There was no thought of receiving lessons from anyone at this time, as it was the Great Depression. I can remember every so often someone would ask me what it was I wanted to do and I might have said I wanted to play the Spanish guitar. They would think I was nuts — just a kid. Segovia had been a very primary influence after I heard him on the radio because we did not have a record player, nor had one been available nearby. I did not hear him play again for many, many years. I'm eighty-five years old now and my memories of this live on quite vividly. I just had this big notion that I would somehow pursue the guitar as my lifetime work and it's still there — it's crazy! What I loved about the guitar was when I was able to play a cowboy song or a folk song and be able to accompany myself.

I used to hitchhike into town almost every week to visit the one music store in Lewiston, Idaho, which was seventeen miles from home, to see if they had any copies of guitar magazines — though I'd had no money to buy anything. George C. Krick of St. Louis wrote a column that came to figure largely in my life because he spoke about playing guitar with the fingers. He did not really give out any real information but this is probably where I'd first read of Segovia. I was not certain if one played with the fingers or if one included the nails as well. I did not even know how to file my nails!

Though I was interested in classical guitar, I was making money playing jazz guitar. My first performance was when they had the county music meeting of high school musicians in this city of 13,000. I was invited to come play my guitar and sing. I sang a cowboy song with my harmonica, and man, I do remember I simply brought the house down. They just screamed! That was the first time I ever played in public and I was maybe fourteen years old.

Fate has been very kind to me and I am so grateful that life has turned out the way it has. I was hoping to do something for people to help them play the guitar. I wanted to create something beneficial because I'd never had a book that showed me how to play the guitar.

Dick Dale

Dick Dale is the King of Surf Guitar, whose breakneck speed and fiery fusion of Middle Eastern and Eastern European melodies and defined tones have set the style for this genre. His song "Miserlou" is featured famously in Quentin Tarantino's film *Pulp Fiction*. Dale is also renowned for experimenting with Fender amplifiers and collaborating with Leo Fender in the construction of the 100-watt Showman guitar amplifier.

I typically don't like doing interviews on account of an issue known as *perceivability*. Whenever you speak, you create a problem. If I say I like chocolate and you say you like chocolate, we're fine and should leave it at that. But if each of us starts to explain how it tastes and smells, that is where we could get into a disagreement. There is a saying, "He who speaks does not know. He who knows does not speak." I believe in living by my talent with love, warmth and a good smile. My music is for helping the elderly and the children who are dying of diseases that they have no business having. My music opens doors to kids of all ages and I play to the grassroots, not to other musicians. I do not put drugs, alcohol, smokes or red meat into my body. Your body is your temple — treat it that way.

I've talked with some of these journalists who say, "Yeah right, Dick." They take my words, twist them around and say "he claims" or they use words like "supposedly." Then they go and write about stuff like "the wet, splashy surf sound" that started in the 1960s. I've got news for you: they were not in the room with me, Leo Fender and Freddy Tavares. And Dick Dale created surf music in the '50s, not the '60s. I am the Last of the Mohicans now, as Leo and Freddy have passed away. Talk to the original and listen to the original.

Leo was a very focused guy. He hardly smiled. The one time I saw him laugh was when he saw me play his guitar upside down and backwards because I'm a true lefty. He was developing the Fender Stratocaster and he took me in like a son. Leo had a saying, "When it can withstand the barrage of punishment given by Dick Dale, it is then fit for the human consumption."

I play the guitar upside down and backwards the way Jimi Hendrix did instead of restringing it as a true lefty would. I discovered Hendrix in a small bar in Pasadena, California, playing bass for Little Richard, but he wasn't called Jimi Hendrix then. Buddy Miles said to an audience, "Jimi used to say he got some of his best shit from Dick Dale."

I've never missed playing a show in my life. Back then, if you did that, it was called a *no show*. The only time I had to miss a gig was one time at Harmony Park Ballroom in Anaheim, California, because I had to have surgery for rectal cancer. I asked Dave Myers and the Surf Tones to fill in for me. At the time, Jimi was recording, and he said to his guys, "I heard Dale did a no show." Jimi's guitar player quickly said, "He's dying." Jimi then dedicated the song "Third Stone from the Sun" (his only fully instrumental song recorded) to me, because he had heard that I was dying, which prompted him to say, "You'll never hear surf music again."

I have a dedication to Jimi on my *Spacial Disorientation* album where I say, "Jimi, I'm still here, wish you were." People have read into that whatever they felt like, but the real reason for it is because of Jimi's earlier dedication to me, thinking that I was going to leave this earth. I dedicated "Third Stone" back to him.

My big musical influences were Hank Williams, Harry James, Ray Anthony, Louis Armstrong and Gene Krupa. I wanted the guitar to sound big and thick like Gene Krupa's drums. Leo gave me the Stratocaster and said, "Beat it to death and tell me what you think." What I am is, a *manipulator* of an instrument. I climb inside an instrument, find its soul then make it scream with pain and pleasure. A critic once said, "Les Paul invented the electric guitar and Dick Dale put the *electricity* in the guitar."

Dick Dale in the 1963 film *A Swingin' Affair.* (*Courtesy Dick Dale*)

I was born in South Boston but I grew up in Quincy, Massachusetts, during the Depression. My father is of Lebanese heritage and my mother's parents came to the U.S. from Poland when they were twenty years of age — White Russian gypsies. I used to stay with my mom's parents at their farm in Whitman, Massachusetts, during the summer, and I would pet the cows and chase the chickens and eat the food grown from Mother Earth. Back then, a gallon of gasoline cost twelve cents and you could buy a house for $6,000. I got paid twenty-five cents a week to clean a three-story house, doing the cooking, ironing and sweeping. I also worked for five cents an hour in a bakery making bread along with setting up bowling pins in the pit at the bowling alley in Quincy.

I saw an ad in the back of a Superman comic book that said if I sold all these jars of Noxzema skin cream, I could get a ukulele with a cowboy rearing his horse and swinging a lariat painted on it. Now, I always wanted to be a cowboy singer like Hank Williams because I used to listen to the cowboy songs on the radio. If you listen, Western music is songs about places and Hillbilly music is songs about people, like, *oooh, she broke my heart*. I ventured out in the middle of a Massachusetts snowstorm — you had to climb out through the windows in the house because you couldn't get out the front door on account of the snow being so deep — and bothered my neighbors at night, banging on their doors to sell them this Noxzema skin cream so I could get this ukulele. They used to yell at me, "Dickie, why aren't you in bed? You have to go to school in the morning."

After sending in all that money I made, I had to wait three months before it came in the mail. When it finally arrived, the uke turned out to be nothing but green cardboard. The tuning pegs were wooden pegs pushed into the holes and they fell out every time you turned them to tune it. I was so disgruntled that I threw it into the trashcan.

I got out my Red Rider wagon and collected enough Coke bottles to earn $6. It's probably what I should have done in the first place. Then I walked to a music store seven miles away to get a plastic ukulele that had real pegs with screws that kept the pegs where they belong. It had nylon strings, and it had a brown bottom and a cream top. I first bought a chord maker that you strap on the neck to make a chord, but it was kind of crappy, as the strings would rattle when you strummed them. I then bought a chord book and tried to put my fingers where the book told me. It was nearly impossible. The book didn't say, "Turn it the other way, stupid — you're left-handed." Ha!

I used to tape my fingers into a chord on the neck of the uke before I went to sleep, hoping that a fairy godmother would come along and tap my fingers and I would wake up with my fingers staying there.

I wanted to play this uke and make it sound full to make my country singing sound good, so I applied a style of strumming that had a rhythm like Gene Krupa playing his drums. What I did was develop a picking style to emulate the rhythm playing the snare, the ride cymbal and the bass drum. I've taught my son Jimmy the same method which gives him the metronome effect in his head to articulate the beat that keeps him right on the note. The first song that I ever sang and played on the uke was "Tennessee Waltz." Jimmy started out playing the uke and drums also. He started playing drums when he was twelve and a half months old, and when he was five, he was playing with me onstage during the Vans Warped Tour and the drummer from Green Day asked little Jimmy for his autograph.

When I was in grade school, my friend Lester and I went out picking swamp berries in the marshes in Whitman, Massachusetts. There is some real swampland out there, and while we were walking through the woods, we heard this spooky sound of strumming coming through the trees. It was like a scene out of *Deliverance* for how this strange sound appeared to come from a ramshackle house with a broken-down front porch with no steps to step up. We found seven guys in there who looked very scary, with cigarette packs rolled up inside their t-shirt sleeves and one tooth inside their heads. They were strumming out the blues on these flat top guitars.

I'd said, "Wow, look. You've got a flat top guitar! All I've got is a uke." One of the guys told me he had a guitar for sale, for $8. I asked if he'd take twenty-five cent payments with twenty-five cents down. He wanted fifty cents down, so we went back and forth haggling like this until he accepted an installment of fifty cents per week. Well, now that I had this thing, it occurred to me the guitar had six strings on it and I was used to only playing four. "What am I going to do?"

He said to me, "Well, kid, just pretend you're still playing the uke. Play the four strings and muffle the others. No one's gonna know."

Basically, I saw the guitar as an exploded version of the uke. My buddy later asked me to play rhythm with him in a talent contest while he played the lead to a guitar boogie shuffle. He played it real plain, and I said, "Why don't you play it like this?" and I put a double-picking rhythm to it. At this point, he stopped playing and said, "Dick, you take it from here." I played the guitar this way until I got to California.

After graduating the eleventh grade from Quincy High School, my father got an offer to take the family to California and work for Hughes Aircraft in 1954. So my dad bought a 1954 Oldsmobile 98 and we drove to California. We settled in southwest Los Angeles and I went to George Washington High School, graduating after my twelfth year. I went to a pawnshop and picked up a solid-body electric that I redesigned to look like a country guitar. Dad took me to some of the local bars, entering me into their contests. I was underage but he snuck me in. I later wound up winning a talent contest on a TV show called *Town Hall Party*, which had also featured Johnny Cash (before he wore black), Gene Autry, Lefty Frizell and Lorrie and Larry Collins.

My dad and I re-opened the Rendezvous Ballroom in Balboa, California, establishing a place for everyone to come and dance their hearts out to the music of Dick Dale and the Del-Tones, (a name my sister Shirley came up with). My dad and I met with the fire department, police department and the parent-teachers association. We told them, "Look, would you rather have your kids running around in the streets not knowing where they are, or would you rather have them in one building under one roof, knowing where they are?" Their kids would be dancing to Dick Dale music. They finally gave in, saying, "Well okay. But they must to wear neckties." They gave me the permits and my dad went out and bought a huge box of neckties. We didn't have any money to promote so I helped get an audience by word-of-mouth through the seventeen kids I was surfing with. They all arrived opening night and my dad handed them each a necktie. They danced barefoot and they had the ties on. This is why, at the Los Angeles Palladium's first Surfer Ball, everyone came wearing black tuxedos and sporting bare feet. It was great — barefoot surfers in tuxedos. Afterward, Colonel Parker called up my dad and asked him to bring me to his office at Paramount Studios because he wanted to see who had the entire California scene "sewed up," as he put it.

Parker had an inner sanctum of three offices. We stepped into the first office and a voice on speakerphone said, "Let 'em into the next office." We stepped into the second office and the voice on the speakerphone said, "Let 'em into the next office."

I saw the Colonel sitting there in his full Confederate uniform behind this huge desk and when I looked down at the two stools we were to sit on, I noticed the chair was made of a real stuffed elephant's foot. My dad asked the Colonel if he would like to manage Dick Dale. The Colonel replied, "I would love to, but I've just spent $80,000 on a boy called Elvis, and I wanted to take a look at this Dick Dale who is packing in four thousand people a night. I like what he stands for." The Colonel then proceeded to show me all his Elvis promotional materials that he had set up. He had a gold bust of Elvis on his desk. It was wild, like a Barnum and Bailey Circus promotion, very colorful and in your face.

Elvis invited me to his home in Trousdale Estates, Hollywood. He was so excited about his new Stutz Bearcat he had to take me out that night for a drive in it. El ran over to the Stutz and discovered that he had locked the keys inside. In a fit, he punched out the passenger side window, splattering glass all over the passenger seat where I was to sit. I brushed away the glass as much as I could as El wanted to start driving, and we took off with the Memphis Mafia following close behind us in the Rolls-Royce. El roared down Hollywood Boulevard and the cops pulled up next to us, looked over at El and said jokingly, "Oh, it's you. Do you need a manager?"

El replied, "Thank yuh very much" and sped off. We drove back to his estate, where he proceeded to show me around his home and view his collections. Priscilla, or Prissy, as El called her, showed me the famous white Eagle Belt that she had made for El for his upcoming Las Vegas show. Then she showed me the home she was designing for them both. Elvis was so proud but yet so scared because he was producing his very first show for Las Vegas. I knew better, telling him that he would kill them. And he did.

Elvis and I studied with the same karate master, Ed Parker, and I can tell you that El loved the martial arts and practiced every moment that he could steal. It was a shame that he had to live his life in a goldfish bowl. Let me tell you the kind of guy he was: he'd found me sitting on the floor inside his closet reading a book I found on his shelf called *This Is Karate* by Masutatsu Oyama and, knowing this book was hard to find and not knowing the fact that I had been searching for years for it, he bought a copy of it for me the next day as a gift. He told Ed Parker there is the book that Dick wants, bought it and signed a very personal note to me when he presented it to me. Elvis, Ed Parker, Chuck Norris and other close practitioners of the martial arts always stuck close together. Many times they would come to visit my menagerie of tigers and lions, eagles and hawks. (I would tell people, if the animals liked you, they would lick you. If they didn't like you, they would eat you.) Priscilla and Elvis loved the cats. When Elvis trained, he used to bring home the soft foam bats that we used in karate and he and Priscilla would bang each other every time they got into an argument. Prissy couldn't stand the pressure of living with the Memphis Mafia living in the same house. She wanted her own privacy, so she had Elvis build another house next door so the Memphis Mafia could move out and live there.

After Elvis died, I had a friend contact the Colonel and we found out that he had moved his office into the RCA Building in Hollywood, where my dad used to have the old Dick Dale Enterprises office. Parker was a carny man from the word go. Thanks to him, Elvis never had to pay any taxes. The Colonel knew how to market and how to sell, to the point of even making the press pay at Elvis' concerts. He told me he'd say to them, "Listen, I know all you guys are going to write shit about him anyway so you might as well pay."

Back then, the guitar was considered the creator of evil devil music and the school bands were horn bands. Art Laboe produced concerts under tents on the grass, and Art had me play at his tent concerts. One night Ritchie Valens sang "La Bamba." The crowd went wild and Ritchie got scared. He ran off the stage and didn't know what to do with the crowd yelling, "Ritchie! Ritchie!" I grabbed Ritchie, calmed him down and told him to get back out there and do the song again. He sang it three more times, ha! I loved it. I have been close with his family ever since.

There were no loud guitar power players back then because there were no power amplifiers. Country guitar players stood still and played with their fingers very eloquently like Chet Atkins and Merle Travis. There was an expression for that type of playing, "I got a sit-down job," because the only thing that moved were their fingers. Chuck Berry also played on these little amps with little six-inch and ten-inch speakers. Freddie Tavares used to play the Hawaiian steel guitar with Harry Owens' Royal Hawaiians, and Leo hired him to take out any of the bugs in the Telecaster guitar. Leo and Freddie were the two main forces for Fender and the Telecaster country-plucking guitar.

Freddie once told me if you could take a telephone pole and put strings and pickups on it, you would get the purest, fattest, thickest sound. But obviously, you can't play a telephone pole. So he made the Stratocaster out of a solid chunk of wood and made a cutaway so it would fit against the stomach. I first met Leo Fender when he was developing amps and guitars and my dad took me to meet him. I introduced myself, saying "Hello, Mr. Fender, my name is Dick Dale and I have no money for a neat guitar, but I am playing at the Rendezvous Ballroom in Balboa with lots of people coming to see me." Leo said, "Here, take this guitar, play it and tell me what you think."

Leo handed me a Stratocaster, and I turned it upside down and started playing it. The look on Leo's face was first one of shock. Then he burst into a fit of laughter. Leo never was one to laugh, as he was always so serious about his creations, but he couldn't help himself and asked, "What are you doing, young man? Turn it around, Stupid. You're left-handed."

That, I believe was the glue that made the three of us forever friends: Leo, Freddy and me. Forrest White, Leo's manager, joined the newly formed friendship as we started experimenting with Leo's creations.

As I started blowing up Leo's amps and speakers, Leo would say, "Dick, why do you have to play so loudly?" I would play so hard, it would heat up the electronic wires to the speaker and the speaker would catch on fire. When I was playing in concert at the London Forum, smoke was coming up out of one of the speakers and my bass player, Ron Eglit, motioned to me, saying, "Look, the speaker is burning," as the smoke rose up in front of me. I'd motioned back to him to shush and keep playing because I knew I had burned it up. Ha!

One time Keith Moon of The Who came up to me onstage, grabbed the microphone in the middle of my song and said, "You're the master. I've been listening to your bloody records for seventeen years and I want you to play on my album. I've got John Lennon and Ringo on it, and if you don't play on it I am going to junk the bloody thing." He said he was Keith Moon from The Who and I said, "Who?"

"Yes, The Who," he repeated. It was a bit like Abbott and Costello's "Who's on First?" Keith was the first person I knew who spent $80,000 on making an album, so I recorded on his last album.

Because Leo Fender was always asking why I had to play so loudly, Freddie Tavares urged him to attend a concert of mine at the Rendezvous Ballroom, where four thousand people watched me tear up his guitar and amp. Leo then said, "Freddy, now I understand what Dick is trying to tell me. Back to the drawing board with reconfiguring the guitar." Using a 10-inch speaker in Leo's Fender amp, we used to sit in his living room listening to Marty Robbins records. I think Leo loved the fact that I loved Marty Robbins and country music. Leo hated stereo sound. He would only listen to his country music monaural, not in stereo, while we were testing out these amps and speakers.

I later wanted to improve the sound of my singing voice, so I got the idea to steal the reverb spring can out of the back of a Hammond organ that I had. I thought it had a nice sustaining sound that made my dry voice sound better. Reverb was really meant for the voice, not the guitar, like everyone thinks.

I still have my original "Fender Champ Amp" put together with nails, and I have the only 600-watt Fender Mixer PA System that Leo build just for me as an experiment. Freddy had the other one as a backup at the factory, so there are only two in existence.

Leo went back to the drawing board every time I blew up an amp. The power, color and sound had to do with the output transformer, and I wanted that sound to come out of my amp and speakers. Leo created the first eight-ohm eighty-five-watt output transformer peaking at 100 watts. This transformer favored highs, mids and lows of the sound spectrum, as this had been my request. Transformers of today only favor highs, mids or lows by themselves. I wanted it all together to get my big, fat sound.

Leo wound the copper wire in an unorthodox way until he finally created a transformer where the sound peaked at 100 watts as the four 5881 tubes built up internal gas. The tubes created the distortion and pumped up the sound until it became bigger and fatter and blossomed in color. We now needed something to plug the amplifier into so we got an eight-inch Jensen speaker, then a twelve-inch speaker. We fried them immediately. I made changes on the guitar as we were connecting this amp to the speakers. Leo, Freddy and I went to JBL speaker company and requested them to build a fifteen-inch speaker with a twelve-pound magnet mounted in an aluminum alloy casting, and I added an aluminum dust cover on the cone on the speaker so I could hear the treble click of the pick as I played. They laughed and replied, "What are you going to do with that thing — put it on a tug boat?" Leo replied, "If you want my business, make it." This speaker was called the JBL fifteen-inch D130.

We plugged the new amp into a speaker cabinet that was three feet tall by two feet wide and twelve inches deep. It had no sound portholes and was packed with fiberglass for creating a tightness of sound. Inside the cabinet we mounted the JBL fifteen-inch D130 speaker. Leo named the amp "The Showman" because I used to leap off a four-foot-high stage down into the audience, sliding onto my knees across the floor whenever I ended a song. "Man, what a showman," Leo would say to me, but my dad would go crazy with scolding, screaming that I would never walk again if I kept doing that. Ha!

Now it was time to fire up this creation that Leo made for me. Bam! When I hit those sixty-gauge strings on that chunk of wood Stratocaster guitar, I experienced a newfound power. I told Leo that I wanted to put two D130s inside the cabinet. Leo replied in shock, "Dick, I will have to design and make a new output transformer." The next week I got a very excited call from Leo, urging me to come to the shop right away. Lo and behold, there on the desk was a four-ohm 100-watt output transformer that would peak at 180 watts. Powering the new Dual Showman Amp and blasting into two fifteen-inch JBL D130s, I plugged the "Beast" (as *Guitar Player Magazine* named it) into the Dual Showman amp and made people's ears bleed.

There had been one more bump in the road, though. I was still freezing and twisting the JBLS. Freddy said, "Dick look at this, how are you doing this?" referring to the twisted speaker cone. I replied, "If the speaker is supposed to move in and out with each note that I strike on the guitar, I think that the heavy staccato picking that I am pushing into the speaker is confusing it, and the speaker is moving in and out crookedly. That might be the reason why it cocked itself and jammed its movement." Leo, Freddy and I went back to the JBL speaker company, and Leo asked them to put a coating of a rubber glue–type material all around the ridge of the speaker. This worked. It kept the speaker pushing in and out in a straight direction. It did not cock and twist anymore. The speaker was now called the JBL fifteen-inch D130F, the letter "F" meaning Fender specifications," as Leo would say.

Fender Company manufactured my guitar strings, and the tech buzz in the factory was that my guitar strings were like coat hangers or telephone wires. Ha! In my thinking, the thicker the strings, the fatter and thicker the color of sound was going to be, and the amp would be working less hard to produce the sound. My strings were sixteen-gauge plain, eighteen-gauge plain, twenty-gauge plain, thirty-nine-gauge wound, forty-nine-gauge wound and sixty-gauge wound. That's why they called me the Father of Heavy Metal. It was the first creation of what's now known as heavy loud power playing.

One performance night I had blown another amp, and Leo was right there to put another one together for me. He had run out of covering material for the wood frame that housed the amp head. He found some cream-colored material in the back of the factory and quickly covered the amp head with that. Leo brought it to me saying, "Dick, do *not* let people see this. They will want it because you are playing through it. It will not be practical as people will get it stained with coffee and cigarette burns. I replied, "But Leo, I love it. It is so pretty and I love the color. Please can I keep it?" Well, the next week Leo called me into the factory and took me to the assembly line to view an entire line of cream-colored amps. I loved it. Every Showman amp that rolled off that assembly line came out with my cream covering.

While I was playing my Beast, I removed the plastic knobs because my wrist would accidentally turn down the volume. But after I pulled off the knobs, the metal shafts kept cutting my wrist as I picked up and down. I asked Leo if he could relocate them to the bottom of the guitar. He said it would cost him $12,000 to make a jig to put them where I wanted. He borrowed the guitar for a few days to check the neck. Then I received a message asking me to report to the factory. Bam! Leo handed me my guitar, saying, "Check it. I want to see how you play it." He'd moved the controls on the bottom. My guitar neck is one quarter of an inch smaller in width, and the Dick Dale Signature Stratocaster comes with a choice of either a three-position switch or the Dick Dale five-position switch. If you want the original neck, you have to ask for it, and I still use the three-position switch.

My advice to people who want to play the guitar is simple: Perfect practice makes for perfect performance. Empty yourself and you will find the humility to ask, how does one learn? You do not play for the acknowledgment — you play from deep within. Picture in your mind that you are creating awareness as you play, for you can create with your talent or you can destroy with your talent.

Albert Lee

Grammy-winning British guitarist Albert Lee grew up in Blackheath, London, and performed on recordings with Deep Purple before he joined The Crickets and Emmylou Harris' Hot Band. Lee has also worked with Eric Clapton and is known for his fast fingerstyle and country, rockabilly and western swing picking style.

I was at school when a good school friend's brother just returned from the Navy with a guitar. We had recently become enamored of skiffle music. This is a kind of folk music that was started in England by a guy called Lonnie Donegan. In the mid-1950s, everyone was trying to learn the guitar as a result — simple songs, like three chords, strumming and so on. A school friend of mine, Max Middleton, and I started learning to play on his brother's guitar. I borrowed the guitar and I might have borrowed a couple other guitars for the next year before I finally got one of my own. I was about thirteen years old at the time, and this guitar was a Höfner President archtop, a cheap one, and of course, the action on it was very high. Looking back, I'm sure it was just horrible and terrible to play, though we did not know it.

I had taken piano lessons for a couple years, so I was already interested in music. A little later on, I heard Jerry Lee Lewis, and I wanted to play piano like he did. But it was the guitar that really got me. I thought, well, I could do that. Once I learned to play a couple chords, it all fell into place. I was very fortunate, really, because it all came to me rather quickly, and I was on the road playing by the time I was sixteen. I didn't have any grand plans. Wish I did, really. I just wanted to play the guitar. My family was very supportive all along the way. In fact, they turned the living room into a band rehearsal room and let me just take over the house. I would just listen to records because there really wasn't anyone to see.

There were visiting American guitarists who came over. I remember seeing Duane Eddy when he came to England in 1958. I'd seen a few people on TV. I was a big Buddy Holly fan, but I never actually got to go to one of his gigs. Bill Haley — I never saw a gig of his but the movies were out, like *Rock Around the Clock* and *Don't Knock the Rock*. All the artists in those films were very inspiring to me. I never had a teacher. I still don't read music. I taught myself really, just by listening to solos and trying to copy them. I started to then improvise my own solos that I'd heard other people play.

I just love the sound of the guitar. It's such a thrill to hear a solo and then realize, "I think I know how he's doing that." And then, to finally figure it out in the confines of your own bedroom where you're sitting, playing away. It was a thrill for a real number of years till it got to the point where it came easily to me. My schoolwork went downhill pretty quickly after I discovered the guitar. I pretty much left school at the age of fifteen. That was the earliest age you could leave school in England. I started working a day job of paint-spraying for a few months, all the while doing little gigs. But at that age, one earns very little doing a day job anyway. I found that I could easily beat that day job pay by playing a couple places during the week, earning one pound sterling a night and, soon, I was earning more than I was with a day job. When I was sixteen, I played my first professional tour.

There was a dance hall near where we'd lived that had a dance band, and we'd roll up with our instruments and beg the manager to let us play. He said, "Okay, boys, how 'bout it? Seven and six a man." This translates as seven shillings and sixpence a person, which I believe was about a dollar back then. So we'd play for twenty minutes while the dance band was having a break. We were about fifteen or sixteen years old.

I've been playing professionally now for over forty years, and I've played with most of my heroes. My biggest hero was Jimmy Bryant. He was a country swing player during the '50s, and I met up with him during the '70s in Los Angeles. His was just a name that I'd heard off a record and to see him in the flesh was memorable — I actually played with him a couple times at the Palomino Club in Los Angeles. That was really a special moment for me.

Here's a story for you, I was playing with The Crickets. Rick Grech, who plays bass with The Crickets, was from Blind Faith. We did a tour together and he's a really nice guy. One day, he said, "I've got a guitar that I'm going to give you. You're really going to love this guitar. Jimi Hendrix gave me this guitar." It was a black Les Paul Custom, with two pickups. Not a reissue but one from the '60s. *Hendrix* had given it to him. My ex-wife needed money and sold it while I was away on tour. So that was the end of *that* marriage. The guy who'd bought the guitar promised me that if he sold it, I could have it back. He called me one day and I went to have a look at it. Apparently, he didn't like the way it was playing so he had the fingerboard taken off and instead of having a camber on it, it was flat, like a classical guitar. I looked at it and thought, "Oh, this is *not* the same guitar that Hendrix had," so I passed on it.

We all have guitars and regret selling them. Of course, in the early days, it's hard to justify having more than one or two guitars. You just had your axe and that was it. But nowadays, people have got lots of guitars. I've got about thirty or forty — though haven't counted them lately. Not all of them are collectible, but people give you guitars and you feel like you can't give it away and sell it, so it just ends up in the closet. I had a guitar that used to belong to Tony Sheridan, who was the guy The Beatles used to back in Hamburg, Germany. Probably The Beatles have played on this guitar. It was a Martin D-28E with DeArmond pickups. They're quite rare. I had this guitar and thought, "This isn't working, I need to get something else." So I sold that and regretted it. But I do have another one of Tony Sheridan's guitars.

My first decent guitar was a Les Paul custom that I owned in 1961. I reluctantly sold it to a friend of mine, only because I'd wanted to buy a Gibson Super 400. I thought this was going to be *the* guitar, for being a top-of-the-line jazz guitar. It was a great guitar, of course, but it was not right for me, given the style I was playing and developing at the time. I always regretted giving up that first Les Paul.

In '79, I'd started playing with Eric Clapton and we were at one of our first rehearsals when he saw a picture of me playing my Les Paul Custom. He said, "I've got one of those at home." The next day, he brought in this '58 Les Paul Custom and he gave it to me. I still have that guitar, so I don't feel so bad about losing my old one because I have Eric's one now. It's pretty much the same guitar, except he had it refretted with heavier frets, which makes it more playable because the original guitars had very thin frets and were a little hard to get along with. It's a great guitar.

The funny part is I did find my first Les Paul Custom again, the one that I sold. It had been sold to Eric Stuart of 10cc. I was in the BBC Studios when I saw this black Gibson case on the floor, quite rare in England because there were not many Les Pauls around. So I opened it up and saw my guitar with a ding on it and I thought, "Ah, there's my Les Paul!" I lifted it up — they're very heavy, Les Pauls — and I discovered he'd cut a big chunk out of it to make it lighter. I thought, "Oh god, why on earth would he do that?" I was just devastated.

I have another guitar that Don Edward gave to me as well, another 1958 Gibson, one of his J-200s with the big black pick guards on it. That's a really famous rock 'n' roll guitar. I'm not home very often to play them, unfortunately, but they're classic guitars that I'd hate to part with.

Jorge Morel

In the '60s, Argentinean classical guitarist and composer Jorge Morel performed nightly at The Village Vanguard, where he shared billing with jazz legends Stan Kenton and Herbie Mann. He is known for his brilliant arrangements of popular songs and jazz standards and had been lifelong friends with Chet Atkins, who had arranged for him to record with RCA Victor, following Morel's work for Decca Records.

My first guitar: my father gave it to me when I was twelve. I had a little Christmas gift of a guitar before this one when I was six years old. It had wooden pegs like a *cavaquinho*. I didn't play much, just learned a few chords. When I went to school to learn, I took this guitar with me. My teacher pointed out it was a toy and not a guitar, so my father bought me a bigger guitar.

One time, in the bedroom that I shared with my brother, I was playing my new guitar while he was talking, but I was not listening. He started screaming at me so I'd said, "Shut up!" He took off his shoe and threw it and I reacted by holding up guitar in defense, but the impact of his shoe cracked the guitar. My brother was crying after that. I was twelve years old and he had been ten.

My brother and I started to learn the guitar together but, six months later, he stopped. "Look, I don't have the talent," he said. "I like it but I can hardly hold the guitar. I could never do that." I suggested that he try. "Why should I struggle so much?" he asked. He was an intelligent man and, listening to me, he said, "You make it sound easy." He quit the guitar. My father didn't push. He said, "One guitarist in the family is enough." My brother became an engineer — a great architect, designing the heating systems.

So my first real guitar was one made in Buenos Aires by Antigua Casa Nuñez. In those days, during the 1940s, they made guitars in the shop rather than by factory. My father was an actor and had a lot of friends in entertainment. He also played the guitar. One day I came home from school and my father said to me, "Go to your bedroom, I think you'll find something there that you like."

I saw the closed case and inside was this gorgeous instrument. Oh, my god. I couldn't get my hands off it the whole day. It was an Antigua Casa Nuñez Diego Gracia, made in 1928. He had bought it from a friend who played the guitar. This friend was about to pawn the guitar but instead, my father offered him $250 — a lot of money back then. I played this guitar for so long. When you are very young, you don't know how to take care of an instrument. We knew nothing of the Dampit for maintaining the humidity of the wood.

I came to New York with this same guitar in 1961 from Puerto Rico to play at Carnegie Hall with the Kingston Trio. We were both on the same bill and had two concerts in one evening. I went to the hotel, the Edison on 47th Street. I was very excited. I placed the guitar on top of a table. It was December or November, very cold outside. I went downstairs, had lunch, took a walk and came back to the hotel. When I opened up the case and touched my guitar, I was surprised that it felt hot. And when I picked it up . . . crack! Crack! Crack! What I had thought had been a table had turned out to be the radiator. The guitar had sat directly on the heater for two hours and cracked in twenty places.

Somebody gave me a Velasquez guitar. I tried to have the top of the Antigua Casa Nuñez replaced in Cuba but it was not the same guitar afterward, so I sold it to one of my students. Of course, I wish I still had it because it was my first guitar. Many guitarists do not still have their first guitars. I revisited the store where that first guitar had been made, and I bought another one but it, also, was not the same. I brought it back to America with me and eventually got rid of that one, too.

I have not played any other instrument but the guitar, though I do have a piano for composition. I just bang on the piano — I don't play it. I think my favorite instruments are the strings. I liked American music and orchestras. I liked traditional guitar music, of course, like Carcassi, Giuliani, Bach and Sor. Bach I learned later when I was seventeen or eighteen years old. I wanted to play Bach's music and nothing else for a while. I had no idea that I might have something inside me that would someday speak musically. When I was maybe fifteen or sixteen years old, I wrote a piece that I liked but wanted to make sure it was mine, that I didn't inadvertently steal from some place. I started to write more and my friends liked it. Then my father said, "Who wrote that? I like it. You wrote that? Are you SURE? Well, I like it. You sure you didn't take it from somewhere?"

Even before I came to America, I liked jazz, the tango, American folk-lore, Argentinian and South American music from every country. But I also liked Benny Goodman and Artie Shaw and their orchestras playing violins, romantic stuff. I thought that the guitar would probably be the wrong instrument because I couldn't play this music on it. But I fell in love with the guitar anyway and realized that I could possibly make some arrangements of this music for the guitar. Not all of it but some of it.

When the sounds of Gershwin came into my life — that was it. I first heard his music while watching a movie about Gershwin's life starring Robert Alda, called *Rhapsody in Blue*. I knew the name of Gershwin, but when I heard his music in this film, it mesmerized me. In those days, the movies used to be replayed from the start. You paid one admission and then if you wanted to see it again, you simply stayed. Well, I stayed for three showings of this film. My father was worried because I'd left at two p.m. and I didn't come home until the evening. Not long ago, they showed this movie on an old movie channel on TV. Gershwin was born in Brooklyn. "Where's Brooklyn?" I wondered. I had absorbed every detail of this movie.

My father was an actor, a very good one, and he took the guitar everywhere because it was his life. He loved the classical guitar and it's why I am playing the guitar. It's important for me to say if there is one person I need to acknowledge, it is my first teacher, Amparo Alvarisa. She taught at the school where my father took me across the street from our house. It was a class of twelve students and some dropped out. I was there with two or three students and, with the class being so small, the school did not think it worth keeping. So she came to my house to teach privately after that. My dad did whatever he could to pay this lady. I had two lessons weekly for two years, then once a week the third year. By the fourth year, we went to Pablo Escobar because he had been her teacher. She said she could not teach me anything further so I took lessons from him.

George Benson

The winner of multiple Grammy Awards over the course of his forty-year career, jazz guitarist George Benson is also known for using a distinctive Manouche rest-stroke picking technique, similar to that of gypsy jazz players, where one string is plucked downwards and the pick ends its run on the next string.

I was nine years old when I received my first guitar. I had already been playing the ukulele for two years at that point because my hands were too small yet to play the guitar. I could not wait for my hands to grow large enough to play! So when my hands grew just large enough, my parents bought me a $15 guitar, something along the lines of a Stella. It was a functional acoustic guitar, nothing electric — it had a round sound hole and, boy, I thought it was the greatest thing that could ever happen. I'd learned a few chords and things and immediately went out into the streets and started making money with it.

I did try to play violin at one point, which had been before the ukulele, and I'd tried to play the piano, too, but again, my hands were too small to be able to play the piano, too. My first electric guitar, my stepfather made for me. We couldn't afford a new electric guitar because they were expensive. I kept crying about this instrument that I saw in a pawnshop and finally, my step-father said, "Let's go take a look at it." We did not go inside the store but we looked at it from the front wraparound window. He said, "You know what? I could make that." So we went home and started cutting up wood around the house and, a few days later, I had my first electric guitar for less than half what they had been asking for at the store! My stepfather was a jack-of-all-trades who knew how to do electricity, carpentry, plumbing, everything.

When my mother met my stepfather, I was only seven years old, and he brought an electric guitar to the house with an amplifier. He also had a record player. Those were the first electric items in our house because we had just moved from a house that had no electricity to a house that did. He went to the pawnshop and retrieved his guitar, amplifier and record player, and he played Charlie Christian records for me with The Benny Goodman Sextet and George Shearing records — those were my first experience with listening to records and it set a high standard from the very beginning.

My family was glad to see that I was happy playing the guitar, but they did not think anything special would come of it until I started making money with it. Then they said, "Oh! Ooooh! Wow!" They did not know how much money I was making but it was three times the amount of money my mother was making every day in the hospital, making pennies. I was making two weeks' worth of her salary within a single day of playing out on the street corner before she found I was making that kind of money. I started making records when I was ten years old, only one year after I started playing the guitar.

The guitar is a personal instrument because you can take it with you and you can play it from different points of view. You can make up your own ideas. It's not like a piano, either; on a guitar you can play the same A on various strings and frets, whereas on a piano each A on the keyboard is a different pitch. Also, with the guitar, you're able to add a couple different kinds of trills, vibrato and tune it down. The biggest challenge I've ever faced with the guitar was with the quality of the instrument because I'd always had cheap guitars in the beginning and they used to literally fall apart in my hands. The strings had edges on them that used to cut my fingertips. This did set my mentality about the guitar neck early on and created the very reason that I play the way I do now — with a very light touch — because I was afraid I was going to run into one of those barbed strings.

That one moment that said I could be playing the guitar professionally for the rest of my life has never come to me. The guitar is merely something that I do. I have found that everything I have done, I have done well. A lot of my friends thought I would wind up becoming a doctor. I used to conceive of things and ideas and then actually make them. I used to be an artist who had studied commercial art in school and also I studied electric power. I was always a B or B+ student in everything I studied. Music is the one area that allowed me to make a living. It was something I did with relative ease, so it began to take over and the money started going to the moon when I left Pittsburgh, my hometown. It wasn't for pennies anymore but serious dollars. When we had a hit record, boy, everything changed, and we found that we could almost buy anything we wanted, so I passed that good success on to my children and my wife.

I went into a store one time in New York on Music Row on 48th Street. If you said to anybody you were heading to 48th Street, they knew you were going to be looking at some musical instruments. I was walking by a brand new store when some fellow saw me walking by and said, "George, come here! I've got something you've gotta see!" He pulled out this fabulous guitar and I knew right away it was very expensive, just an incredible guitar. He'd said, "It's only a thousand dollars." I said, "A THOUSAND DOLLARS? Get out of here! I ain't got no thousand dollars." He said, "Why don't you just charge it to your record company?" And jokingly, I'd said, "Yeah! Do that! We'll charge it to the record company!" So he packed it up, put it inside a case and let me walk out with it after saying, "Just sign right here."

I just walked out the store with it. And sure enough, the record company paid for it. This guitar is made by one of the most famous luthiers in the jazz guitar world — his name was D'Angelico. I still have this guitar and every time I pull it out, I make a hit record with it. I pulled it out eighteen years ago and then it was in my closet for fifteen years after that, and I pulled it out two or three years ago and every record I have used this guitar on has become a #1 hit for smooth jazz. Now it is worth about $150,000. I'd had three or four other D'Angelico guitars later that I have auctioned and wish that I hadn't done that now, but I've always kept this one because it was special.

Roger McGuinn

Chicago-born guitarist McGuinn is famous for his jangly electric guitar playing in songs like "Mr. Tambourine Man" and "Eight Miles High" by The Byrds. He creates that signature sound using a technique based on banjo finger-picking he learned at the Old Town School of Folk Music.

I was fourteen years old when I received my first guitar for my birthday because I had been turned on by Elvis Presley's "Heartbreak Hotel" the year before. This guitar was a Harmony brand and, though I do not remember the model number, it was one of those f-hole guitars with action that was about an inch high. I always say that guitar was better for slicing hard-boiled eggs than playing music. I did not realize that the action should have been lowered. Instead, I did the best I could with it. I couldn't really play any chords because the strings were too difficult to press down so I'd figured out some single string music and copied the lead break from a song called "Woman Love," on the flip side of Gene Vincent's "Be-Bop-A-Lula." Some years later, when I'd met George Harrison and compared notes, it turned out that he and I had learned to play the same lead breaks of that song around the same time. That was the first song we both learned to play on our guitars.

My little brother had a toy accordion that I would mess around with, but that was really it in terms of my playing any other musical instrument. My brother and I both took guitar lessons at the Old Town School of Folk Music in Chicago, but he did not wind up pursuing music. Rockabilly is what fascinated me — Elvis Presley, Gene Vincent, The Everly Brothers and Johnny Cash. My family was fine with my playing the guitar, but they did not like Elvis Presley at all. They didn't trust him. I guess he just scared them for being too wild. So I used to have to secretly listen to rock 'n' roll on my transistor radio with an earphone. They were fine with the idea of me playing music, though.

I love the way the guitar looks, feels, smells and sounds. I love everything about guitars. It's a sweet-sounding instrument and, once you get over having calluses on your left hand, it's pretty easy to play. I never really understood the piano, which feels like playing a typewriter. I know how to figure out the notes on it but I never really liked the sound of a traditional grand piano — I love the sound of a guitar. I played a nylon-string guitar when I worked with The Chad Mitchell Trio for a couple years. I had a nice little Martin 00-21 that I bought in Chicago, and I had offered to play that behind them, but they said no, saying they felt the Martin was a little thin sounding. They'd wanted the fuller sound of a classical guitar.

I still find the first position F Major chord challenging to play because it is so close to the nut. So I cheat on that chord by using my thumb like a lot of rock guys do. I don't like the F Major chord. If I had my way, there wouldn't be any F Major chord. When I got into playing the 12-string guitar, the B strings were always difficult because they might be in tune if you are tuned to E and you play an E chord, but when you play a D chord, it would be a bit sharp. It's tricky. A lot of the early 12-string guitars did not compensate at the bridge, so the B strings would not be in tune up the neck. Marty Stuart, the country guy, once said, "When you get to heaven, there will be no B strings!"

My first real performance was at my high school, the Latin High School of Chicago. I did not get paid for it, though. My first paid gig was when I played at a coffeehouse in Chicago called Café Roué on Rush Street at Oak Street. By that time, I had been excited by folk music when I was attending the Latin School because our teacher had invited Bob Gibson over to play a set for us. He had played really cool music for us on the five-string banjo, and he'd been excited by Pete Seeger. Gibson was like a younger version of Pete Seeger, doing more souped-up folk music than Pete — not quite as traditional — and I had liked that a lot. So I got into folk music and played a lot of Pete Seeger and Bob

Gibson songs on the five-string banjo. By that time, I had acquired a five-string long-necked Vega banjo like Music Man and I also had this little Martin 00-21 guitar that my teacher Frank Hamilton at the Old Town School of Folk Music played. I saw that Josh White played a five-string banjo, too, so I'd thought it was a good instrument to have.

I followed Bob Gibson's career since he played at my high school and I went to see one of his shows at the Gate of Horn, a really great folk and jazz club in Chicago. This club had been active from about '56 to '63 and all the folk singers like Judy Collins and Bob Dylan played there, as well as Peter Yarrow, before he was in Peter, Paul & Mary. It was owned at the time by Albert Grossman, who later managed Peter, Paul & Mary and later, Dylan.

I was at this club when Bob Gibson was playing. I was walked into his dressing room and saw that he had a Vega 12-string guitar, which had been an unusual instrument because nobody was making commercial 12-strings at that time, in the late '50s. You could find some old Stella 12-strings, like the kind Lead Belly played, and some others by other low-end manufacturers like Harmony — but Bob had this great Vega 12-string. I couldn't resist the temptation to pick it up. I took the capo off this guitar, tuned it and played a little bit. Then I put the capo back on just as I had found it. What I did not realize is that this completely knocks the guitar out of tune. Bob walked into the dressing room, grabbed this guitar, went onstage and proceeded to play. And the guitar's tone was really sour. He walked right by me, roaring, "WHO was playing my guitar?!" It was me but I did not confess to it. Now that he has passed away, I can tell that story.

Once, back in the day, I took a flight from Paris to New York on the Concorde. The flight personnel claimed they would treat my guitar with kid gloves, saying they would wrap it carefully in plastic with assurances it would travel perfectly fine. When we arrived in New York, I found that my guitar had not been wrapped in plastic. I didn't open the case until we arrived at the hotel. My wife took one look at the back of it and gasped because it was all crushed in. If they had put kid gloves on anything, I'd say they'd probably put kid gloves on the forklift before they drove it straight through my guitar.

There is a happy ending to this story, though. Because it was a 12-string guitar, a signature model that Martin Guitars made about ten years ago, it inspired me to go back to Martin and request an entirely new signature model 7-string guitar, one that Martin Guitars continued to manufacture afterward. My reason for creating this new guitar is that I'd wanted a high G and a low

G like a 12-string has, but the rest of the guitar would be a 6-string so it had the flexibility of a 6-string guitar with a distinctive bite on the G-string tear, which I use to play leads up and down from the 0 to the 12th fret. The sound of a 12-string, when I played lead breaks on it, like the break in the songs "My Dear" and "Turn, Turn, Turn," is all done on the G string, but with this seven-string guitar, you can bend it, play bluegrass runs on the bottom, and it has more flexibility, like having a Swiss Army knife on the guitar. So that incident from Air France ultimately prompted me to do something good.

Taj Mahal

Henry Saint Clair Fredericks, a.k.a. Taj Majal, is a blues guitarist whose career has spanned nearly fifty years. He uses a flat pick to play blues leads, and when fingerpicking, he leads with his thumb and middle finger rather than using his index finger. I interviewed Taj Mahal in his dressing room backstage at the first Wall-to-Wall Guitar Festival at the Krannert Center in Champaign-Urbana, Illinois.

My stepfather came after my dad died during the early 1950s, when I was about eleven years old. About three years later, when I was fourteen, I discovered this guitar sitting inside a closet and learned that it belonged to my stepfather. That was the beginning and the end. I was already guitar crazy. I was music crazy. From every direction, I'd wanted to hear music. I also became acutely aware of when they were trying to fake the public out with some version that did not feel like real music. This was back in the '40s. I used to ask myself, "Why does that feel so, hmmm? I cannot put my finger on it." And then the other stuff I loved had been wild music captured live by tape and that was exciting. Then it was like, "Well, the notes are there, but I'm not getting it." I couldn't figure it out, but then later came to realize this was the sound of people who had figured out patterns, which they were trying to market.

I had my stepfather's guitar and, as luck would have it, some new neighbors moved in next door with two brothers in the family. One of the brothers was about six months older than me, nearly fifteen at the time, and he was playing. See, I never had to go through that whole Robert Johnson thing in order to find the door that mattered. By the time I got to Robert Johnson, that was the weirdest sounding, most far-off thing to my ear because I'm talking about having a live guy who is the same age sitting in front of you playing, and processing Blind Lemon Jefferson, Muddy Waters, Blind Boy Fuller, Lightnin' Hopkins and Johnny Lee Hooker. Those guys are huge musicians. These boys down the street said Muddy and all those musicians came from Clarksdale, Mississippi, but they really came from Stovall, Mississippi. These boys came from deep in the Delta.

The young girls who came recently from the South liked this music, but the ones who had been up North longer started having a taste for more sophisticated music and shut the door on it altogether. It was a great thing for a couple of young, crazy boys to have grownups come up and say, "We'll give y'all a coupla dollars if you come on up here. Now y'all can't drink but you can play that music." And we'd make all this money, drinking our sodas and just whangin'. These brothers were so exciting. And of course, it was all because of that Silvertone archtop guitar I'd found inside the closet. It had flaming maple grain with a sunburst and f-holes — a huge find for a closet.

When I asked where to get strings, I was told by the older brother who lived next door, "Go to the drugstore." The drugstore?! Not the music shop? I went to the drugstore to get these Black Diamond strings. He showed me how to unwind the third string, because the third string is always wound, and we'd take a pair of pliers and pull that wrapper off — that's how you get a bendy, winding string. And then we'd never tune the guitar up because we wanted to build our hands up. That would hurt your hands for a while and then he'd say, "Tune it up some more." We were probably at E-flat or D when playing in the 8th position, except when we played with Ernest and them, because Ernest played harmonica as well as they played guitar. The police used to come and tell us to turn that stuff down. They were outta sight, that clan. They played "Boogie Chillen," which was a huge song.

I had another friend named Garland Edwards, and he played more R&B and funky blues. All of us agreed on Chuck Berry and Bo Diddley. I loved

Johnny "Guitar" Watson and Albert Collins and Noble "Thin Man" Watts, Billy Butler, Nicky Baker, Banjo Ike, Freddie Greene, Nat King Cole, Oscar Moore. Oh god, I loved those guys. And later, I liked Wes Montgomery. I stretched out because my father was a bebop composer with West Indian roots, and a lot of people at that time contributed their rhythmic patterns. But yeah, the *sound* of the guitar just killed me, coming from any direction. I still love it a lot. It's just this instrument. Sometimes I could not play three notes of what this guy was playing, but I could go there and listen to what he was playing all night long.

My mom did not like my obsession with the guitar. She and my friend Garland's mother called the guitar "a starvation box." "You still up there playing that starvation box?" It did warn both of us. Garland went to Canada and I kind of drifted on. My purpose for playing music was not so much to be popular, as much as it was something I needed to do for myself.

It would not have mattered whatever kind of job I had, as I was really interested in agriculture. I spent about ten years working on two different farms when I was working my way through school. I worked at one farm, a dairy farm, briefly and the other for a longer period of time. And I still check in on the dairy farm to this day. Working there is how I got my money to go to school. It gave me a chance to think about what it was I wanted to do with my life. I've never been afraid of work. I worked my way up to foreman at this place. I learned that while city music sounded good, it had nothing to do with lifting them bales and cleaning that barn. So the kind of music that I knew I wanted to play was music that accompanied this situation.

As I got older, after a couple of years spent picking tobacco, I went back home to my old neighborhood and found my friend Lyndon Perry, and I'd sit down with him or the Nichols, who lived up the street — Junior, Alex, Mary. They were all just into playing. It had nothing to do with anything. These are people who played music from the heart because they loved it and wanted to pass it on to another generation. I didn't know how lucky I was because these were just people I knew in the neighborhood. Years later, all those guys had bands but this is where they started.

I still have that Silvertone. It's missing one of the tuning pegs but I can get a new set. Back then, nobody knew you could do that. We'd use a pair of pliers to tune the guitar. The hard thing for me about the guitar had been singing and playing at the same time. I just worked at it. The guys who always killed me were the bass players who were in the pocket with the drummer and singing. Larry Graham from Graham Central Station and from Sly and the

Family Stone is an amazing player. He's in the pocket, kicking the pocket while he's singing the melody over the top. This is the way people played. If you had to do it, you did it. I was *determined*. Pretty soon, you just let go and there it is.

I played a National guitar on *The Natch'l Blues* that came to me from a guy who had freaked out on acid during the '60s. He was kind of a weird guy who had this beautiful guitar but he could not play it. While he was tripping on acid, he'd had a vision that he needed to give this guitar to me. I was wary, but it was a really good guitar. The sound of that National on that record! The guys who had founded the original company, the Dopyera Brothers from Chicago — I'd met *all* of them plus their sister and nephew. They used to fix my guitars and this one guitar had the biggest sound you could possibly imagine. It was an early '30s guitar. That album was recorded in '67 or '68. In 1971, this guy came back around because he knew what that guitar was worth. And you know what? I just gave it to him. He was freaking out, and when I say freaking out, he knew that I was bigger than he was because after giving a guitar to somebody, I would never ask for it back. Some people live in a paradigm. Whenever it's like that and it's crazy, my thought is to just let it go. More times than not, if I let it go, it comes back around. I'm not hassled and brooding over it. I tell myself, "Hey, how much time did I have with that instrument!" as opposed to thinking how bad I feel because it is gone. It's a hard one to work out but you'd better work it out, because it will take years off your life and turn you into some sad, self-pitying thing. My brother freaked out because he couldn't believe I did that. He wanted me to put pressure on that guy, but I said, "I don't know, man. Right now that guy's got pressure on him." I'd tried to find a comparable instrument and have to say that I have not found it.

Another story I'd have is that I was playing in Arizona when a young guy came in with his dad. He said that he knew I played this kind of guitar and he had an instrument that he had tried to take a blazing torch to in order to cut out a space. This was a Dobro, an old fiddleback grasp with the round holes and square crosses. This was an old, old, old guitar, like 1921. He had tried to take out the faceplate to put a pickup inside. It looked like someone had taken a can opener to it for all the sharp edges where he did the cutting and he was upset that he did this. The kid said, "I will trade you for any other guitar." We went back to the West coast, where I had a Martin 00-18 that I could never get the sound I wanted from it. We decided that he would put this Dobro inside a guitar case and send it up to me and I would swap it out with the Martin and send it back to him. I took this Dobro guitar down to the Dopyera Brothers and they were horrified to see what had been done to it. They cut that piece out, put a brass piece in and buffed it. They cleaned up that instrument so good that, when I walked into the shop, I walked right past my own guitar. Never in my life have I walked passed my own instrument. It had old patina to it, from when brass gets dull. There's a picture of me with it on the *Fuh Ya' Musica* album where I'm sitting there in a white suit, barefoot with this guitar.

John Hammond

Blues guitarist and songwriter John Hammond, the son of record producer John H. Hammond, has recorded with Jimi Hendrix, Eric Clapton, Dr. John and Duane Allman. He is a recognized blues scholar who hosted a 1991 U.K. television documentary *The Search for Robert Johnson*, the legendary Delta bluesman.

I met John and his wife, Marla, backstage at the First World Guitar Congress, where we did this interview. A year later, we caught up in New York City so I could write a cover story on John for *Acoustic Guitar* magazine. I had the chance to play the Stubbs guitar that he mentions here. John would play a riff, hand the guitar over and ask that I play it back exactly to prove that I got it. I realized he had two advantages — forty years of playing and larger hands.

I got my first guitar at Antioch College in 1960 from a girl named Carlotta Jones. I bought it from her for $10 — a Gibson J-100. I think they called it "The Sailor's Model," from the 1930s or '40s. It was an old guitar, black with white trim. It had a hole punched into the top to serve as a sound port, but this did not seem to alter the sound all that much. I thought it was a beautiful guitar. It

John Hammond, age seventeen. (*Courtesy John Hammond*)

had this great fingerboard, and this was the first guitar I learned to play, when I was seventeen. I was nineteen when I started playing professionally.

I'd have to say I was attracted to the guitar because it was for sale. I could afford it and it was right there. My roommate had a Martin 12-string guitar that was like a work of art. I was so reluctant to play his guitar that I bought the Gibson. I was basically an art student at the time and not particularly happy about being in school. Everybody seemed to have an acoustic guitar that they played at parties. I used to say to myself, "I could do that." I guess I took it a step further.

I don't think my family realized at first how serious I was. My mother was more supportive than my dad, but when my dad saw that I was actually making a living at playing, he eventually came around. My first musical inspiration has always been the music of Robert Johnson. I love blues in general and country blues became a passion for me in 1957, when I picked up an album called *The Country Blues*, a compilation of '30s masters like Leroy Carr, Scrapper Blackwell, Blind Boy Fuller, Blind Lemon Jefferson. And then Robert Johnson had one song on the album that galvanized me — it's not like I wasn't inspired by others but he was my main inspiration. The song was "Preaching Blues." Other artists who inspired me are Howlin' Wolf, Muddy Waters, John Lee Hooker and Little Walter Jacobs. They were truly motivating figures in my imagination.

I do not have my first guitar anymore. I went through about four other guitars before I got a 1947 Gibson country western model in 1967, once owned by Josh Graves of Flatt & Scruggs. And I played it for eighteen years until it became a little fragile.

What I love about a guitar is hard to explain in words. It's just something that has to chime inside of me. The two guitars I travel with today are a Stubbs acoustic guitar that was made in England and a 1935 National Duolian. The Stubbs guitar was made in 1992 by Vinnie Smith from Kendal, England. It has koa wood back and sides with an ebony fingerboard and a cedar top. It has a beautiful balance with a deep bass and a very strong high end. The hardest thing for me about the guitar is that I've been robbed twice on the road of all my instruments. It's why I've had so many guitars over the years, I think.

My first paying gigs were in the Los Angeles area, where I migrated in the spring of 1962. I had a job at a gas station and would travel to coffeehouses to audition on open mic nights. I was pumping gas one day, and a convertible Porsche drove up with a Martin D-45 in the back seat. The guy driving the guitar wore a big cowboy hat and told me to fill it up while he walked into the garage. When he came out, he found me ogling the guitar, and he asked if I played. I told him I did and he asked me to play a song. So I did. He said, "I can get you a gig." And he did, at a club called the Satire Club in South Gate, Los Angeles. It was my first paying gig. It turned out this man was Hoyt Axton, whom I eventually came to know very well. It was 1962, and the beginning of my career.

Seymour Duncan

Seymour Duncan is a legend among guitarists for his life's work in engineering critical elements of guitar tone and nuances within electric guitar pickups. He has manufactured custom pickups for artists like Jeff Beck, Peter Frampton, Eddie Van Halen and James Burton, to name a few.

My first guitar was a Sears Silvertone Jupiter 1423L model. I was twelve years old when I spotted this guitar among the pages of a Sears catalog that came in the mail. When the Christmas catalog arrived, I had started making endless drawings and doodles of this one guitar that looked like a Les Paul, though it was a Sears Silvertone. On Christmas Day, I saw a giant box standing in the corner and asked if I could open it. My family told me I had to wait and first open gifts sent by my uncles and aunts, which had been neckties and socks and all that. Finally, I was able to open up that one big box. I was in shock. My family had bought me an accordion.

I was distressed because I had been expecting a guitar. A neighbor who knew my mom had observed that I liked to watch *The Lawrence Welk Show*. I used to watch this weekly program for Neil LeVang and Buddy Merrill, the two guitar players on the show. My neighbor told my mother that since I was watching so much of *The Lawrence Welk Show*, I must really like the accordion, which is what Lawrence Welk played.

My uncle, Bid Furness, had a little acoustic guitar, which he let me strum on from time to time. The guitar was in his attic, so every time my family would visit him, he would bring it down and let me look at it. My dad's brother, who had an old Martin and a Dobro and played country music, he showed me my first D chord. He showed me how to alternate between the D and the A string by hitting the D note and the chord and then the A string and hitting the chord. That was actually my first experience with holding a guitar and figuring out how to place my fingers and gain calluses. The following Christmas, when I was thirteen years old, I finally received the Sears Silvertone. And I played it *every day*. They got me the little Silvertone model 1482 amplifier, too.

When I was thirteen, I made my own lap steel guitar out of an old dresser drawer, which was a nice piece of mahogany that I had pulled apart. The front piece was about an inch thick and this became the top part of my fingerboard. I mounted tuning keys to it and made an apparatus for the tailpiece. It had six strings and I tuned it to an E chord. I had recovered the tuning keys from an old, broken guitar that I found in the trash. I used to ride my bike around and pick up old radios and try to repair them when I was a little kid. I used to love that. Every Saturday, I'd get up at six a.m. and zip around the neighborhood before the trash men arrived. That is how I came across this broken guitar with the neck separated from the body and the body had been smashed. But I managed to salvage the keys. I made this lap steel guitar because I loved the group Santo & Johnny, who had made records called "Sleep Walk" and "Tear Drop." I remember around Christmas of 1963, they had a single called "Twistin' Bells." All of it was played on slide guitar and I wanted to play it. I no longer have this slide guitar. My dad's family might still have it back east, but I am not certain because that was a long time ago.

When I grew up, my uncle gave me two records. One was Jimmy Bryant and Speedy West. It was a little EP called *Two Guitars Country Style* and then the other record was by Chet Atkins. I used my allowance to buy a tape recorder so I could record the Neil LeVang and Buddy Merrill from *The Lawrence Welk Show*. I listened to The Ventures and Duane Eddy. Those two guys were probably the most influential on me because Jimmy Bryant and Speedy West were too far beyond what I could even play at that time. But The Ventures were playing songs with melodies in them and Duane Eddy was, too. The Ventures did "Walk, Don't Run" and they were playing songs that you could play a melody along to. I always like music that has a strong melody and it is one of the reasons why I enjoy instrumentals so much.

I did not get a whole lot of support from home about playing the guitar because I had another uncle who was a drummer and who was always getting himself into trouble for cheating on his wife and drinking a lot. Back in the '50s, many jazz musicians were involved heavily with drinking, women and drugs. Being part of the nightclub culture, I think musicians can develop a bad reputation. So there I was, this happy little kid, announcing that I wanted to become a guitar player and my relatives went, "Aaaaah, boy. Not again." They were worried. My dad said to me, "Seymour, if you ever get into trouble with drugs or wild women and drinking, I'm going to take your guitar away from you."

To me, the guitar was the most important thing that I had. I was an only child so the guitar was my role model. My dad was very understanding about how much I liked my guitar. They eventually came to see I was this straight kid who really just loved the guitar and made every effort to learn everything about it. The best thing for me was a report that I had to write for school when I was sixteen. Many of my classmates chose to write about their father's work, if he happened to be a policeman or else they wrote if they wanted to be a fireman or a farmer. I wrote about my guitar. I did an entire report on the guitar with drawings diagramming the function of each part. I wrote instructions on how the guitar was tuned and how to play a guitar chord. I also showed the teacher how to play a guitar chord. That was the first time in my life that I ever received an "A."

I used to write letters to the Fender guitar company all the time, and my family knew that I was getting letters back from Fender, and they said, "This little guy loves his guitar! He's getting these letters back from guitar companies answering his questions." I was very involved in wanting to learn more about the history of the instrument, so I would write Fender and ask them when the first Jazzmaster was made, the first Jaguar, the first Stratocaster — and they would send me back a complete list of all the years those guitars had first been made. I still have these letters. They were written to me by people like Bill Carson, who was one of the first who helped to design the Stratocaster for Leo Fender. For me, having all that history helped me in the future when I started writing guitar articles for *Vintage Guitar* magazine. My family came to realize and accept that I was really serious about the instrument, not only how to play it or performing, but the history of it, how it was made, what kind of wood was used and what pickups.

What I love about the guitar is how you can have your own personality

Seymour Duncan, age seventeen. (*Courtesy Seymour Duncan*)

when you play. Every guitar player has created their own style, and you learn to appreciate what other players are doing with their techniques, such as how they pick and how they strum and how they play their chords and what kind of strings they use. I would make note of amp settings and how the pickups were adjusted on their guitar. I always wanted to learn how to get different sounds out of the guitar.

I was so fortunate to have worked with Jimi Hendrix, Duane Eddy, and The Ventures, making pickups for them. All these artists that I grew up admiring, I wound up working for, which is just so incredible to me. I have listened to the work I have done with bands — I worked for Michael Sembello, who had a song called "Maniac," which was used in the film *Flashdance* and became song of the year. I worked on the *Thriller* album by Michael Jackson with a guy named David Williams, who was the guitar player who performed all the rhythms. I had made these new stack pickups and he was one of the first to use them. He played on "Beat It" and "Billie Jean," which is still one of the bestselling records of all time. I learned from playing guitar enough to know what other guitarists were describing of the sound they envisioned and hoped to conceive from their own guitars. I understand the guitar and I know how to play it and get different sounds from it. Having this ability allowed me to create different pickups for people. It's like its own language.

There are many people today who make their own pickups. They buy the parts in kits and put them together like constructing a model airplane, but they're not really manufacturing every component. We make every part. We create our own injection molds. We do our own stamping. We do our own designing of the pieces we use. We have thousands of pieces of slotwork that we use to make different pickups with and we designed them. And that is the difference between manufacturing and being a boutique hobbyist. I have wound so many pickups. We are making something like 30,000 pickups a year at the factory. Maricela Juarez and I in the customs shop are the ones doing all the custom fabrication. We do a lot of custom work for artists like The Eagles and Gloria Estefan and Chuck Berry and so many others.

I love playing guitar because of all the people I meet and the camaraderie we develop. The neatest thing for me about making guitar pickups is the connection I have with other guitar companies. Being able to make something for Fender or Gibson — I never thought I would be doing something that far out when I was a thirteen-year-old. So for me, I've been very honored and I've helped to write books for Fender and Gibson about all these artists.

It can be challenging at times with manufacturing because you want to be able to use the right material but sometimes we have issues with this because of all the regulations that exist. If we made something, say, in Mexico or Arizona, it would be okay. But when you're manufacturing in California, you are not allowed to use certain lacquers or paints because of certain restrictions. You want to make a neat product and lacquers are one of the best products for a guitar because they allow the wood to breathe. But so many polyester finishes are being used today, which makes it hard for the guitar to have a good sound because this is almost like having a plastic coating on top of the wood. Fender has a fantastic facility with a new center for people to visit. I respect what they are doing and feel proud that we make pickups for them, too.

When I heard a guitar sound, like "Walk, Don't Run" by The Ventures, for example, I was always trying to figure out what guitar they were playing. I would see photos of Bob Bogle, who was playing with The Ventures at the time, holding a Fender Jazzmaster so I figured that sound he was getting in that song came from a Fender Jazzmaster. I would put that idea together. Then I would watch Don Wilson from The Ventures, and he was always playing a Strat for the rhythm parts. So whenever I heard a rhythm guitar from The Ventures, I knew that was the sound of a Stratocaster. When I heard Duane Eddy play, I would recognize the sound of a Gretsch guitar with Gretsch pickups or HiLo'Tron pickups or DeArmond pickups, so I would put that together. When I heard James Burton playing together with Ricky Nelson, I knew that twang from James Burton's guitar was a Telecaster. I learned early on, when I heard something, what kind of guitar it was, at first. If I heard a sound, I would write a letter to a record company and try to find out what kind of guitar the artist was using. Usually, about fifty percent of the time, the record company would respond with an answer, which was so neat. I put all this information together so that when a guy would come to me and say, "I want to sound like James Burton or Ricky Nelson," I would say, "Okay, well then you need to play a Telecaster and this is the kind of pickup you would want for it."

When I was sixteen, I was playing a Saturday afternoon jam session at a club and at one point, I allowed someone to borrow my guitar. Somehow, they managed to get the high E string hooked under the bridge of the pickup, which really messed up the pickup so I had to rewind it. I had to figure out what to do, so I took the pickup with me to school. I put my pickup under the microscope in biology class so I could examine the damaged part. I could see that the wire inside the pickup had broken when the guitar string got snagged under the edge of the pickup. I proceeded to remove the wire turn by turn in order to arrive at the point of the breakage. I gave the wire to my uncle, who told me that it was forty-two-gauge plain enamel, which was the kind of wire that was used back then for Fender pickups. I got a spool of this wire and made my first winding machine when I was sixteen years old and subsequently got into learning how to make pickups.

My first official performance was at a cousin's wedding. I was fourteen years old and had a three-piece band called The Adventures. It was our clever homage to The Ventures and gave the message that we were curious and exploring new musical ideas. We maybe knew five songs — "Bulldog," by a band called The Fireballs; "The McCoy," by The Ventures; "Quite a Party," also by The Fireballs and one instrumental that I made up in the key of E that might have been called "Adventure." We played these songs over and over again for two hours and I made $3, which was a lot of money back then. I could buy ten sets of guitar strings with that.

When I turned sixteen, I bought my first Fender Stratocaster. I ordered it from a music store in Woodbury, New Jersey, and the Stratocaster at the time was a tremolo with a sunburst that cost $126. I had helped a neighbor clean out his garage and he gave me a coin, saying, "Son, here's a coin for you that you will really like to have some day." It was a 1793 half-cent, issued during the first year of the U.S. Mint. My uncle, who heard that I had this, offered me $100 for it. $100 for a coin had seemed like so much money to me. I couldn't even fathom how much money that was so I said, "Oh man, I guess, yeah." I knew I could buy a Fender Stratocaster with that kind of money. I put the $100 down on the guitar and borrowed the remaining $26 from my dad. The guitar came with a case, a strap and guitar chord manual. The first day I had this guitar, I took it to band practice. I had a band at the time called The Flintones, which was a nod to the cartoon. It is kind of a silly name but we had found it funny at the time. My bass player and I were going to show each other our instruments and trade off playing them. I handed him my guitar just as he handed me his bass, and we were not paying attention that our amplifiers inside the basement of our drummer's house only accommodated a two-prong cable. When we touched each other's guitars, we both were electrocuted. I dropped my guitar to the floor. He dropped his bass onto the floor. I always remember that it was like an omen to me not to let anyone borrow your instrument because it had felt as if the guitar was saying, "Don't give me to him!" We both got zapped in this hot, humid basement that did not have much air.

I've had so many great experiences with guitar when growing up. I knew Les Paul and Mary Ford when I was a little kid. Les was so kind to me, showing me what the pickups were about. This is what really inspired me to get involved with making pickups. Everybody I spoke to, I was asking how their guitar was set up and what the switches did on the guitar. Everybody was so kind and helpful to me, and that is why today I enjoy helping young kids and inspiring them to learn how to play guitar and learn how to do things. I think it is important to give back what has been given to me my whole life and I really appreciate all these young kids who are out there playing and practicing all the time. If I can do anything to help them get a better sound, that is what I am here for.

A Guitar on the Make

At an early age, I viewed the guitar as suspect because I associated it primarily with war-protesting hippies of Madison, Wisconsin, where my parents had attended school in the late '60s. Guitar as I knew it seemed to be a vehicle for protest or seduction, or a seductive protest. I did not have the insight to be able to articulate this at the time, other than to say, a piano felt grand sitting tall and proper in the corner, that a plastic whistle inside a box of Cracker Jacks was a lucky prize — but a guitar always felt like it had an ulterior motive outside the realm of music. A guitar was on the make.

My theory that people with guitars tend to have some *modus operandi* was confirmed when my mother and I moved, after her divorce, to my grandmother's Chicago rooming house when I was seven. A prospective tenant figured he could improve his odds by turning up at our front door with a pawnshop guitar. My grandmother, tough and discerning, grilled every renter who crossed our threshold. Because she had grown up on an Iowa farm during the Depression, she was steeped in austere frugality — with one exception. Her most outrageous and baffling expenditure had been a 1924 Apollo baby grand player piano, which sat in the front room, unused. She kept an enormous collection of player piano rolls stacked floor-to-ceiling in one narrow corridor of the house. She had purchased many of these rolls for a song with her sister from an estate sale in a California desert town, and they awoke the next day in an itching frenzy because the rolls had been teeming with bed-bugs, which, in hindsight, probably explained the great bargain.

I used to spy on these tenant interviews by crawling beneath the piano. I had a test of my own for them, to ascertain their rent-worthiness: I would push the pins from the underside of the keyboard to make it appear as if invisible fingers were taking a stroll. If the prospective tenant jumped, they flunked. One man, an itinerant musician from Hawaii, had been the first not to jump. He was slim, olive-skinned with jet-black hair, dressed neatly in khakis and a pressed white shirt.

I lay on my back under the great belly of the piano and listened to my grandmother chirp through her usual spiel. *No cooking utensils, no hot-plates, no hi-fis, no visitors.* She emphasized the word visitors with a certain delicacy and followed it with an abrupt cough. At some juncture, I pushed a series of key pins from underneath the piano. My grandmother jumped up, berating me to get out from under the piano before the entire thing collapsed and crushed me to death.

He unzipped the long, soft black case he'd brought with him that had been sitting at his feet. "I've seen you jumping rope out front," he told me. "I picked up this for you. Figured you might like it." For a guitar, it was odd-looking — homemade with a thick, U-shaped neck, a rainbow-stained back and grimy strings bowing away from a warped fret board. My first reaction was dismay because it suggested I was going to have to be one of THOSE people — up to something. And it was entirely up to me to figure out what.

Taking advantage of our stunned silence, this man seized the chance to express his admiration for the baby grand player piano. He caressed its keyboard and asked my grandmother if he could play it. She let him. He was only an ear-trained musician, he told us, hinting that we should not expect much. I noticed that in spite of his neatly dressed appearance, he had open and oozing sores all over his fingers. But my focus soon shifted to the astounding sound pouring out of the piano. When he started to sing, his voice filled the room and soared like a canopy of birds in flight. For a moment, I forgot where I was, and when he finished, his music soaked into my skin with a chill.

Not to be outdone, my grandmother pulled out a Scott Joplin piano roll manufactured by the Duolian Company and demonstrated how it snapped into place in a drawer that pulled out from under the keyboard. My grandmother flicked a tiny brass switch and stood back as a gust of air pushed through the piano and commenced the wheezy works and grinding gears. The old piano thundered out a loud ragtime melody as an impossible splay of ivory bobbed up and down all at once.

Before the last chord died away, this man had been granted the key to the basement room, #19. My grandmother considered herself the household expert when it came to music, though her knowledge of it seemed to begin and end in 1925. She sang a song called "Flat Foot Floogie with a Floy Floy" but liked to sing it as "Flat Foot *Floozie* with a Floy-Floy." Her other favorite was "I Don't Want to Set the World on Fire," and she had mixed admiration for Peggy Lee's "Is That All There Is?" Though she claimed to hate the song, saying it was too modern for her taste, I heard her singing it often enough that I couldn't resist breaking the reverie of her warble with my own hound-dog howl of the chorus. My grandmother tersely informed me I couldn't carry a tune if I tried, which my mother chimed in was no surprise since she couldn't, either. So I had better find a way to play this new guitar while keeping my mouth shut.

My mother reluctantly sent me off to a night class at an Evanston grammar school to learn chords from a college girl who taught us tunes about dead American rebels, like Jesse James, Bill Bailey, Tom Dooley and John Brown. After a few weeks, she recommended I study with her bearded boyfriend, a music student at Northwestern University. I met up with him at the school's ivy-covered practice hall known as The Beehive for the dissonant drone of heavy-footed pianists, belting trombone players and shrilly opera singers, all of them racing up and down their scales in a battle for supremacy between rest notes.

If I showed up early and found a practice room, I would read the graffiti left on the wall, spiraling riffs of debate on Philip Glass versus Steve Reich versus Arvo Pärt, followed by the virtues of sopranos versus mezzos, pianists versus violinists, who played their instruments best in bed, who didn't and why. These messages would start out with a biting spider of wit that attracted progressively stupider comments until all of it became painted over in white. If I showed up early and could not find a practice room I became a hallway freak show — the kid with the funny-looking guitar. Even the Italian janitor would ask me, "Bella bambina, let's see you do a G chord."

I learned to sight-read and, by the summer's end, my Northwestern student teacher sent me on to luthier Richard Bruné's studio where I studied with guitar instructor Len Novy. Bruné's studio was built to look like a white-plastered, Spanish hacienda, with ironwork grilles and an arched wooden door, and it smelled of sawdust and cedar inside. If I arrived early, Bruné would show me his latest project and pull down enormous sheets of cedar and spruce to point out their wood grain and color. I tinkered on his latest harpsichord and admired the ivory doily inlay of one of his guitars that was going to be shipped off to the Smithsonian. During my lesson, my teacher would spend the first few minutes answering his phone or else discussing his crush on Olivia Newton-John in *Grease,* the moment she breaks into singing "Hopelessly Devoted to You." Then we'd finally launch into the intricacies of a Sor study while the last minutes ticked off under the orange glow of his prominently placed Westclox alarm clock. Two years later, with the help of Sonia Michelson, I was playing "Recuerdos de la Alhambra" by Tarregá, études by Brouwer and Villa-Lobos.

Room #19 didn't stay around long enough to see any of this. Three months into his time with us, he set the house on fire with a sock balled up inside an electric popcorn machine and disappeared in the middle of the night. I smelled the smoke and woke my family, who then roused the twenty-one other tenants and shepherded everyone to safety through the thick velvety black plumes of smoke spewing into the back hallway. Firemen in masks with tanks on their backs stampeded through the front and back doors, shouting to each other as they tromped through the house, swinging their axes at the windows and shattering them. In the panic, the one possession I had thought to grab had been my warp-necked guitar.

Eli Kassner

Eli Kassner established the guitar program at the University of Toronto and the Royal Conservatory of Music in Toronto. His more notable classical guitar students include filmmaker Atom Egoyan, Liona "The First Lady of the Guitar" Boyd and Norbert Kraft, who is the producer of the Naxos label's guitar collection.

To tell you the truth I do not exactly remember when I received my first guitar. I was probably about seven years old. My oldest sister played mandolin and wanted an accompaniment so my parents bought a cheap little guitar with nylon strings. I went to a local teacher around the corner who did not know much about playing the guitar. That is how I started learning the guitar, by learning to play chords, perform accompaniment and read music. I had that guitar for only a very short time.

I stopped and started with playing. As a kid, one will have these fluctuations in interests. But then I had to leave my parents in Vienna, Austria, to flee from the Nazis and I had no guitar. Just before I left, my parents bought me another guitar, which I took with me on my back.

I did start on the violin, and I had a quarter size violin at four years old but, again, it was an issue of time, money and teachers. When I came to Israel, there was a very good violinist in the kibbutz who saw that I had talent, good pitch and intonation. In the kibbutz, we had a very famous cellist, Joachim Stutschewsky. I played Mendelssohn for him, and he asked me to come to visit him in Tel Aviv, which I did a year later. He gave me a violin, which I've had all these years. But my love has always been the guitar.

The sound of the guitar is what attracted me. I loved the harp as a kid and also the cello, but with the guitar, I knew I had the instrument that could emulate both of these sounds. The guitar is cheaper, more portable. The harp is too big. I played guitar all those years but not seriously — I just played. The one really good classical guitar I had, I bought once I arrived in Canada in 1950 and started working at a music store. I was playing guitar as people browsed through the sheet music, and one man came up to me and asked, "Would you like to teach me that?" And I said, "Well, if you'd like to be my guinea pig, I'll be happy to teach you." So I was teaching him and, before long, I had twenty students. It did not take long for word to spread quickly, and teaching became a source of income.

I had no family left once I left Vienna — all of them had been killed. They were shipped to Russia and executed there. Once I came to Canada, I started studying the guitar seriously and attending the guitar societies. The guitar society had Segovia come every year to play, and at one party he asked me study with him at Santiago de Compostela. I went a couple of times. He was definitely my idol and inspiration, but then I'd also had the good luck to get in touch with other people whom I could study with, like Ida Presti. At that time there were no teachers available so readily, so one learned and picked up what one could. There was no such thing as a school or university. Teaching was a very neglected and unavailable commodity. Some great players became so scared that you might lift secrets from them.

Whenever I hear the guitar, it gives me great pleasure. When I went to Segovia, Bream or Presti concerts, to hear them play was a great experience. I met Odair and Sergio Assad at a party in Rio de Janeiro. Sérgio Abreu held the party. The Assads were such young boys and their playing was fantastic. It's an ongoing thing. I still derive great joy from listening to my students.

I always knew the guitar was my calling.

Paco Peña

Flamenco guitarist Paco Peña has had a forty-year career that includes sharing the stage with Jimi Hendrex. Peña found a spare moment during the First World Guitar Congress at Towson University in Maryland to do this interview in the front lobby of the Marriott Hotel, with the coffee cart perking aromatically fresh brew nearby and giant cicadas buzzing ferociously outside in the sultry summer heat.

I suppose I had about three first guitars. The first memory of a guitar that I have is maybe from when I was six or seven years old. My brother, who was older than me, had a guitar, and this was the first one that I picked up to tinker with. It was a big Miguel Rodriguez guitar from Córdoba. I had wanted to do what my big brother was doing.

Very soon after that, in school, I encountered a group of kids playing music. Some of the music they were playing was melodic, like the *bandurrias,* and folk-type of music. I wanted to play so the teacher allocated a guitar to me. It was a horrifying instrument, very dark and very cheap, with steel strings. I didn't know better, and I was really keen about wanting to learn. It was a remarkable time for me because the teacher encouraged me. We did not have much money so I had to wait until I was eighteen before I finally had a guitar of my own, a Manuel Reyes from Córdoba. It was amazing. Emotionally, I suppose, I feel attached to those three guitars in different stages.

For me, the guitar was the normal thing to play — not only was it in my home but it was the instrument that was most accessible in my community. A lot of other kids might have chosen violin or piano but I did not belong to that class — we were not a cultured family. Flamenco is a music medium much more popular in poorer communities.

I was so fascinated by the guitar. I used to spend hours and hours and hours playing it, late at night doing the *patio* there, just for myself. My ambitions were not ambitions, as such, but dreams. I did not know much about flamenco or any other type of music, but I used to watch shows featuring parties with a singer and guitar. I used to dream someday about the possibility of me being famous like those successful people in music. I was just a kid. I was dreaming, never thinking it was something I would do. It was fantasy.

My school was very interesting because we did not just play flamenco — flamenco just was not done in that group of kids — we played light Spanish music in the folk tradition. It was rather more about learning to play harmony and subtlety than playing guitar. There was melody, second voices, third voices, accompaniment and a discovery about the arrangement of music. It was very constructive.

I started teaching soon after that. We were very poor, so I started teaching groups like that. I was about twelve or thirteen years old time and earning a little bit of money for it. When I really fell in love with flamenco, I certainly had great idols — Niño Ricardo, for one, for his great emotional output. I looked up to him like all the young kids did from my generation. Also, in town, there were other people who were able players in town and we looked up to them as well.

Obviously, my mother was very concerned with my education and hoped I would not neglect it. Everybody wanted me to travel and play with their group, and more often than not, I would be out late. So my mother was very concerned I would be working with the right people and that I would not waste too much time given the other things I had to do, like school. We were a family of nine children. I had one other brother and the rest were sisters, so my mother was working. She owned a market and she earned the bread for us. But she was also very active in looking after us.

My family felt my guitar playing was cute and wanted me to play with them. There was concern also that life had to be kept in check because I used to go out and play in different directions with flamenco companies traveling to little villages around Córdoba with flamenco companies and then bigger places like Madrid. I was really quite young but I think they appreciated me because I was clever with the guitar and my playing made people happy.

Music is beautiful. It is a beautiful feeling when you can express and move people, even move yourself, when things are moving right with your playing. Being a professional, as I am, doing what I like to do — to sit on the stage and have the responsibility to transmit these emotions and feelings to people and see that it works — is very, very rewarding, indeed. This is the aim of it, to become emotionally involved and touched to the very fiber.

Of course, I have had moments where I feel I have not mastered all that I hope for — one day I would *love* to be able to play the guitar! It is very demanding to be on top of technical difficulties. Those are terrible moments, really. There is faith on my part that things will get better and usually, they do.

I like all kinds of music so I am tempted to go off into many different directions. It is a challenge, yet it is softened, because I do not have to be a professional in any other form but for flamenco. So my true challenge comes from within world of music, and for that I like to be myself and have something to say. I make sure that shows are choreographed and I arrange a portion of the theatrical production. I look forward to making a convincing contribution.

Solo guitar was not done where I grew up. Solo flamenco guitar came later. You could play it but nobody was interested. I was very young when a company came in from Madrid — it was not a flamenco company but a company of young, beautiful girls. They did some dancing, humor — a variety show, essentially. They wanted me to play a flamenco act with a girl singer. We traveled together through Andalucía, sometimes in atrocious conditions. That was memorable because I was young and surrounded by these young, beautiful girls in the company, you can imagine. It was a good moment. Also, I got the chance to see places I had never visited before.

Once, I was to play a concert using a beautiful guitar and, for some reason, the top of the empty case fell onto the guitar and broke it just minutes before my program. It left a dramatic crack. This had been a brilliant guitar, my first real guitar, the Reyes. Thank god I was actually wise enough not to say anything. I played with a terrible-sounding guitar and made the best of it. I did not tell anyone that it was broken because I was used to a really good-sounding instrument and this guitar lost a lot of sound with that big crack. It was a terrible moment. However, I went through with the concert. At the end, I said, "You must excuse my sound. It's not really as good." Had I not done that, a lot of people would have been disappointed. I felt strongly about saying the quality of sound had been my fault rather than blame this flawless instrument.

Pat Martino

Jazz icon and guitarist Pat Martino was faced with relearning to play the guitar and re-establishing his career after undergoing surgery in 1980 for a nearly fatal brain aneurysm. A recording artist for the Prestige, Muse and Warner Bros. labels, Martino is renowned for his fusion of avant-garde jazz, rock, pop and world music played in the bop idiom.

My first guitar was purchased by my father from a pawnshop in Philadelphia. I was twelve years old at the time, and it was a child-sized guitar. It was not really a serious instrument. In fact, my father bought it for me to see if I really was interested. He said, "If you can do something with this, then I will get you a serious guitar." This guitar had no name on it, but in two weeks, my father bought me a Les Paul Standard.

My father was a guitar player and he really loved guitar music. So I guess before I was really even conscious, I was absorbing Eddie Lang and Django Reinhardt. Their playing filled my environment — I was surrounded by it. My first intention with playing the guitar, as it is for every child, was to become well known. Children want to be noticed. I would think that was my first intention, as any child. This brought me to the music business.

Pat Martino, Bobby Rydell, Joe Lano. (*Courtesy Pat Martino*)

After so many years and the events that took place within those years, I became an established musician in the jazz community and suddenly I forgot all of it, including my guitar playing skills. I'd had a brain operation for an aneurysm, and when I had to relearn the instrument — my intentions were totally different. My intentions were totally focused on one thing, as they are today. That is *now*, the moment: to be able to enjoy my life. That is what it finally evolved into.

My father was always very happy about my playing the guitar. My mother was a little disappointed. She was very scholarly. She would have been happier if I was involved with education, as she had been a teacher in Italy. My father was the happiest, though, because to him, my playing was a dream come true. I did not really have a teacher — I've always had a basic understanding of the instrument that was innate, almost like this is a second life and the instrument is an old friend. I never had any trouble with it. In fact, being self-taught, the instrument revealed itself to me. Due to that innate intuition I had of how the guitar should be played, when I was brought to certain individuals for guidance in those early years I wound up studying *them*, not particularly what they were teaching. I learned faster, playing my way. When I would return for a lesson, I would have it together and they would be under the impression that I did my study and that I'd learned from it. I did what I did so that I could continue the social interaction with them. The music was secondary to that potential.

I was studying their character. I was studying the person and seeing how they survived and how they made a living doing this. I was envious, as a child, of the adult. The last teacher I had studied with, as a teenager, was Dennis Sandole, and my observation of him had been even more intense because I was interested in why he had a Van Gogh on the wall. I was interested in why there was a piano in the studio and why the guitar was there up against the wall in a corner, covered with dust. I was interested in why he always wore a black suit and a black tie with a white shirt. I was interested in why he always wanted his payment to be placed in a glass on top of the piano and why he never wanted to touch it. I was interested in things like that. As far as what he'd instructed me, I couldn't read it, primarily because his handwriting was similar to a doctor's.

The initial joys I felt about playing my guitar as a child is something every child feels. It is the reason children feel happy: it's playfulness. I had always been interrupted by one adult or another saying, "Stop playing and do your homework." This happens for every child as preparation and training for the system that is in play within our culture. The enjoyment came from the same reason I was happy playing — that I was interrupted. Once I went to New York at the age of fifteen, I came back to playing as I had been as a child — with no interruptions. That's why I left school.

Every time you play, there is always a problem. Even today we had a problem. There is always a problem with sound checks. It is something that is separate from the ecstasy of collective rapport. In fact, there is an elusive expectation, and every time, expectation will lead to disappointment. So that is a challenge in itself. It is an ongoing challenge that never ends. It reveals the polarity of reality itself — to prepare for something that is not, in total, communication as it would be, prior to itself taking place. As you saw for yourself today, we just completed the sound check one more time. It's done every time. So you get a general idea of what you would like it to be, with the hope that when all of the people come to hear you play, then that will get close to what you'd really love it to be. Sometimes it works, sometimes it doesn't. But I think it is due to expectation. I think *all* challenges and all of the impacts of everything that takes place, takes place similarly to that. Even when I had my operation — there were many things that took place. It is very difficult to pinpoint any one of them, especially now because that was the past and I really don't think too much about the past. The only thing I really find interesting is the present. Now. The moment.

Bob Margolin

"Steady Rollin'" Bob Margolin served as a backing musician for Muddy Waters from 1973 to 1980. He has also performed with Pinetop Perkins and is a columnist for *Blues Revue* magazine.

My younger sister started taking guitar lessons and my folks bought a $30 Stella guitar from her teacher in 1964. I picked it up and said, "I can play this," and I started taking lessons too. Not for long, though — they weren't teaching what I wanted to play. I was fifteen years old at the time.

From 1957 on, I listened to the radio and the wide variety of pop songs of it offered. It was Chuck Berry's guitar playing that really made me want to pick up the guitar. I also appreciated The Beatles and then the guitar heroes — first Mike Bloomfield, then Eric Clapton and then Jimi Hendrix. A few years later, I started listening to the blues intensely.

Muddy and Jimmy Rogers were my main inspirations but I've also been strongly influenced by Robert Lockwood Jr., Hubert Sumlin, Magic Sam and Luther Tucker. For slide guitar — Tampa Red, Robert Nighthawk and Earl Hooker. Past Chicago Blues players: T-Bone, B.B., Freddie and Albert King,

Albert Collins. Among modern guitarists, who inspire me, I would have to name Jimmie Vaughan, Ronnie Earl, John Mooney, Derek Trucks and Junior Watson. For acoustic guitar: Robert Johnson and Lonnie Johnson. For rock: I still love Chuck Berry and Scotty Moore and Carl Perkins. As you can see, blues on a guitar is what moves me.

My family was very supportive. I imagine some guitarists have families that discourage them, and that's very sad but understandable, as it's not a pursuit that brings in a lot of money, except to a few at the top.

Bob Margolin, age sixteen.
(*Courtesy Bob Margolin*)

Guitar playing and the music itself are sensually exciting. Having a gig go well feels great. I've also found that having a tone on the guitar and/ or amp that feels right inspires better playing. If I have any challenge with the guitar, it's in making the best music I can. I have to play my best possible each time. When I was in Muddy's band, there was a time near the beginning when he let me know with looks from the bandstand when my playing was not pleasing him. I tried to get him to show me what he wanted and one night after a performance, I followed him back into his room with my guitar and asked him to play it for me. He wouldn't do it on the guitar, but he tried to describe it and sing it at me while I fumbled around on my guitar. In sympathy, he told me that trying to play it right would "hurt like being in love." Most guitarists will understand that.

I've played in bands since I was in high school. Toward the end of my college years, I was in a band that was starting to work often and I found that my gigs were conflicting with my school. The bass player in the band, who was a year older but a lot wiser, advised me that if there wasn't time to do both well I should at least choose a deliberate priority. For me, that priority was music, and from that point on I judged every course of action by whether it would lead me to have a good time on the bandstand. This attitude didn't come from a gig or a performance directly but from trying to understand myself. It was an easy choice because those gigs gave me so much pleasure that I knew I wanted to pursue playing more.

My guitar story is about a lost love: the first really bluesy guitar I had was a '50s Les Paul Special that I bought used in 1968. A friend refinished it beautifully. I loved the sound of that guitar, even though it was so heavy that in '71, when I was playing six sets a night in bars, it was making my left shoulder lower than my right. One night, someone broke into my apartment and stole it. I still dream about that guitar.

Richard Thompson

Born in Notting Hill, London, Richard Thompson is a well-known British songwriter, highly regarded for his acoustic and electric guitar-playing techniques. He was named for his service to music on Queen Elizabeth's 2011 New Year Honours List as an Officer of the Order of the British Empire.

My father was a policeman in the Metropolitan Police Force in London. He worked in the West End where all the music shops are located, along Charing Cross Road and Denmark Road. For the last fifty years this area has been full of music shops. One of my dad's old army buddies was the manager of a shop called Lew Davies, and he gave my father a nylon-string Spanish guitar to bring home since it had been part of inventory broken in transit to the shop. It was a pretty basic, nasty cheap model. My father was a fairly good carpenter so he repaired it with the idea that he was going to play it. Yet he did not really get around to playing it. My older sister was going to play it but she did not really get around to it, either.

The guitar was just sitting there so I had a go because I really liked guitars and I loved the idea of rock 'n' roll. The guitar for me was a seductive thing, so I started to play it. I then started to play together with my friend, and

Richard Thompson (right), with his bandmate Malcolm Fuller and Richard's sister Perri playing his second guitar. (*Courtesy Richard Thompson*)

together we had formed a little band of two guitars, bass and drums when I was twelve years old. I'd been asking for a guitar since I was about five years old but instead, I'd received all sorts of toy versions, like really bad plastic ukuleles. My parents did not believe I was serious about the guitar.

Even though my father was a bad amateur guitar player, he'd been playing dance music and jazz since the 1930s and he had great records, including recordings of Les Paul and Django Reinhardt. So on the one hand, I grew up listening to his music and on the other, the stuff that grabbed me was my sister's records. She was buying rock 'n' roll records. I'd thought that was the coolest stuff, to hear Scotty Moore playing on Elvis Presley records, Buddy Holly, Duane Eddy, Cliff Gallup playing with Gene Vincent and Hank Marvin and the Shadows. Hank got such a great sound out of a Fender.

This is the stuff we wanted to play as kids — this was my dream at age twelve. My parents had liked it at first that I played the guitar, and I did have classical guitar lessons for a year. These lessons were great because they shoved me up a lot of new avenues and gave me a lot of possibilities. When I was playing guitar a bit more loudly at sixteen, my parents were not so keen on that. I think this was really frustrating for my father, who loved music and loved the guitar — but he did not like The Who. I think it took my parents a while to resign themselves to the fact that I was a musician.

I think any instrument is a voice, not unrelated to the human voice. You try to find a tone and a sound that expresses the voice you want. It becomes a joyous process to be able to make these sounds and play these notes and summon up these emotions, seemingly out of the ether. Music is such a strange, elusive thing. It's not like architecture. You can easily see the steps that go into building a skyscraper, such as starting with pouring a cement foundation — but, with music, the construction process is a bit slipperier and trickier.

For me the more challenging aspects of playing were with the acoustic guitar as opposed to the electric. I had not played onstage solo when I started playing at folk clubs in the early '70s. I had to find a way of being more orchestral on the acoustic guitar, and this is where my classical training became very useful. I used alternate tunings to make the guitar sound bigger. I obtained a new classical guitar of a German make with a mahogany top after that first guitar, as my parents took pity on me for struggling with that first Spanish guitar. I had this German guitar until I was eighteen years old, when I obtained a proper acoustic steel-string, made by the English maker John Bailey, who was well known in the mid-1960s. He had made guitars for The Incredible String Band and Jimmy Page.

I was thirteen years old when I had my first performance and we were opening for another band at St. Aloysius High school, a Catholic high school in London. We were really bad — the audience threw things at us. In fact, it had been so traumatic that I've blocked out what it was we had played past "Twist and Shout."

I was walking along Charing Cross Road past a music shop when I was nineteen years old. I saw a Gibson 120T in the window, a thin hollow-body guitar with f-holes and a big plastic scratch plate. I'd thought this would be fantastic to have, as I was into playing slide guitar. I paid about £75 for it, which was a small fortune at the time. I took it home with me and started using it to play gigs.

When we were driving home from a gig one evening, the back doors of the van opened unexpectedly. And of all the instruments to fall out, my guitar went out the back. The driver immediately realized something had happened so he stopped the van and hopped out to retrieve it. But it was already gone. Another car had come down the road and someone had grabbed the instrument before they took off. This guitar was insured so I bought another Gibson 120T from the same shop and paid another £75 for it. Almost immediately, this guitar was stolen from my dressing room. I realized I was cursed and doomed. I was not going to bother to get another guitar of that same make ever again. Had I gone through this three times in a row, I might have had to go into therapy.

Steve Howe

British guitarist Steve Howe is known for his guitar playing with English progressive rock group Yes. Gibson guitars produced a Steve Howe Signature
ES-175 guitar in his honor in 2002.

At Christmas 1959, I was given my first guitar. My pestering of my parents had
started two years earlier, and finally they gave in as they began to believe that
I really was going to take it seriously. A week before Christmas my Dad had
taken me to King's Cross, an area of North London that was fifteen minutes
from our home in Holloway. "Freemans" was the name of the shop, I recall.
There were many different styles of guitars on display. A Spanish guitar did
not fit the bill, nor did a flat top folk guitar. An electric guitar was unthinkable,
mostly due to the anticipated amplifier and the noise levels. I chose an archtop
acoustic guitar, which seemed to catch my eye. It was from Germany but not
made by Framus. I do not remember a maker's name, only that it was brown
with plain cream plastic tuners and it had f-holes.

Although rock 'n' roll was certainly one reason I desired a guitar, I had
imagined that one of the steps I would need to take was to become a dance

band guitarist! I had spotted these "slaves to the rhythm" and enjoyed the syncopated strumming they had to maintain along with the occasional guitar breaks they were given. I liked the concept in these bands where there was only one guitar, one bass, a drummer and then the rest of the musicians. The real action seemed to come from this tight unit called the rhythm section. I'd been listening to rock guitar for two years before that, as well as musicians like Les Paul, brass bands and war music. But rock 'n' roll seemed to reach out to me. I got more into The Shadows, particularly the instrumental aspect. I was learning from listening to Hank Marvin and Duane Eddy. I was entirely ear-trained, never forced to take a lesson but thought I'd like a lesson if I could.

The only book that helped me learn about music was the Eric Kershaw dance band chord book. I studied it long and hard, but I never could get along with method tutor books. Method books always said, "You are now ready for the next page," but I wasn't! At the time, no teachers seemed to be around so I drew what I could from the players around in Holloway, yet the mystery of the fingerboard layout and the potential of what one might do with more knowledge, appeared to be beyond reach.

So I set about learning as many of the chords as I could remember the names of like c Major 7 + 5, changing to f diminished flat 9. This was an education I welcomed, unlike school. There were usually three inversions for each chord as the shape got higher up the fingerboard. My first guitar sounded at home doing this sort of music study, and this method of study was to influence my style throughout my career.

As far as my family goes, I suppose at first my playing was irritating or a strange misconception, as I would play along with records. My brother had played clarinet but gave it up, mainly because our family was living in a small flat in London and my brother and I shared the same bedroom. By the time I was nineteen, they got used to me being there and practicing "Tea for Two" until gradually, something started to gel.

I remember getting a Chet Atkins record, sitting at home with the guys and remarking, "This *can't* be one guitarist!" There was no overdubbing. We were in awe. Same with Scotty Moore, who played with Elvis Presley. I was sixteen years old when I first saw Albert Lee play. He used to play at the Ronnie Scott Jazz Club, and I'd seen Wes Montgomery playing there with a smile on his face. Later I met Chet Atkins, Segovia and Steve Morrison was friendly, too. All these people get around the guitar in different ways.

I often refer to acoustic guitars as the starting point that I will return to, as

I write, arrange, practice and prepare music on one still. I kept my first guitar until it got lost around 1968 after it had suffered the indignity of having pickups crudely screwed to it and being decorated with colorful images of "flower power" during 1967! It just disappeared as I began collecting other guitars. Now I use a Gibson L-4C as my archtop acoustic guitar.

Like any "first" in your life, you never forget it. In my mind's eye, I can still visualize that first guitar, even though it was quite inferior and unyielding. Perhaps the same term used for our first car, an NSU RO 80, might apply to that guitar — it was just a "Beautiful Lemon."

Peter Frampton

From Beckenham, England, Peter Frampton was eighteen years old when he joined the band Humble Pie. His fifth solo album, 1976's *Frampton Comes Alive!*, which features his famed talk box guitar effect, has turned platinum six times, making it one of the top-selling live records in history. His instrumental album *Fingerprints* won a 2006 Grammy Award for Best Pop Instrumental Album.

I was eight years old when I got my first guitar but, before that, I played my grandmother's banjolele, which was a small, ukulele-sized version of the banjo with four strings on it. Christmas 1957 is when Santa brought me a guitar. It was a cheap 6-string, steel-stringed guitar that my father bought from a local music store. (Yes, I was onto Santa Claus by then.)

The first people who inspired me were ones I saw on TV, Americans like Buddy Holly and Eddie Cochran. I was into the guitarist/singers and not interested in the singers who just stood there at the mic. I liked lead guitarists, like Hank Marvin, who was the lead in The Shadows. They were The Beatles before The Beatles came along.

I learned to play mostly by ear until I was about eleven or twelve years old.

Peter Frampton's first electric guitar, a Hofner Club 60, bought in or around 1960. Peter would have been ten years old. (*Courtesy Peter Frampton*)

That's about the time my family noticed I was becoming obsessed with the guitar and they figured, "You might as well do it right, then, with some lessons. I had classical guitar lessons for four years, which I did not like, if only because it took time away from my learning rock solos. At the time, classical guitar seemed a bit pedantic and uninteresting and I was not paying much attention, though I wish now that I had, because it did help me broaden my knowledge of the guitar — and I still use classical techniques today. The pieces I learned in classical guitar had Italian-named composers, which I forget, but I could still play them for you.

It was during these lessons with Miss Graham — god, I still remember her name — in Bromley, South London, where I grew up, that I met another one of her students, Terry Nicholson, who would become the bass player for our band, The True Beats. We hit it off right away, sharing the same taste in music. He introduced me to Roy Orbison's music and more. We also played some songs by The Shadows, like "Apache."

I met all these other people of like mind, a bunch of other musos — it was great to see how many other people were into music and we formed our first band, the True Beats, within a couple of weeks. We played a combination of surf music, like The Ventures and The Shadows, *The Good, the Bad and the Ugly* theme and everything Elvis. Then The Beatles hit and changed everything — they just ruined it for us, because now we had to sing! The True Beats did well enough to capture the attention of a few London agents who were interested in taking the band pro. My dad, a schoolteacher, didn't see eye to eye with the other parents of the bandmates, who basically saw the opportunity as a leap to stardom. He said to me that I had to finish school. I was only twelve years old. (The rest of the band had been between the ages of fourteen and sixteen and they were nearly done with school.) I was not going to argue with my dad, so I dropped out of playing to finish school instead.

There was a television program at the time called *Ready Steady Go!*, which had a *Star Search*–type format called *Ready Steady Win!*. The True Beats made it onto that program and won. I think they might have had an album, too. But they never broke out beyond that. (Did my dad have the right idea taking me out of the band, you ask? Come to think of it, if I'd stayed, they most likely would have had a hit!)

What I love about the guitar — where to start? It's an extension of my hands. Ever since my formative years through adolescence, I've seen the guitar as an escape. It kept me occupied. I didn't realize it at the time, but I played guitar instead of dating, let's say. I was uncomfortable around other people and, really, the guitar is what I knew best, so I was not going to let go of that. I enjoy playing and cannot imagine *not* playing. In fact, I play more now than I did at other times because I realize this enjoyment I get from playing. It's a gut feeling, a pleasant twinge that comes from just picking up the guitar.

Of course, when I was ten years old, I was obsessed with getting an electric guitar. I would do nothing but doodle pictures of them on my books during class. I was eating, sleeping and breathing the guitar. I have small hands, so I prefer a thinner guitar neck. I do not have the left hand stretch as easily as people with longer fingers do, so I've had to work on that. I've had to make changes and modifications. Django Reinhardt played with a supreme handicap — he had two usable fingers and his thumb. Apparently there'd been a fire in his caravan and he raced in to rescue his wife and child. His leg was burned the worst and his left hand was withered, with his little finger and ring finger paralyzed. What he did was shift and at least press down with these fingers. I listen to Reinhardt's music every day. I'll be taking my daughter to school and running around doing errands with Django Reinhardt playing on my iPod.

My first show, as I recall, was when I was eight years old. It was at the end of the school year and I was a Cub Scout. I had already won my badge from passing the musical proficiency test by playing my guitar, and I was asked to be an accompanist at the local Ed Sullivan–type variety show that was mainly put on for our parents. I said yes and cut a deal with them to give me my own spot to play a couple numbers at the end of the first half of the program. I played my two numbers and they went very well, to say the least. So I stepped forward into the mic and said, "Seeing as you like me so much, I will play you another — one that I wrote myself."

Now, I cannot tell you the title of what I played, just that I wrote it and my mother helped me with the lyrics, which had something to do with falling water or a waterfall. The audience loved it — here was this precocious eight year old — meanwhile they were giving me the hook from the wings, jerking their thumbs and whispering sharply that I had to get me off. But it was a resounding success.

My guitar story is sweet and sour. When I played with Humble Pie in '69 in San Francisco, supporting The Grateful Dead, I was playing a Les Paul Gibson SG, a solid-body guitar. I had recently swapped it for a semi-hollow body Gibson but found out the hard way that semi-acoustics played at a high level give a lot of feedback, especially when turned up for a solo. Nothing came out of my guitar but a *waaaaaah-waaaaaaah* sound. Needless to say, it was very frustrating.

After a show, a guy named Mark Mariana came up to me and said, "I love your playing, and I couldn't help notice your little problem."

"Yes, thank you very much," I said, muttering, "my little problem, indeed."

He told me, "I've got a Les Paul that I've been doing some work on. I've sent it back to Gibson and had a three-pickup custom put on there." It was gorgeous, like something out of Smokey Robinson & the Miracles. He let me play it for a show, and it was like this guitar had been made for me. I met him for breakfast at a coffee shop the next morning. "I don't want to seem crass after all the work you've put into this guitar," I told him, "but would you be willing to sell it?"

He looked me in the eye and said no. "I'm not selling the guitar, sorry. I am going to *give* it to you."

This is the guitar I used on *Frampton Comes Alive!* and on all my solo albums from '69 through '80. This guitar fit me like a glove — not O.J.'s glove! My only other guitar was a '55 red Fender that I used on "Show Me the Way."

During the '80s we did a tour of South America through Argentina and Brazil. In Caracas, Venezuela, we had a mini-riot during our visit, which was unpleasant. But then we had a day off before going to Panama. Because we had this day off, our instruments were placed on a cargo plane and the band flew separately. Prior to this, we had been traveling with everything together on one plane.

The plane carrying my guitars and the entire stage crashed upon take-off, killing the pilot, the co-pilot and the loading guy. Needless to say, given the loss of these men's lives, the loss of the guitars cannot be compared.

I tried playing other Les Pauls, but they were not the same. It was not until I moved to Nashville during the '90s that I started hanging out at Gibson and they asked if I would like to have a custom guitar built in my name. I thought they were kidding me! Mike McGuire over there is my hero because he helped build *exactly* the same guitar like the one I'd had. We worked together on this for a year. It's not a cheap guitar because it comes from their custom division. Basically, I can fly to Paris or London, walk into a shop, pick up this guitar and it is the exact same guitar. We are currently working on a second, more afford-able Peter Frampton model guitar, which is like a Les Paul Junior with different pickups from my original model.

Frederic Hand

Classical guitarist and composer Frederic Hand has performed the guitar music in the Academy Award–winning film *Kramer vs. Kramer* with Meryl Streep and Dustin Hoffman as well as the film *This Boy's Life*, starring Leonardo DiCaprio and Robert De Niro.

When I was six years old, my mother took me to see Andrés Segovia perform at Town Hall in New York City. I was totally captivated by the experience, enough to announce immediately after the concert that when I grew up, I wanted to become a classical guitarist. I asked for a guitar for my birthday. Though my mother was pleased with my enthusiastic response, my request for a guitar was not taken seriously. My seventh birthday came and went . . . with no guitar.

I asked again a year later and this time, I was offered a ukulele. My parents, being frugal, reasoned that a ukulele was less of an investment for an eight year old. I refused the ukulele and kept my sights on obtaining a guitar. Finally, as I approached my ninth birthday, three years after initially hearing Segovia, my parents gave in. My mother had been singing in an amateur chorus whose conductor was studying classical guitar. He recommended a three-quarter-size guitar made by Tatay.

Frederic Hand, age ten, sitting on a park bench in New York City. Says Hand, "Everyone who sees this photo thinks the man is my dad but he had just been some stranger sitting there, listening to me play." (*Courtesy Frederic Hand*)

On a bright September day in 1956, my mother and I took the subway from Brooklyn to the Spanish Music Center in Manhattan. The proprietor, a man named Gabriel Oler, picked out a guitar for me with a price tag of $90. I don't know what $90 in 1956 would be worth today, but for my family, this was an expensive purchase for a nine-year-old. It was impressed upon me this was a real musical instrument, not a toy. As we were leaving the store, Mr. Oler looked me in the eye and said something extremely odd. Not knowing at all of my interest in baseball, he said, "Now don't put a baseball bat through that guitar." My mother and I laughed and headed back to Brooklyn.

Two weeks later, I was playing one of my favorite games alone in my room. I lived and died by the exploits of the Brooklyn Dodgers and would create imaginary games between them and their hated rivals, the New York Yankees. There I was, as Mantle, stepping up to the plate with my baseball bat and a rolled-up sock for a baseball. Mickey was batting from the left side that day. I threw the rolled-up sock into the air and, lacking the control needed to be a real switch hitter, I swung and missed the sock completely. Instead, the bat swung straight through the side of the guitar, which was lying out on my bed, shattering the wood into dozens of little pieces.

It's forty-seven years later and I remember that moment vividly. For a few seconds, I was stunned silent. I couldn't believe or accept what had just happened. I wanted to shout "do over" like my friends and I did when we played together. The truth was I was struck numb and didn't know what to do. I screamed — I had just put a baseball bat through my guitar.

My mom and I went back to the Spanish Music Center and then on to numerous shops along West 48th Street. No one could help us. They all said that my guitar, which had a gaping hole in its side, could not be fixed. I was completely despondent. After we exhausted every repair possibility, I showed the guitar to my fifteen-year-old cousin, Stevie Robin.

Woodworking was to Stevie what music would eventually become to me. He was undaunted by the fact that every guitar repairman in New York had said the instrument was unfixable. He steamed and bent a piece of plywood to the missing piece on the side of the guitar. Then he glued dozens of little fragments of shattered wood back onto the plywood. This created an almost patchwork effect. The repair was completely successful and the guitar sounded as good as new, maybe better. And, I had the most unique-looking instrument, a curiosity to everyone who would encounter it.

This guitar served me well for the next four years until I outgrew it. I still have it. Though I've owned many guitars since, this one remains the most special, mainly because of how my cousin Stevie had saved it . . . and me.

Richard Bruné

Guitar builder Richard Bruné is renowned for his guitar craftsmanship and restoration work on many valuable, historical instruments, including Marie Antoinette's guitar, Agustín Barrios' 1927 Simplicio guitar, Julian Bream's lute (originally crafted by the late David Rubio) and Charlie Byrd's guitar. One of Bruné's Baroque guitars has been displayed at the Smithsonian Institute and he has also drafted the technical details of Andrés Segovia's 1937 Hermann Hauser guitar, currently on display at New York's Metropolitan Museum of Art.

I was about thirteen or fourteen years old and I was playing the violin at the time I became interested in the guitar. I started playing violin in fourth grade but I grew up listening to flamenco because my dad had many recordings. I'd loved the sound of it. Other music I grew up listening to was various *primas*, or gypsy violin soloists, and Sándor Lakatos. Dayton, Ohio, was very heavy with Hungarian immigrants, and on Sundays, there was a Hungarian radio hour that was actually done by Sándor Lakatos, rebroadcast from Hungary. My dad did not go to church but he tuned in to this radio station and played these records, and that is why I had wanted to play this music more than anything, and this is why I first took up with the violin. For someone of that age, trying to master this kind of music, I'd realized, man, I was kind of out of my league here. The violin teachers in Dayton were into the Sevcik Violin Studies, and I thought it was going to be a very long time before I would be able to play any of *that*.

My mom took me to a music store in Dayton, and the only thing they had that I could afford was a nylon-string Brazilian Giannini that was practically all plywood. It was very much a Spanish-style instrument and I was already starting to play flamenco. My influences were Sabicas, Niño Ricardo, Carlos Montoya, but particularly Sabicas was my influence for flamenco guitar.

My family took my interest in music in stride. My dad died when I was fifteen so he was not around, but my mom was still trying to eke out a living, and I think she saw my interest in the phonograph and my father's records as a way of keeping me out of trouble. When I looked around for a new guitar that was better than the Giannini that we'd paid $75 for, I realized we could not afford the kind of guitar I wanted. And this is what prompted the decision to try to make my own guitar. I was convinced that the knowledge I had of what a good guitar would be meant that I could create a better guitar than the one I had. A few friends owned Spanish-made instruments that were of course beyond my means but they'd let me study these guitars, and that is how I got started.

I'd made my first guitar out of a dining room table that dated from the '30s, when my parents had gotten married — and this dining room set had been retired to the basement long ago. My dad, before he died, had taken on the project of renovating our basement into what they called, back then, a "recreation room." That's what people did back in the '50s. They turned their basements into recreation rooms where they'd have highball drinks with their neighbors. So the dining room table did not have a function within the context of the basement except keeping stuff off the floor whenever it flooded down there.

When I mentioned to my mom that I wanted to make a guitar, she suggested that I use this dining room table because we knew it was aged wood. Back in those days, cheap furniture had been made out of real wood versus cheap furniture these days, which is made from wood byproducts. The table was made of American poplar, which is a rather bland, soft wood. Actually, it's not too bad. It's sort of like cypress in color and texture but if you hold up poplar sides and backs and give it the traditional tap test that luthiers like to do in order to test the tone of a wood, cypress has a nice tone, whereas poplar is flat without much of a tap tone. That wood from the dining room table

Made from his parents' dining room table, the first guitar ever made by Richard Bruné. (*Courtesy Richard Bruné*)

was cheap and available and was therefore perfect for a seventeen-year-old kid who did not have much money or even tools. I finished making that guitar in the summer of '66. It was better than my Giannini but still, it was not what I envisioned until I made my second guitar with better tools and materials.

I love the guitar because it speaks to me and I can express my emotions with it and that, in a nutshell, is what it's about. It was unusual for me to have this interest in flamenco early on, especially for not being someone born into that culture — but it was the style of music I started playing rather than rock. I faced challenges in terms of absorbing the fundamentals of this art form for this reason — the techniques of flamenco, which incorporate classical guitar on top of techniques like the *rasgueados*, thumbwork and tapping that are indigenous to playing flamenco. All of this I had to figure out on my own without having a live person in front of me whom I could learn from. I was self-taught, by ear, from listening to vinyl LP records.

We did not have a TV in our room — we had a Magnavox record player. On one side, it was a monster cabinet with a turntable and the speakers were underneath and on the other side, you stacked your records. Whenever I had some money, I'd go to the record store and search for flamenco records that I did not own, and then I would visit the library in search of more. I lobbied to get a reel-to-reel tape recorder that allowed me to copy these borrowed records from the library. That had been a real revelation because I could then play these recordings back at nearly half their original speed.

My first paid performance had been at a coffeehouse called The Lemon Tree in Dayton, Ohio, right next door to the arts theater and movie house, which showed what we called "art films" for the eighteen-and-older crowd. Some films had the pretension of being European art films and others were just flat-out jiggle films but, at any rate, the coffeehouse was located right next door and served as the hangout for the local intelligentsia, which was comprised of what was left over from the beatnik crowd with the burgeoning hippie crowd intermixed. Being underage, I went in there and performed solo and, much to my amazement, actually made money from doing this. Later I was asked to appear on a local TV show called *Rising Generation*, and, immediately afterward, I was hired to play on an advertisement and do a voiceover in Spanish for Vic Cassano's, which was a big chain in Dayton. I wondered why she wanted me to speak in Spanish for an Italian pizzeria, but I thought, "Hey, it's paying." I think the lady who had hired me felt that Spanish and Italian were the same. That was the era we grew up in. I did this whole spiel of playing the guitar and then saying, "*El pizzeria de Cassano es el mejor in el mundo!*" in my seventeen-year-old voice, of course. Somewhere out there in the world there is a tape of that floating around, and thank god it has not shown up on YouTube!

Many years ago, in about 1978, Northwestern University started their classical guitar concert series and hired Julian Bream to perform. Len Novy and I became involved with selling tickets, and we did a great job, using mailing lists and selling out the hall, which was a no-brainer at that time. We were then asked to take care of hospitality and asked to pick up Bream from the airport, which we of course obliged, saying, "Sure!" We picked up Bream and, during the ride, he came to realize I was a guitar maker, so he asked to visit the shop. I said, "Sure!" which, of course, had been the intention all along. We walked into the shop that, at the time, had the storefront windows and I was also making harpsichords in addition to guitars. Julian asked if I had a guitar available and I said, "I do! I have one that I made about ten years ago."

Immediately, Bream said to me, "I don't like cedar." So that kind of slammed the door on that and I'd thought, oh, okay. At that point, he walked over to the harpsichord, which was parked in front of the storefront window, right next to Len's teaching studio. Bream then asked, "Did you make this harpsichord?"

I said, "I did, actually."

"Is it English?" he asked.

I said, surprised, "Very good! It is an English model. I didn't realize you knew so much about harpsichords."

"May I play it?" he asked.

I said, "Be my guest."

So Bream sat down to play the harpsichord and started exclaiming, "Lovely tone! *Very* fruity!"

I said, "Really? You like it?"

"It's so colorful," he said.

"Indeed — thank you," I said.

"It has a French coupler, does it not?" Bream asked. "It is a French instrument within an English case."

I said, "Wow, you really know harpsichords!"

"Well, I studied this in college, you know."

"Great," I said. "So you really like the sound?"

"I *do*. It's *very* colorful."

"Well, you know, it has a cedar soundboard."

"You're leading me on now!"

"No, look! It's a cedar soundboard!"

He said, "I don't like cedar!"

I thought, "Oh man, he's got to be like this with Brussels sprouts, too."

So he never played the guitar that I had here. That 1977 instrument was the first instrument that Segovia received from me, and he did not even want to try to play it. I told Bream that Segovia had played this guitar, but it did not faze him one bit. He told me a story of how he went to take a lesson from Segovia and became so nervous that he forgot his guitar.

This guitar I had made came into Segovia's possession through a fellow who grew up in South America from Montevideo whose name is Carlos Mendez Bower, who was head of the gynecology department here for many years at Cook County Hospital in Chicago. When he was a kid, growing up in Montevideo, it was at the time when Segovia had fled Spain during the Civil War to relocate in Montevideo, and Segovia had been one of the best teachers in the city. Carlos' family was originally been from Spain as well and fled for the same reasons. Carlos studied with Segovia when he was a boy so they had been lifelong friends.

Carlos told me, "El Maestro would like to try one of your guitars." This guitar I had was the only one I had lying around, available, and though I had not made it for him and it did not have the features or specifications I thought he would want, I sent it along with the offer to drop everything and make a guitar to his specifications and measurements if he liked it. To my surprise, he came back with a payment, stating that El Maestro (as he always referred to Segovia) wanted the guitar. This happened in 1984, though the guitar had been made in 1977. That letter with Segovia thanking me in Spanish is framed and hung in the alcove of my studio. In 1986, Carlos came to my shop and told me that El Maestro would like to try my Hauser model guitar. What Hauser model?

Carlos supposed that Segovia meant he wanted to try a spruce version of what I had made so I said, "Well, I've got this guitar here that is due to be delivered to a client this week and it is made of spruce. Why don't you take it and just have him play it and try it. If this is what he likes, I'll drop everything and make one for him." Much to my shock, a payment arrived from Segovia for this guitar, so it was the second guitar he had obtained from me. He had it for only six months before he died. He bought this guitar in December 1986 and died in June 1987. That guitar came back to me. Segovia willed that spruce guitar to Carlos as a gift.

Carlos, who had retired at this point and moved from Chicago to Madrid, returned to my shop in Evanston and said, "Richard, I know you would really like to have this guitar." I bought the guitar back from him and have it in my cabinet here in the shop.

Carlos Barbosa-Lima

A native of São Paulo, Brazil, Carlos Barbosa-Lima is famous for being an expert arranger of popular tunes for the classical guitar. He has collaborated with numerous artists, including jazz guitarist Charlie Byrd and Brazilian songwriter and composer Antonio Carlos Jobim. His style ranges from classical to contemporary and Brazilian to jazz.

I've always enjoyed performing in public because it gives me an "up" energy. As a performing artist, you have to enjoy it — it is not just a job. The highest aim of music is to be able to renew yourself. I am very impressed with the great Brazilian architect Oscar Niemeyer. He is 104 years old, and not only is he alive and well but he is still challenging everything possible. He has renewed his interest in architecture with new styles. We have many artists who also approach music in this way.

I first played at Agustín Barrios' grave in El Salvador in 1993, accompanied by guitarist Rico Stover. The last time I visited Barrios' grave in 2010 was a different experience. It had been poured rain every day so they scheduled the visit right on his birthday, the fifth of May. I had said, "Wow, good luck, because it is soaking." We took a chance and the afternoon turned beautiful. Every day

CMG-1004

O Menino e o Violão

ANTONIO CARLOS BARBOSA LIMA

Uma gravação em Hi-Fi

Carlos Barbosa-Lima, age fifteen,
featured on his first recording.
(*Courtesy Carlos Barbosa-Lima*)

following that, it poured rain. Very wild. There must be something otherworldly to it. I would love to go back to El Salvador because it is a magical place.

Montevideo I have very strong links to, not only because of my teacher Savio, but because it was the first place outside of Brazil I visited, when I went for a series of concerts in 1960. Don't forget that since I started playing very young, many people were still living who had once known Barrios. Those days they did not have much mixing but I met a mixer who knew Barrios and a conductor who thought Barrios was the greatest, Maestro Sousa Lima. The image of Barrios had been so alive that it was unbelievable. Attilio Bernardini had studied with Josefina Robledo back in the early 1900s, and she was a pupil of Tárrega so he and a guy in Rio had been the first major guitar teachers in Brazil who claimed to come from the Tárrega School, though we know today no such school had existed. Each student had his or her own views of what he did. In principle, you could see more or less what his ideas were. Anyway, my father had a good way to smooth down Bernardini, and he made me study counterpoint and write out four against three. He did not know I was sight-reading already at fourteen. I played for Bernardini and played one of his pieces.

It was an interesting beginning — I was about seven years of age when my father had the interest to learn the guitar, just to have fun. He hired a local teacher named Benedito Moreira for nine months but found that he did not make any progress with the guitar. My father walked home tired from work. He was busy as a salesman for a pharmaceutical company and had no time to practice. During those months, I had been watching the lessons and became inquisitive about many things. My parents have told me that one day I surprised them by picking up my father's guitar and playing what was supposed to be his lesson. At that point, my father told the teacher to continue with the lessons but to teach me, instead, because I seemed to be very interested in the guitar. That is how I started playing the guitar. My parents told me when I was two years old, when they were playing 78s of popular Brazilian music, big bands, classical music, opera — they noticed when they tried to get me to sleep my eyes would open to the size of a night bird's upon hearing the music.

I continued playing on my father's guitar, which was a gift from the Di Giorgio Company. The old Mr. Di Giorgio was still alive, the man who knew the legendary Paraguayan composer Agustín Barrios. His son Reynaldo, who was adopted into the Di Giorgio family, is the one who gave the guitar to my father. So this guitar was my first guitar. My teacher had, incidentally, studied under Isaias Savio, one of the great teachers of classical guitar in Brazil. I made huge progress within three years and practiced maybe just an hour to an hour and a half daily because I was doing other things like playing soccer. We lived near São Paolo, though my parents came from the hinterlands and had met in Rio. I think I was called to this world in Rio.

I had a huge repertoire simply from picking up music I heard on the radio. When I was ten, I needed a little spark in order to progress to the next level, a crucial point in my life. My father was concerned that I needed to become more organized with my repertoire. We were in a music store in downtown São Paulo, which, today, is totally different. We are talking now about the 1950s. Luiz Bonfá pretty much owned the scene there in the Delvecchio store, which was a central meeting place for musicians. They called me to play for Luis Bonfá, who happened to be in town. This was an important moment in my career because, once they heard me play, they told my father that I urgently needed to study with Isaias Savio. They insisted I do this right away in order to cure bad habits like biting my fingernails — I had been playing without fingernails as a result. You have to let the nails grow. That was a lesson for me right there about the nails. My father's solution was to put some hot spices on my fingertips so that if I slipped to chew my nails, boom! Yet, as a result, I developed a taste for hot food!

The next evening, I met Savio and found him to be very stern and full of conditions. He said that he was going to treat me as an adult student, not as a child student, which is very interesting. He made that point and I committed myself. I took everything seriously. I had not played any other instrument besides the guitar but must make one exception: when my father brought home the Di Giorgio guitar, he had bought a *cavaquinho* as well, which is like a very small guitar. I had always liked the sound of a *cavaquinho*. He had wanted us to become good enough to have a little father-son jam session. But as would have it, I drifted toward playing the guitar. Prior to my studies with Savio, I do remember visiting a music store and trying not the electric guitar, but an electrified acoustic. I liked the sound of these guitars. But then, the lights went out in the shop. Perhaps that had been a lucky moment because it defined my choice to play the unelectrified acoustic. There had been a touch of destiny there.

When my father had to tell my first teacher, Benedito Moreira, that I was going to be studying with Savio, he was nervous. He did not have the guts to tell him that I was going to make a switch so my mother told him. There was a bit of a scene there because Moreira felt hurt. He did not understand that I needed to make this switch in instructors in order to improve my playing. Years later, when he began to follow my career, I saw him two or three times at concerts and he acknowledged this had been a positive choice for me.

We had a very good radio program in São Paulo that was focused on the guitar, run by a wonderful director who programmed everything from Brazilian to classical music and acoustic guitar. I heard recordings of Segovia and Laurindo Almeida and Dilermando Reis on this radio program. Luis Bonfá had been very much on the regular radio and television scene. There had been a great wealth of music during the 1950s as big companies sponsored many acts. Unfortunately, this kind of funding was cut in 1964 when the military came into power. It seemed as if Brazil took a step back by about twenty years in progress.

But we had very good music like Duke Ellington's jazz bands and Nat King Cole, which made a big impact. Symphony orchestras came in later. In the months soon after I began studying with Savio, my father came home with some recordings because he traded free samples prescribed by doctors in exchange for items like this. He brought home a large collection of music from Segovia, which was really fantastic so I was exposed in a more direct way to classical guitar music. My career started soon after this. It was in November of 1957, when I was about twelve or thirteen years old that I performed and then I made my first recording at age fifteen.

My parents encouraged me to study the guitar but to do other things as well, like reading and schoolwork. I was a huge soccer fan because Brazil won the World Cup for the first time in 1958. As far back as I can remember, I was involved in soccer and I used to play until I became more serious about the guitar. I had to quit playing soccer at thirteen because one can get hurt, even with riding a bicycle. I have always been a quick learner and Savio reinforced the merits of practicing with quality time, not quantity time. Almost immediately, my father took the advice of Theodoro Nogueira, who suggested I extend my learning into theory and arrangement. Nogueira was an important figure for me because he was self-taught. He had studied music to its depths and had worked as an arranger. And he was very much into the national movement, which had been led by composers like Heitor Villa-Lobos. He had taken lessons from Guarnieri. He was a good mentor. I loved other subjects in school like the Humanities and humanistic studies and I was not so good at mathematics.

Savio fixed my right hand technique and you know my hand was better when he gave me "Las Abejas" and "Estudio Brillante" to play. Don't forget that certain habits stick with you. Because I was ten years old when I met Savio, the guitar was bigger than me, so I had my right hand slightly falling to the right. Then Savio taught me to hold it at a proper perpendicular angle, with the wrist at a natural angle and not held too high. Savio claimed this technique came from Llobet, whom he studied with during the 1920s when Llobet lived in Buenos Aires and made frequent trips to Montevideo where Savio lived until he left for Brazil in 1931. It took me about four or five years to conquer my bad habits.

What I love about the guitar is its sound, portability and the beauty of the instrument. What I love the most about the guitar is that it has a piano-type shape to it but I never played the piano. The guitar allowed me to explore my own inquisitiveness and find chords along the fretboard right into the music. When I brought home a new record that Savio introduced me to, he gave me a new spark of enthusiasm and taught me big left-hand jumps. I studied with Savio's own rare method book that incorporated left-hand stretches. As one grows more mature, you find what works for you but sometimes you are in haze. You have to let yourself go and usually, this works.

My first performance was at the Teatro São Paulo when I was twelve. It does not exist anymore. It held close to 2,000 people. My father and his friends promoted the concert well, and I was put on TV Tupi in São Paulo prior to the concert. There were only two television stations at that time. I did well on television, and the concert sold out as a result. I performed three pieces that one must have in their repertoire to play no matter what — which included "Las Abejas" and a shortened version of Chopin's Nocturne Op. 9, No. 2, a guitar transcription by Tárrega with a cadenza that the left hand plays alone. This was a cadenza created by the great violinist Sarazate and Tárrega had incorporated it. On television, one must play a shortened version and this left-hand cadenza had a very showy, visual effect. And I played "Tico Tico," which had been on the list of pieces, including those by Dilarmando Reis, that Savio wanted me to stop playing but I did not. I always played that stuff for my friends. They're such beautiful pieces.

When I came to the U.S. in the autumn of 1967, I was not quite twenty-three years old and had brought a Brazilian-made guitar that did fine for ten years in Brazil. Then, my tour within the U.S. became extended by three months. I gave my first recital at Carnegie Hall after Washington and the Spanish Institute. The weather grew colder and central heating kicked in, those buildings had been so overheated until the first oil crisis of the '70s. The guitar did not hold up well. My first trip to Ottawa in Canada, the guitar just gave up with big cracks all over. I actually had to borrow a guitar to play a concert in New York. I say that I think that guitar committed suicide. You know how some people just give up? This guitar gave up. It did not like the Northern climate.

Juan Martín

Born in Málaga, Spain, Juan Martín has studied flamenco with Niño Ricardo and Paco de Lucía. He has recorded with Herbie Hancock and Rory Gallagher and performed with Miles Davis. He is the author of two flamenco guitar methods and has been voted one of the top three guitarists in the world in *Guitar Player Magazine*.

I started to play when I was six years old and my first guitar was a Conde Hermanos flamenco guitar made of cypress on the back and sides with old pegheads called *clavija de madera*. It was not a first-class model, but it had a good flamenco tone. In fact, it was so used, so secondhand, that it had a big dip between each fret. The strings were very high so you had to press down a long way. It was very tough to play. But someone gave it to me, and I was so keen to play that anything was great. Just the look of the guitar and its sound attracted me. In the end, the difficult features of my guitar proved to be a strengthening thing, because when I eventually got a good one, it felt very easy to play. It was good thing to have done. I am not sure I would recommend it for children. You shouldn't have to fight an instrument. But I was so passionate to play that it just didn't bother me — I just thought, well, somehow, I will make a sound.

My grand plans at the start were to just to learn anything I could. I'd exchange what we call *falsetas*, short melodic variations, in the way people trade stamps. So I'd meet with one guy and say, "I'll trade you this variation in *soleá* for that one you've got in *bulería* or *alegría*." In this way, I built up a repertoire of material, just to learn. And then, just to hear as much as possible, I played at baptisms and weddings when I was very young. I thought nothing of walking six or seven kilometers just to play somewhere in Málaga, in the south of Spain. I would find very knowledgeable singers and other guitarists, and in this way, I was picking up things.

When I was seventeen, I went to Madrid and mixed up with the great players in the capital. I used to listen to a record of the great flamenco guitarist Niño Ricardo, and I would do this by slowing down the old 33 rpm LP to the speed of 16, making the music one octave lower. This way, I could more or less work out what I was hearing. So when I traveled to Madrid, I went to the Conde Hermanos shop with the hope of finding a better guitar than the Conde I had or at least to see if they could make it better for me. I played this Ricardo material and there was an old man in the shop, listening. He said to me, gruffly, "*¿Tu quien eres?*" ("Who are you?"). I said, "Juan Martín." "*¿De donde aprendido estoy?*" ("Where did you learn this?"). I told him I learned it from Niño Ricardo.

"Yo *soy el Ricardo!*" he growled.

At this point, I was so small and he was a maestro. He was very nice. He was flattered that I had bothered to learn so much of his material by ear, so he would advise and correct me, saying, "No, that's not an open E there, it is played on the second string." And he would go by the Conde Hermanos shop, which was on Calle Gravina No. 7 in Madrid, every day at about five o'clock. He'd then say to me, "C'mon, let's have a glass of red wine." We'd order *tintorros*, as he'd call them. And this is how I became close to this man who was the number one flamenco guitarist in Spain. It was very exciting. He would correct me, and I'd go back and practice in my *pension,* or apartment.

Subsequently, I met Paco de Lucía in Madrid also. Paco lived on Calle Ilustracion No. 17. I'd go there and he gave me a lot of material. I studied with him enough to develop a base. From here, a flamenco guitarist has to find their *proprio sello* or their own voice on the guitar, and I think I did that. This is the most difficult thing about flamenco. Not only do you have to play, but you have to compose your own material. It takes a long time.

The flamenco guitar just has a certain intense resonance. And the

Juan Martín as a teenager working at the dance studio Amor de Dios in Madrid, Spain. (*Courtesy Juan Martín*)

technique is amazing along with the sense of rhythm and melodies. There is so much to it. When you're working with dancers, you have to follow their feet, not have them follow you. It just seemed to me to be such a world of variety. You have three elements: the guitar, singing and dance and on top of that, *jaleo*, which is the handclapping. Just to be involved in that fascinated me — and the characters involved in flamenco, the people are such interesting people to be with. It's a beautiful life and you can go to bed very late. For young people, it's not ideal, particularly if you have to go to school. It's like a potent drug — *flamenco*. You can't lose that passion.

I listened to a lot of records at home of classical music and jazz, and I thought about flamenco guitar and its technique, thinking it would be wonderful to have a record where flamenco could stand on its own. Even though I loved accompanying, I thought the guitar could grow so much more. In London, I attended a concert at Wigmore Hall and heard wonderful guitarists.

And I gave my first really important concert there without a microphone. I did not think the guitar should be covered up, after hearing a lifetime of handclaps and footwork. I wanted the beauty of the guitar and the stability of flamenco technique to be developed. I made seventeen albums. The first were dedicated to solo flamenco guitar. Then I became involved in fusions.

I made an album with Mark Isham, who is a well-known film composer in America for RCA and BMG, and an album with a jazz pianist and an album with the Royal Philharmonic Orchestra. All of this was a tremendous learning experience. I recorded at Abbey Road Studios in London. I was a bit overwhelmed by it all. Now it comes full circle, with my return to flamenco. It was very educational to be open to all those things.

I played a concert once for a Spanish association. It was overnight, by the embassy. And everybody clapped at the end of the pieces but for one person. This one guy in the second row looked rather miserable. I thought, normally, in a formal concert, I would not say anything. You never know. They might be critics. It's amazing how vulnerable you feel onstage. I mean, this guy just sat there. He never moved. So after a number of pieces, I said, "Excuse me, sir, but do you not like flamenco? Do you not like my playing?" He just lifted an arm, which turned out to be encased inside a plaster cast all the way up to his elbow. I felt terrible. *That's* why he looked miserable. He couldn't clap. His wife came up to me afterward, yelling at me: "You had no right to chat up my husband like that." I just had no idea.

But it just goes to show how, in a way, we're all so dedicated, insecure and transparent onstage, so that if you are really open to the audience, it affects you. The more you are reactive, the more I feel they can join you. It only takes one or two people to do that.

Dennis Koster

Dennis Koster is an American concert-classical flamenco guitarist who studied with flamenco legends Mario Escudero and Sabicas. He is the author of a bestselling, three-volume flamenco method published by Mel Bay Publications.

I started out studying violin but, when my teacher died, I lost all interest in playing, which greatly upset my parents. I was about thirteen years old when I became interested in the guitar. However, my parents did not want to buy me one, given they had already invested in a violin that I now refused to play.

So I wound up borrowing a guitar from my dentist's son. It was a Danelectro, a solid-body electric guitar made of Masonite. The pickups were made out of old chrome lipstick tubes. Apparently, the Danelectro factory bought up 50,000 lipstick tubes from a company that went out of business and converted these things into the pickups used on their guitars. You plugged the guitar into the case, which had a built-in speaker, and away you'd go — it was great.

When I proved to be fairly serious about the guitar, my dad picked up an inexpensive guitar during a business trip to Spain. It was a mahogany Juan Estruch, made in Barcelona. Basically it was a Fleta knockoff. I was about fifteen years old at the time and started studying with Howard David, one of the first American flamenco guitarists to write a method book, under the name of Juan Grecos.

My big hero was the gypsy flamenco guitarist Mario Escudero. I was thirteen years old when I first heard flamenco on a tinny radio, and I just flipped out. To me, it was a way of playing guitar that captured all the expression in the world. I got the chance to see Escudero perform at the 92nd Street Y on a magnificent guitar and thought to myself, "If only I could some day play a guitar like that!"

A month later, my teacher told me he was packing up and moving to Spain. I almost fainted. "But you're my teacher," I told him. "You *can't* go!" He told me not to worry because he had a teacher lined up for me already. I told him did not want to study with anyone else. When I found out my new teacher was going to be Mario Escudero, I nearly fainted again.

Mario did not speak much English at the time, and I did not speak Spanish yet but for a few basic phrases I was learning in high school. So I started learning by copying what he showed me. A year later, Mario needed to sell his Ramírez guitar because he needed to buy some furniture. I worked at the shipping and loading dock of a table and lamp factory all summer — this was 1965 — in order to save up $700 for his magnificent concert Ramírez.

Two years later, at age seventeen, I had my first Carnegie Hall recital with a Spanish dance company. Carlos Ibañez, the director of the dance company, asked me to dress up wearing a frilly shirt and Cordoban hat. Minutes before I was due to go onstage, I went into the hallway to get a drink of water. I opened a door and found myself standing in a stairwell as the door locked shut behind me. Making matters worse, there was no doorknob on my side of the door.

I ran down the steps and stepped outside onto the corner of 57th Street and 7th Avenue in the pouring rain. Here I was with my guitar in hand, wearing this ruffled shirt, Cordoban hat — instantly wet. I had to go back in through the front door with the rest of the crowd, and a couple of my high school buddies snickered at me. Once I got backstage, I used my shirt to frantically dry off my guitar. Then I went on and played. Everything went fine. Playing in Carnegie Hall, under any circumstance, is an unforgettable experience.

Guitar can be a tough field but I can't say there has ever been a day where I did not have one in my hands. My parents, who are in their eighties, still wonder what it is I am going to do with myself when I grow up. I wonder about that myself from time to time. But then I put that on the back burner to go play.

The Assad Brothers

The Brazilian-born brothers Sergio and Odair Assad are a legendary Latin-Grammy-winning classical guitar duo that sounds uncannily like one guitar whenever they perform. They have expanded the repertoire of music for guitar duos and have collaborated with renowned artists Nadja Salerno-Sonnenberg, Yo-Yo Ma and Paquito D'Rivera. Odair Assad, who also has his own solo career, teaches at the Ecole Supérieure des Arts in Brussels, and Sergio teaches at the San Francisco Conservatory.

Odair Assad: The story is that Sergio is the one who first wanted to play the guitar.

Sergio Assad: I was twelve years old when I received my first guitar, which I wanted to play very badly. Our father is a mandolin player who plays traditional Brazilian *chorinhos,* and because he was bringing musicians to our house all the time, we were very accustomed to listening to music from a very young age. When I was about eight or nine years old, I first asked if he would teach me to play, and he said, "No! Not for kids!" So I was very disappointed.

Odair Assad: [Laughing.] Poor Sergio!

Sergio Assad: I felt as if our father would never teach me! When I was twelve, an uncle of mine, came by our house and played a bit of guitar. He was much more accessible, so I immediately asked if he could teach me a few chords. The first chord he taught me was D Minor. He also taught me a simple progression of Dm, A7, Dm, and then he showed me G Minor, which is very awkward because you have to do the barre, but I could do it! I know for many people that chord is difficult and challenging, but I could do it and this made me excited.

I then asked my mother, because I was accustomed to hearing her sing in the house, if she would sing songs so that I might be able to play and fit in these three new chords. She hesitated and balked, and I begged her to give me a break, "Please sing that song! Sing that other one!" In these days, our father used to be gone much of the time. He played serenades with his friends, so he would never be home during the evening until very late. When he returned from his work one day, he heard me play and said, "Wow!" He immediately picked up his mandolin and taught me my first major chord — D Major. A7 was the same, and I learned the G Major chord. He was very impressed with my effort and played a waltz, saying, "Great!" He was so excited, more excited than I was! The following day, a long gray day, he wanted to repeat the experience to show my mother. "Listen to this!" my father told her. I played my guitar in their bedroom and my dad played along his mandolin — and there was Odair, eight years old, standing in the door watching.

Odair Assad: I came to watch. Jealous!

Sergio Assad: Odair said, "I want to do that, too!"

Odair Assad: I was just jealous. I saw that my mother was in tears, too. I knew I had to play the guitar.

Sergio Assad: I said, "Give Odair the guitar." And it turned out to be a walk in the park for him. Whatever had taken me ten minutes to learn, it took Odair about one minute to learn. We had one guitar in the house, only one — a Di Giorgio. Odair and I shared this one guitar. Our father immediately brought home a second nylon-string guitar, a Giannini, which is another really bad kind of Brazilian guitar. We played on these guitars for at least three years. We lived in a city in the state of São Paulo at the time, and one year after we had started playing with our father, we learned his entire repertoire of *choros* within the space of a year, which was amazing because this numbered about 300 *choros*. We played everything with the same intricate passages that he had showed us and, by the end of one year, a friend of his came to the city and heard us play. He was a friend of Jacob Bittencourt, whose stage name is Jacob do Bandolim, a huge *choro* figure in Brazil, one of the most famous musicians of all time. He told Jacob about us! And word came back that Jacob said if we were as good players as this friend had assured, that he would invite us to come play on his television show. So one year after we had only started to play guitar, we found ourselves playing musical accompaniment in one of the biggest, most prestigious venues in São Paolo with Jacob do Bandolim. This was a huge feat for any Brazilian, to say you had played with Jacob Bittencourt!

Our father was recording all his friends early on. He had some friends who played classical guitar. We did not know of Segovia or any of the big names in classical guitar because we lived in this small town in the state of São Paolo. But our father's friends played quite well. They were not professional musicians but amateur players who played at a very high level. We started playing guitar solos because our father encouraged us. But we could not read music and there were no teachers available. It was very tough to find someone who could teach us.

We had simple recordings of my father's friends playing Barrios, which had been the first classical music we had ever heard. My father obtained the scores for these Barrios pieces, and we tried to figure out where the notes were in addition to listening to the recordings and copying the rhythm in order to learn how to play. This is what we did for a year or so. Then it became serious because both Odair and I entered competitions in São Paolo, and we both won. For Odair, it was a walk in the park. He was playing all this Barrios with "Choro de Saudade." He was nine years old and playing this stuff.

Odair Assad: Our father had recordings of this music, that's why!

Sergio Assad: This event was the first guitar competition ever in São Paolo, and I did not want to compete with Odair because he was too strong for me. So I moved to a category that was higher actually, according to age, for teens at the time. Odair entered the category that was for children and won — but I had won my category, too! I simply did not want to compete with Odair. For us, the guitar was not an obsession at all. I really wanted to play but Odair was starting to skip playing because our father wanted us to play all the time.

Odair Assad: He'd started to say to others, "Look! Come and hear my kids play!" It was a nightmare. I hated it because we started to play at eight p.m. and were still playing at midnight, and I was only eight years old. He would have us out playing through two a.m. some mornings, and I would start faking that I was sleeping.

Sergio Assad: Odair had his fee to stay awake. It was chocolate.

Odair Assad: Generally, we were not allowed to have chocolate. But if

I stayed awake and played more again, our father would say, "I promise you chocolate!" At three a.m., I was eating more chocolate, right before going to bed, which is not very good for you but . . .

Sergio Assad: The guitar, from the first moment on, became our life. The guitar had been a surprise, and we were totally devoted to it. The guitar is family and a great companion, because with it you are never alone. I discovered this very early on because I always liked to imagine music in my head. You can spend hours and hours by yourself with a guitar. We were happy with playing traditional music and learning a bit of classical music, but we never expected that our lives would turn out the way they have.

Being two kids from a town that was not the capital of Brazil but a small city, we pretty much had an idea how life was going to go. Maybe we would earn a degree in some field, but then you never leave that town. Most of our friends from those days still live there. Nobody left. Or, if they left, they left for São Paulo as the bigger city but they never left the country. We have created a life outside the country yet had no idea at the time where the guitar would take us. No idea at all. When we were exposed to classical music three years into our playing, our father, who is a bright man, knew he had two skilled children and gave us opportunities. He was not prepared and did not know where to take us or what to do with us but he was constantly seeking what was possible and had received advice that the best teacher to be found resided in Rio de Janeiro — Monina Távora, teacher of the Abreu brothers, Sérgio and Eduardo. She said she would coach us. Because we lived far away, my father asked how many lessons she felt we might need and when she answered, "Once a week," he moved us to Rio so we could have the lessons.

Odair Assad: That's a good father!

Sergio Assad: He did that for us. It was a challenge for us to present a new face of music because before this, music to us had been the *chorinho* and a little bit of Barrios. That was our world. When we had Monina as our instructor, this was a revelation to us. The first time we met her, she saw us play all this traditional music and said she could teach us but handed us a bunch of scores. She said if we could come back to her in one week playing this sheet music, then she would coach us. Odair and I locked ourselves into this apartment in Rio.

Odair Assad: It was the first time in our lives that we never saw the ocean.

Sergio Assad: We had learned all this Renaissance music, and we did not have a clue what this was. She wanted to test our grasp for it, and she was very pleased. Our challenge with the guitar was to learn classical music.

Odair Assad: Our challenge with the guitar was to have pleasure with playing. I always seem to have pleasure playing because we are doing new things. From the beginning, Sergio was always striving and reaching and thinking in new ways, first to have a second guitar and now he is composing. We are always doing different projects and have done so many already and will be doing more. I tell my students not to follow this classical guitar path. Nowadays it is so difficult because there are so many incredible players — so where is there to go? When we started playing, there was no other guitar duo. Now there are many guitar duos.

Sergio Assad: We have been so faithful to our guitar maker Thomas Humphrey, and we still play his guitars today as when we first did, twenty-five years ago. When we first met him here in New York in 1979, he showed us his guitars at the time but we did not like them. They were nothing special. But then we started talking — and he was a good talker. He had this new idea for an elevated fretboard on his guitar. I said to him, when you make it, I want to try it. It was his Millennium model guitar, which everyone is now copying.

It is just amazing to me how many people have copied and are copying his guitar all over the world. When I first saw the Millenium, I asked him, "What do I do with that?" We bought it immediately. I think we have the second set from the first thirty guitars he made of this model. People tried to play down what he created. So many methods had been tried from the eighteenth through nineteenth century, many innovations. It is true that there is someone who did make an elevated fretboard, but why did no one else do this? Humphrey was criticized for creating this guitar with the elevated fretboard because he was the first to do it, and then everyone else jumped on the idea later and copied it without giving credit to him.

Odair Assad: I was especially happy with this guitar model for my role in the duo because I play all the high notes and they are much easier to reach on this guitar. Nowadays there are so many incredible guitar makers.

Wings on My Fingers

Room #19 never turned up again, yet the blaze he'd kindled in me with the guitar continued to intensify. I played because it put wings on my fingers and freed my mind. I probably played too many pieces dashed with *rasguea-dos* in the minor key, but when I did, whatever troubled me spilled out into the air and dissipated into a sweeter sound.

I entered a city-wide musician's competition at age 14, playing against a coat-tailed pianist who could make the keyboard sound like rolling thunder and a man who could make a bent saw wail like a storm of ghosts. I had no idea that such an ugly, brutal-toothed piece of hardware was capable of pro-ducing such a shimmering and ethereal howl. I was not convinced that the century-old piece by Tárrega that I'd prepared could even compare.

Each park district held its own competition to winnow down the talent pool to its first round. One lady pianist, dressed in a bright, floral prairie-style dress with a lacy doily collar, was rumored to be a cheating carpetbagger who was trying to sneak in a second shot after losing in her own district days earlier. I didn't think I stood half a chance against anyone, as I could barely croak out the name of the two pieces I was going to play, "Lágrima" and "Romanza." It didn't help that I was following a hyper middle-school kid who sang a hoarse, frenzied version of "My Sharona." The audience, sitting on folding chairs inside the Indian Boundary Park Field House, squirmed uncomfortably when his pubescent voice cracked out the racy lyrics.

Staring into the dimly lit front row of folding chairs, I noticed one of the judges smiling at me, and I forgot about the overwhelming sea of faces in the room and played for him. As soon as it was all over with, I scrambled back to my safely anonymous seat beside my mom.

"You're *not* going to win," she snapped.

I know she said it out of her own anxiety, but it left me stung and surprised. I swallowed my hurt and returned my attention to the stage. All this just reaffirmed my own certainty that all the glory would go to the man with the saw. It took me a minute to register the judges were calling my name to present me with the gold medal.

Both DePaul University and Roosevelt College sent letters offering music scholarships though I was only a freshman in high school. I performed at the Daley Center and Grant Park, where the cooler-by-the-lake winds detuned my guitar and swallowed up its sound. At guitar society gatherings, where men twice my age labored through elaborate fingerings, I played the same compositions with slouchy nonchalance. I did not know what to say to these much older, *muy macho* men who painstakingly Krazy-Glued sliced-up ping-pong balls onto their broken fingernails and made everything out to be ten times more difficult and mysterious than it really needed to be. I half-listened to their tales of note-hitting prowess; obsessions over details and technicalities seemed to be more vital to them than just losing themselves to the joy of the music. It felt weird to me because we loved the same thing, the guitar, yet I felt troubled by their extreme possessiveness and strange need to dictate hierarchies, pecking orders, rankings — who was the best player, the fastest player, what was the most difficult piece, the most beautiful piece. And, most importantly, who was better than whom. Music in discussions like these felt dominated by ego rather than spirit.

My teacher, Sonia, sent me traveling to competitions in remote and wealthy suburbs, where I wound up winning, but it always somehow felt stolen or tainted by someone else's disappointment. One competition left me feeling like a toy poodle at the Westminster Dog Show. After the announcement I had won, a teacher of a competitor approached Sonia and said to her, "Nice left hand." It took me a few minutes to realize he was referring to my left hand, ignoring me despite the fact I was standing right there. The guitar was my one sanctuary where I knew I could be myself, but my distaste for the culture of competitions made me feel like a Woolworth's dime-store parakeet escaped from its cage, flapping wildly out of control without a clue as to where I was going to land.

When I play, it feels, for a brief moment, like I am immersed in a different time, a different language, a different sensation, a different part of the world — anywhere but here. Time hangs and my fingers seem to have their own memory that allows every emotion inside of me to resonate through a Villa-Lobos prelude. My right hand flies while the left glides as I let loose all that I would like to say and feel but cannot or should not.

My bedroom curio shelf filled quickly with a series of fluted plastic trophies topped with golden lyres. My mother complained to my grandmother that she had created a monster. People advised her that I should audition for Juilliard but my mother, with her Master's Degree in Art Education, remained convinced that pursuing anything that smelled of art could only lead to a schmucky day job that eventually turned into your full-time, schmucky career. Both my mother and grandmother agreed on this much — playing a guitar did not make money. Playing a guitar would not get you anywhere.

It was their usual crabbing, I figured, a sort of faint but permeating scent that I'd grown used to, like the smell of bleach and Murphy Oil flax soap part of the rooming house routine, where someone was always making a mess to clean up, paying the rent late or finding another unexpectedly devious way to break the rules.

When I first started lessons, they demanded I practice at least thirty minutes a day because their hard-earned money was on the line. But I never practiced. I assured other aspiring students that I had, in fact, *never practiced*. When all their little faces brightened at the notion of being liberated from the daily drudgery of having to sit alone in a room with their guitar, I told them that rather than practicing, I played. I could play all day. It drove my mother and grandmother nuts, playing and replaying the same pieces over and over to the point where my grandmother finally laid down an ultimatum that I had to stop because she couldn't think straight and her scarlet-fever sensitized ears were ringing and I might cause her to lose her hearing altogether along with the remaining tenants in the house.

Not long after the fire, I had stumbled across a treasure trove of record albums stashed on a narrow bookshelf behind the door that lead from the small den off the living room into the piano roll corridor: there was Shirley MacLaine in fishnets as Irma La Douce, a ruby-lipped Connie Francis, Dave Brubeck in a sky blue suit and skinny tie, Sammy Davis Jr., whose photo I scrutinized for a sign of his glass eye, and the exotic Yma Sumac, the

Julia Crowe, age thirteen, performing at Indian Boundary Park, Chicago, Illinois. (*Courtesy Julia Crowe*)

five-octave Voice of Xtabay. I found albums by Cannonball Adderly, Johnny Mathis, Sam Cooke and Chubby Checker interspersed with orchestral recordings of Stravinsky's *Rite of Spring* and Tchaikovsky's *Nutcracker*. I became mesmerized by an album photo of my grandmother's Peggy Lee, where she looked like a pudgy Midwestern version of Botticelli's Venus, dressed in a snug spangled white sheath under a solitary spotlight.

Each album contained a paper sleeve covered with liner notes written lovingly by experts, critics and producers. They all spoke of slinky smoky legendary jazz clubs attended by gods of music who performed their most memorable concerts long before I was born. The other side of the paper sleeve offered miniature previews of artwork for at least a dozen other forthcoming albums, which in almost all cases, we did not have. The jaunty lettering and garish, fading colors of these cardboard album covers suggested an intoxicating blend of fun, sophistication and glamour that did not exist in my household. Finding this music was like stumbling over a secret time capsule that promised to spirit me back to another time of this house, a life that once revolved on a record turntable.

This curiosity about nightclubs and theaters inspired a girlfriend and me to sneak into the Apollo Theater on Lincoln Avenue to prowl and root around for a potential souvenir. We were caught within minutes by the stage manager. To throw him off guard, we broke into a song by Tom Lehrer, a snippet of "The Masochism Tango," which charmed him into suggesting that before we leave we take home some flyers from other shows around town. We complied, mostly out of relief not to be in any real trouble.

When I cleaned out my backpack, I discovered that one of these flyers showed a 1940s-style comic book rendering of a haggard man in a loosened necktie, office papers slipping from his hands, looking as if he had utterly given up on the world. The Practical Theatre logo was same stencil script you'd find stamped on munitions box. Art Is Good, it read, along the bottom. The theater address, 703 Howard Street, was less than three blocks away from my house.

Across the street, past the am/pm minimarket; past the Smiles! Dental Services, past the medical prosthetics store with its walkers, canes and portable potties; past the blue-and-white trim of The Cottage diner and a new storefront travel agency with its special one-time airfares to Kingston, Port-au-Prince and Mexico City — I cupped my hands over the plate glass storefront window of 703 Howard Street and saw a blown-up black-and-white photograph of John Lennon in an army jacket. Along the bottom of the photo someone had scrawled, "The John Lennon Auditorium." Wanting a closer look, I pushed through the red wooden door and stepped inside. A wastebasket sat pushed up against the wall with a brass plaque above it that read, "The Official Practical Theatre Wastebasket, Stolen from Wisdom Bridge."

Wisdom Bridge was a more respectable theater farther down the block on the other side of the Howard Street elevated station. They were one of those edgy venues, putting on shows like *Kabuki Macbeth* and an adaptation of the murderer Jack Henry Abbott's *In the Belly of the Beast*. Really edgy, but without a spot for their trash. I was starting to like Practical Theatre.

I quickly ingratiated myself by offering to help build sets, and once the theater crew discovered I played guitar, they asked me to perform during intermission. With several actors whisked off to New York as new cast members of *Saturday Night Live*, the theater became a hive of activity and, as a result, I had met all kinds of artists, cartoonists, actors, musicians, film stars, playwrights and authors. William Burroughs eventually warmed up in his crepuscular way, once he knew me as the kid who could recite the complete lyrics to "Mairzy Doats," which I had memorized from the printed lyrics unfurled like hieroglyphics on one of my grandmother's piano rolls. He was also impressed that I'd read his novel *Naked Lunch* in Spanish as a way of slipping it past the nuns' radar at my Benedictine high school. Allen Ginsberg once returned my call from Barbara's Bookstore and informed me that yes, Bill was in Tangiers, and that no, I should be reading Dostoyevsky and Blake, all while my grandmother kept screaming at me to use the white rotary phone in the front room instead of hogging up the 2988-extension where the calls from potential roomers came in. Meeting these people made an indelible impression on me because, as with composers, I had always assumed the first requirement of any real artist was to be dead.

My mother was at her wit's end that I was associating with older people, with questionable theater people, with artists. I found it all absurd, as I was already living with needle junkies, schizophrenics and the sporadically suicidal. The literate junkies I met had at least advised me to read works of classic literature and encouraged me to attend college.

My mother persisted. As far as she was concerned, my obsession with the guitar would be my ruin. It was hard to figure how much worse it could be than what already staggered up and down the back staircase outside my bedroom door and woke me in the night with a jolt to discover an inebriated roomer ferociously rattling the doorknob until I screamed through the keyhole for them to leave me alone.

So at age fifteen, I had to make a choice between home and the guitar. This was the profound contradiction — the instrument was everything that resonated joy in me. It gave my fingers a bold voice that I could not yet muster any other way. How was it possible that something so beautiful could also incite so much fear in my mother? Given that this was Chicago, Home of the Blues, I already knew that life was never intended to be easy. I knew that the ideal place for me would be with my guitar, outside this house.

Carlos Santana

Carlos Santana is legendary for his forty-year career of fusing rock, salsa and jazz, melding blues with Latin and African rhythms into a distinctive style that has won him ten Grammy awards and three Latin Grammys.

I started playing the violin in '55, when I was eight years old. My father moved to San Francisco for about a year and I was not practicing violin anymore. My mother did not want me to stop playing music, so she took me to a park in Tijuana to listen to a festival of musicians playing, and I heard someone play electric guitar there for the first time. I definitely knew I was hearing someone play the electric guitar the way B.B. King plays it because that gentleman who had been playing, Javier Bátiz, was into B.B. King, Little Richard and Ray Charles — that is all he would do.

But for me, hearing someone play electric guitar for the first time, with the sound of the guitar bouncing against the trees and the cars and the church and the park because it was an outdoor festival, was mesmerizing. It felt like I was watching my first UFO, and my mom saw my eyes and she immediately sent a letter to my dad, telling him, "Carlos does not really want to quit music, but he does not like the violin. He likes the guitar!" So my dad was gracious enough to send me a guitar. I had a big fat electric guitar, a Gibson, kind of like Wes Montgomery's. It was a dark-colored guitar with a little bit of brown and yellow in it. My mom knew that music would keep me out of trouble and keep me from hanging around the wrong people in gangs or anything like that because I would just stay in my room and practice.

The guitar is shaped like the body of a beautiful woman and you get to play with the neck, too, and pull the strings and bend them. So the whole experience is very sensual and spiritual. Being a teenager, those are the two things that make the most sense in terms of where to invest my energy and concentration. My father was my main teacher when he came back. He would teach me chords. But I also learned a lot simply by listening to records, like most people, and going to concerts and watching how performers stand and get a tone out of their guitar. Most people do not realize that you do not get tone from the pedals but from your physical body, how you stand. For example, when you look at Segovia, there is a certain posture that he has and if that posture is not correct, then he would not sound like Segovia. What's beautiful about the guitar is it allows each individual to imprint his or her own fingerprints on the sound. You know how to breathe and how to think with intensity because your thoughts are the first notes before you put them on the guitar. You have to invest intensity into the notes.

I think the only challenge for me on the guitar has been playing odd meters, like 7/11, 19ths — and after a while, there are very few people, like Ravi Shankar or John McLaughlin, who can play odd time signatures and make them sound like breathing, as natural as taking a deep breath. For me, I always gravitate toward just playing music from the point of a beautiful melody that gives you a full-on hug. I was never really that attracted to speed or showing off how fast or how clever or how many chords I knew. I just want to, and please excuse the expression, "penetrate" inside that note and give myself chills so that I can give you chills. If I don't feel it, you're not going to feel it. The first rule of music, from Manitas de Plata to Wes Montgomery or everyone — the first rule of music is if you do not feel it, your audience is not going to feel it. So you have to learn how to access the center of your heart so when you play a note, you see people laugh, cry and dance at the same time — like when a woman has a baby — that's when music is music, when people cry and they do not even know why and when they are laughing and crying. And if you can put it like that as a musician, then I believe you. Otherwise, I do not believe you.

My first official performance was at a competition in the park in Tijuana. Again, I was playing violin and my sister was singing. Out of about fifty people, we were the last ones standing, and I remember I won over her. She was a little sad, but I won and they gave me a trophy, a big Pepsi-Cola bottle and $20, which was a LOT of money back then. With guitar, I think the first time I had my validation with it was when I was a hippie. I had just left my mom's house and I was playing down at the panhandle, the same place Jimi Hendrix had played in the park. I closed my eyes and when I opened them, there was Michael Bloomfield and Jerry Garcia smiling. And I was like, "Oh my god! I am onstage and I just got out of high school." So it did not feel like it was going to be a challenge to be onstage with Eric Clapton or John McLaughlin. All of a sudden, it felt, excuse the expression, like I "belonged" there with them.

I like to smell a guitar before I play it — I got this from my dad. I look at them, smell them and once you get past the factory, there is something really beautiful about equating this to when my dad bought shoes. He always smelled them first before he put them on. So it is a habit for me that I got from him, to connect with the guitar with all my all my senses, from sight to smell. I won't lick it, or anything like that, but this sensory exploration is important because humans are connected to their senses. Intrinsically, it is important to really connect with the guitar. For example, like a spoon gives you honey but a spoon cannot taste the honey. I do not want to be a spoon. I want to taste the honey before you do. I think if you approach music from that perception, then it is five things: genuine, honest, sincere, real and true. And then people will claim you around the world as part of the family.

My treasured guitar right now is a new guitar made by Paul Reed Smith as a gift from my wife. The guitar is creamy-looking but sustains like a Stradivarius forever. The wood feels like it is made out of granite, although it is African wood, very dense and thick. The tone is different and the approach is different. My wife and I were just married December 19, 2010, and on the back of the guitar, it is engraved, "The first time ever, everything." My wife is an incredible drummer in her own right, probably among the top three in the world. She's a serious Bruce Lee type of drummer. She keeps time but not like a time-keeper. She's like a hummingbird so I am very grateful that I married someone who, like Bruce Lee, is deeply invested in higher standards of excellence.

Jimmie Vaughan

Jimmie Vaughan, the older brother of the late Stevie Ray Vaughan, is a Grammy-winning blues guitarist and singer from Dallas. Vaughan is the founder of The Fabulous Thunderbirds.

When I was twelve years old, friends of my mom and dad had a son who was a musician, and he happened to be away on the buddy plan in the Navy. His parents and mine would get together on the weekends at their house to play dominoes, and I'd go into their son's room and play with his drums and a guitar. That was the first time I picked up a guitar.

About a year later, I was playing football at school and broke my collarbone. I was a terrible athlete and didn't understand sports. They told me I would be laid up at home for a month and I had a rolled up tube of a cloth bandage around my arm that was meant to hold my collarbone in place. One of the guys gave my dad a guitar to help me pass the time, saying, "Here's something that won't tackle him." It was an Old Kraftsman flat top guitar with four strings on it — the E and the B strings were broken.

The first thing I learned to play on it was Bill Doggett's "Honky Tonk," and

Jimmie Vaughan (left), age fourteen, in a band called the Swinging Pendulums, 1965.
(*Courtesy Jimmie Vaughan*)

basically it hasn't changed any because I'm still playing the same music. My brother Stevie was eight years old at the time, and he had a little guitar with cowboys on it and plastic strings. The Kraftsman flat top was one sold from the Spiegel's catalog. I played it every single day and I am fifty-four years old now. Thanks to football, I found my career.

At one point I had tried to play drums and could play simple beats, but six months into getting that first guitar, my dad bought me a three-quarter-size Gibson with one pickup and no cutaways. It was like a 335 in thickness and had binding on the sides. He'd picked it up at a pawnshop for fifty bucks and we got an amp from a friend.

I started out playing a lot of Jimmy Reed and Bill Doggett's "Honky Tonk," hits from the '50s and a lot of blues. I learned to play from what I heard off the radio in Dallas, and we had one black music station there as well. My uncle Joe also taught me some country-style playing. It was an exciting time to play because the English guys were also trying to play the blues.

My dad liked to play dominoes with some of his fellow workers and a couple of these guys also happened to be musicians. One of them had a

Telecaster and another guy had a custom-made guitar that looked like one of the big, thick, jazz Gibson guitars with his name, Leonard, inlaid on the neck in ivory. Stevie and I used to watch these guys play in our living room for hours, and they taught us to play Chuck Berry, John Lee Hooker, Jimmy Reed and some country tunes.

As an artist-type kid, it was beautiful for me to look at. I loved drawing pictures and the guitar looked like a rocket ship or a ray gun with knobs on it. It came as such a wonderful surprise when I found out I could play it. The guitar is all I thought about. I also knew it was my ticket because if I got good enough at it, I could be a big guy and have a car, too. By the time I heard B.B. King and Eric Clapton, I knew that was it.

When I was fourteen, I had my first gig during the summer playing in a band six nights a week at The Hobnob Lounge from eight p.m. to midnight and eight p.m. to one a.m. on Saturdays. We had no PA system and had to sing through a mic plugged into the jukebox. The place was a real dive with a go-go dancer and, being in Texas before they had mixed drinks, it was a BYOB kind of place. The dads of our band members had to alternate taking us to the gig, and of course they protested, insisting they *hated* it — all the while the three dads would be gathered there at the same time to listen to us play songs from the Rolling Stones, The Kinks, "Boney Maroney" by Ritchie Valens and "Wine, Wine, Wine" by The Nightcaps, a band big in Texas at the time. We played mostly bluesy songs.

At one point, my dad said to me, "Son, you need to learn your majors and minors, so I'm thinking you should go to guitar school." I was hesitant because I already felt like I knew how to play, but I agreed to take the bus into town in Oak Cliff to Boyd's Guitar School, along a road lined with pawnshops that had guitars for sale.

My guitar teacher insisted I was going to have to learn to read notes. I would go home and play a few notes, but after those few, I could immediately tell what the melody was, like "Mary Had a Little Lamb" and I could easily sound out the rest from there. So I didn't really bother with reading. I didn't want to read because that was like studying and to me the guitar is about playing. By the third lesson, my teacher basically fired me. He said, "You're far gone." I thought he was complimenting me, that he'd meant something like, "You're way out there and advanced beyond the pack." I was happy to quit.

I used to stare in the windows of shops nearby and admire the guitars inside these beautiful wooden display cases with velvet holders sitting behind the clean glass. The cases looked like a gun rack but for guitars. I used to practically drool over the Stratocaster and Les Paul SGs with the double cutaways.

I left home at fifteen to be in a band and left a Telecaster behind for Stevie. I had a hard time forgiving him for cutting it up and putting pickups on it, but that's what people did at the time. It was after I'd left that he became serious about the guitar and, in a couple of years, he started to play around Dallas.

What I love about the guitar is that it's straight from the heart. I never dreamed I'd grow up to be in the Fender catalog or meet Les Paul. The guitar has been amazing. Without it, I'd probably still be in Oak Cliff.

Pat Metheny

Pat Metheny is known for reinventing the sound of jazz guitar, expanding its palette of sound with alternate tunings on a 12-string guitar and playing with digital signal processing and guitar synthesizers. He also plays an unforgettable 42-string Pikasso guitar made by Canadian luthier Linda Manzer.

My first serious guitar was an electric Gibson ES-140, which was an odd, weird guitar. I was about twelve and a half years old when I got it. Before that, I had a cheap little toy guitar that I don't really count. I grew interested in playing the guitar as it became a cultural icon of the youth movement, starting with rock 'n' roll and The Beatles. I was about ten years old at the time, had little knowledge and a transistor radio. That's how I became interested.

The last thing my parents wanted me to do was become interested in the guitar. We were a trumpet-centric family. My dad played trumpet; my mom's dad played trumpet professionally; and my brother, Mike, who is five years older, was a trumpet prodigy. I started playing trumpet myself at age eight. To my parents, the guitar represented everything they thought shouldn't be allowed into the home. This was like throwing gasoline on the fire — it made me want a guitar all that much more.

When I was about twelve, I made a deal with my parents that their Christmas gift to me would be their *permission* to buy a guitar, if I could work and earn enough money for the guitar. This was about August, so it gave me plenty of time to work like crazy and save up. I helped my mother with a garage sale and earned a percentage from that. A week before Christmas, I had $80 saved up. This was in 1967. My dad and I pored over the want ads in the *Kansas City Star* and found an ad for a $100 Gibson guitar, so we drove the twelve miles in from Lee's Summit over to Raytown. I can remember this so vividly, like it happened just yesterday. The man who was selling this three-quarter-sized Gibson hollow-bodied ES-140 also had a solid-body Gibson Les Paul that would be worth a lot of money these days, but he wanted $150 for that one, which was out of our price range. But anyway, I was more interested in the hollow-bodied one. That was the guitar for me, that three-quarter-sized Gibson. My dad, being a car salesman, talked the guy down to a price of $80.

Now, there's an asterisk to this story: six months later, I checked the guitar on a flight to Manitowoc, Wisconsin, to go visit my grandparents. The guitar was smashed. It was incredibly traumatic. Ozark Airlines reimbursed me — this is back when airlines still did that — and my dad and I checked the want ads again in the *Kansas City Star*. This time, I picked a full-sized Gibson ES-175 that I've played ever since. This has been my main guitar for over thirty-five years.

Lee's Summit, where I grew up, was a basic Midwestern farm town in those days, although it has grown quite a bit since. There were really no guitar teachers, which was an advantage in the sense that I had to teach myself how to play by learning to listen. Since I had already rebelled against my family's musical taste, I decided to push it one step further and rebel against my friends by becoming the world's youngest and biggest jazz snob. I had nothing in common with the greasers and the jocks and the 4-H Club kids who lived in my town. Jazz was and is the ultimate rebellion because it requires that you draw from every source and really look inside. I was lucky to find that out at a young age.

At fourteen years old, I'd become good enough to start working with a few of the best players in Kansas City. I learned from them and from the experience of playing in real-life situations. The music I was listening to was Charlie Parker, Miles Davis, Sonny Rollins. I was listening to mainstream jazz music every waking minute of the day. Because of my trumpet background, with the guitar I felt like I could breathe instead of pick, in terms of phrasing. Music was the zone for me. I always loved musicians and wanted to know what they were doing and how it was done. It was incredibly exciting playing in actual gigs, and it's where I learned the most about playing.

As far as jazz goes, the guitar is a bit problematic. There are two issues — one is with the dynamic range and the other is the actual nature of what the guitar is and isn't. It's a difficult nut to crack when it comes to being a fluent, expressive jazz tool. Yet the guitar offers an amazing versatility and variety of texture — from nylon-string players to the guy from some heavy metal band with his eighteen Marshall amps. Everyone will call both musicians "guitarists," though their sound is completely different. The range of expression and what you can do with it is what makes the guitar always new and exciting.

About eight or nine years ago, I retired my Gibson ES-175, which I played nonstop from the time I got it in 1968 without ever having any work done on it. It was becoming too rickety to take out on the road, so I use it at home for practicing and playing or sometimes for recording. What I take out on the road now is a signature Ibanez Pat Metheny guitar, which is a model loosely based on my Gibson 175. A team of Japanese specialists had taken my Gibson for one afternoon with the idea of creating this new guitar, and the idea sounded good to me because I did not want to take the Gibson touring any longer. I'm not a materialistic person but I am emotionally attached to that one guitar.

Christian Frederick Martin IV

Christian Frederick Martin IV is the great-great-great grandson of luthier Christian Frederick Martin Sr., a German cabinetmaker who became the apprentice of guitar maker Johann Georg Stauffer of Vienna, Austria. Martin Sr. had immigrated to New York City in 1833 after a bitter legal dispute in which the Violin Makers Guild attempted to limit competition by seeking an injunction prohibiting cabinetmakers from making musical instruments. Martin Sr. opened a retail music store on 196 Hudson Street in Manhattan (now the entrance to the Holland Tunnel) before moving to Nazareth, Pennsylvania. There he established C.F. Martin & Company, where his great-great-great grandson serves as current CEO.

My parents were divorced so I grew up with my mother in New Jersey, away from the family business. I asked my father and grandfather for a guitar for Christmas when I was about eleven or twelve years old, and I received a nylon-string 5-18, which is a little Martin guitar, a model that goes back to the 1800s. What was great about this one is that it had a plate on the back of the headstock that read, "To Chris, from Dad and Poppy." Poppy was my grandfather. I wanted a guitar because I had gone to summer camp and heard the counselor playing chords and singing songs, and I thought, "I could do that."

My other grandfather was a doctor, and one of his patients was a guitar teacher named Mr. Conrad. Mr. Conrad taught out of his house in Lyndhurst, New Jersey, in a little studio in the basement. He did not know of my connection to Martin Guitars at the time. All I know is he opened up my guitar case, stared at the guitar, looked at me, stared at the guitar again and said, "That's a Martin. I've never had a beginning student show up for their first lesson with a Martin guitar before. Your family must have a lot of faith in you."

I said, "Oh no, my dad owns the company." At that point, a little light must have gone off in Mr. Conrad's head — he was going to turn me into the next Segovia. He pulled out a footstool, propped my left foot onto it, opened up Mel Bay study book number one and started me in on scales. Scales! He told me I was going to have to learn to read first.

I never connected with Mr. Conrad, sad to say. I wouldn't practice all week until a half hour before my lesson, when I would then practice the scales. He was so polite and never said to me, "Look, this isn't working out." I was lazy and not inspired, though ultimately, I did learn to read and play scales very well. I went to summer camp and was unable to play the chords I had wanted to learn. When you're sitting there at the campfire in the dark, you can kind of feel out chords, but you cannot really pull out a piece of sheet music and start playing.

My brother, Doug, on the other hand, borrowed a guitar of mine years later, holed himself up in his room for six months and came out having taught himself to play the guitar just by listening to the radio. Later on, I had a Martin electric guitar with a Fender amp and had learned to play some Beatles music very loudly. I can also bang away on the piano in what some might call strange, improvisational jazz.

I really got into making guitars by late in high school. Grandfather Martin influenced me with his dedication to both quality and commitment to his coworkers. He felt if he treated his craftsmen with a great deal of respect, they would be inspired to make the best guitar of its kind.

The first guitar I made was at summer camp. One of the things you could do at camp was woodworking. The counselor said to me, "Chris, I think you've moved beyond Popsicle sticks and are ready to further your art." I'm not sure whether it was his idea or mine, but I decided to make a guitar. I called up my dad and said, "Send me a kit."

He was baffled, telling me, "We don't have kits."

I said, "Well, just put some parts in a box and send them to me." As luck would have it, the company was experimenting with a trapezoidal-shaped guitar so I received a box with a blueprint but no instructions. I was happy to have the parts and said, "Let's go!"

What I learned much later was the sides are the first thing to be built on a guitar. Then the top and back are cut larger so you have some overhang to trim and fit. What I had done was cut the top and back first after some very careful measuring. And when I tried to fit the sides, it didn't fit. I used *lots* of wood putty

Christian Frederick Martin IV in his childhood with a Martin GT electric guitar. (*Courtesy of C. Martin Archives*)

to fill in those gaps. In the end, I did win a prize because no one had ever attempted to make a guitar before. I still have this guitar and it doesn't sound too bad. It has a mahogany body, and it's a little hard to hold with its shape, as it tends to slide off the knee. There's no upper or lower bout.

For Martin's millionth guitar, we had Larry Robinson, an extraordinary inlay artist, help us develop a steel-string showpiece. We wanted to create a guitar that gave the feeling of Europe about two hundred years ago, and we wanted the guitar to tell a story based on European designs. Larry's first blueprint came back with a crown on it and I said, "Wait a minute, our family is not descended from royalty." We scrapped that idea. The inherent risk with this project was all the shipping back and forth. Larry would do some inlay, send it back to the plant and so on. With all this shipping, the millionth guitar was starting to live up to its name in cost. We had thought about pricing it at one million dollars, thinking it would be a neat idea to say Martin's Millionth guitar goes for one million but I stopped to think about it — we're not elitist. We just decided the best thing to say is this guitar is priceless. Which it is.

I've always found it difficult to play in front of other people. There is always that feeling that your playing is not quite good enough. I think my biggest concern is that younger generations might not want to play the guitar because it is not an easy instrument to learn. When I was younger, my mother gave me a 35 mm camera, and I had to learn to figure out all of the buttons and shutters in order to get a good shot. These days, you can just buy a camera and it does all the work for you. Throughout all the years, guitar has been in existence, it has not become any easier to learn to play, and my concern is kids are going to say, "This is hard. I'm not used to this!"

What I do find inspiring are those kids who stick with it. They are so into playing they are willing to slog through their lessons. They'll start to become interested in their music heroes, researching their influences and discovering that Bob Dylan plays a Martin guitar. Johnny Cash, a Martin. Eric Clapton, when he plays acoustic, plays a Martin. When I consider that, something tells me this company will continue to be around for some time.

Ralph Towner

Jazz guitarist Ralph Towner plays classical, nylon-string guitars and 12-string steel-string guitars and tends to forgo amplification. He has collaborated with Egberto Gismonti, Larry Coryell, Keith Jarrett and Gary Burton and is known for his work with the group Oregon, which mixes folk music, Indian classical forms and avant-garde jazz.

I was a twenty-two-year-old graduate in music composition from the University of Oregon, and I went to the music store to get some valve oil for my trumpet. There was this hotshot salesman — and I'd heard something about him playing the classical guitar and thought it sounded kind of nice and even kind of difficult. I went to get the valve oil and did not even have enough money, really. Yet amazingly, this guy at the music store sold me this Martin classical guitar, which is all shaped wrong — but it was a Martin! It cost $100 and it took me a year to be able to pay for it. It's true!

I took one or two lessons with this guy, and he really was not a very good teacher. In fact, later I heard he was put in prison for molesting an eleven-year-old boy student, oh my god. At least I have him to thank for selling me the guitar, even though it was not shaped right, but I did not know this at the time.

Once as a composition student I wrote a piece for flute and guitar with a difficult flute part and a really simple guitar part because I was still trying to teach myself a month after I had bought the guitar. I really wanted to play this guitar properly and very well, so I asked a professor at school who was kind of a Germanophile to recommend a good classical guitar teacher for me. He said, "Oh, Karl Scheit in Vienna," and I said, "Where's THAT?!" Well, I got there and I did not speak German, but they accepted me though I could hardly play.

I love the guitar because it is a polyphonic instrument and I was really into piano. It struck me that the guitar shares many similar qualities as the piano for the ability to play multiple notes and obviously harmony. It is a colorful instrument with so many possibilities, which I discovered as I continued evolving and learning to play with this great teacher. It's a great instrument.

I've been a musician since the age of three and could imitate records on the piano. I was kind of precocious and lived in a very tiny town so I had a real American life of playing baseball. One radio station in town played nothing but country-western, which I'd hated, but I grew up listening to Duke Ellington and Nat King Cole and World War II vintage records with swing and big band music because I had some older brothers and an older sister. So that is where I had heard sophisticated music as a child.

I had a musical family. We were all obsessed. My mother was a church organist and piano teacher and all my family played instruments, so I was not a freak but perhaps just a little freakier than the rest. From the beginning, the guitar was not joyful at all — it was so difficult. I think it was the most difficult instrument I've learned to play and to sound good on. For a while it just felt like a bunch of wires snagged under your fingers. It took a while to feel comfortable on it.

Being a professional musician is not being a musician but someone who tries to make a living at it, which is always tough and risky. Playing music is one of the greatest things you can do for yourself and for other people, too. It's funny — my wife is an actress in theater who has just completed a six month-long tour, if you can imagine (not me!) but they had a party at the end of the tour and a couple of actors picked up the guitar and they knew every Italian song written in the past 400 years, from pop songs, Neapolitan songs and standard Sicilian songs. It was incredible. They were just strumming, but it was perfect for that. I would have been a bummer in that party. I know my place and *that* wasn't it. Everybody was singing out of tune and of course, in Italian. What a joy — what a great thing!

Sonny Landreth

Louisiana slide blues guitarist Sonny Landreth plays with a slide on his little finger to enable other left hand fingers to work the fretboard. His right hand technique also incorporates tapping, picking and slapping. Landreth has recorded with Jimmy Buffett and collaborated with Eric Clapton, Mark Knopfler, Eric Johnson, Robben Ford, John Hiatt and Vince Gill. He brings a distinctive flavor of Cajun music, slide blues and rock to his playing.

When we were little kids living in Mississippi, my older brother Steve and I would entertain our relatives by yowling Elvis songs and flailing away on plastic "Elvis" guitars that had been popular toys at the time. That's how I got the guitar-playing bug, and I carried it with me when my family moved to Lafayette, Louisiana, in 1959. Though my first real experience playing music began with the trumpet when I was ten, it was in 1964, when I turned thirteen years old, that I got my first guitar. Somehow I convinced my parents that it'd be the perfect gift for my birthday even though they had already paid for the trumpet that I was still playing in the school band. I remember walking into the showroom at Prof Erny's Music Store and seeing rows upon rows of guitars. Man, I was excited! But that excitement soon turned into confusion as I was

Sonny Landreth, age fourteen. (*Courtesy Sonny Landreth*)

hit with the dilemma of which one to choose. Mindful of the $50 budget I'd been given, I proceeded to take the rest of the afternoon to make my choice. Eventually, I settled on an acoustic Kay with a sunburst finish that seemed to say, "Get your folks to kick in ten extra bucks and take me home." They agreed to the $60 plus tax but said I'd have to actually wait for my birthday to get it. The Erny's staff put it aside on their store's layaway plan and that sealed the deal.

After what seemed like an eternity of anticipation, my birthday finally arrived and, after school, I caught my dad coming out of my room smiling. Sure enough, on my bed I found that big, beautiful Kay guitar. It wasn't wrapped up or anything and my dad had simply written, "Happy 13th!" on the back of a small card he'd slipped through the strings over the neck. I'll never forget that. Of course, I couldn't play a single musical note yet, but I loved the way this guitar looked, felt and smelled. Plus, I'd gotten a fake tortoiseshell pick and a leather strap that came with it, so that was cool. Learning how to unlock the magic and play the songs that had me all fired me up was still very much a mystery. I just *had* to figure it out, and that became my mission.

A whopping six months or so into this journey, I realized I had a problem with my beloved Kay, as the string height from the fretboard made it difficult to play. (Ironically, as I would eventually become a slider, and higher action creates better sustain and sound.) By then, José Feliciano had hit the scene on national TV and radio with a new album that included "Muleskinner Blues." I was amazed by his virtuosity and fell in love with the sound of his flamenco style guitar with nylon-strings, so I decided to make a course correction. My brother donated yet another $60, and with that I traded in my Kay for a Gibson c-o model acoustic guitar with nylon-strings. It was sweet sounding and much easier to play but, as it turned out, I wasn't done with finding the right axe just yet.

About a year later, my dream-come-true mojo was really peaking when I got my first electric rig for Christmas. This time, the guitar was a red Epiphone solid-body called the Olympic Double because it had two pickups. Since I was into reading Greek mythology at the time, having a guitar with "Olympic" in its name was a hit with me before I even plugged it in. And, well, it was red. As part of the package, I also got a little Epiphone amp with a ten-inch speaker. Meanwhile, with my best friend Tommy Alesi on drums (who went on to play over thirty years with the legendary Cajun band Beausoleil), I started my first band playing instrumental songs by The Ventures. We had to hold off on The Beatles and The Stones because I had neither the microphone nor the nerve yet to sing into one. My folks were always encouraging about my playing.

However, when I plugged the guitar in everyone, including my dog, suffered in the early stages. It was THAT loud. In fact, at one point, when Tommy would come over to my house everybody would leave and take the dog with them. Then we'd get out into the carport and blast out. On the next weekend, we'd switch houses and his family would take us into the kitchen and they would all leave. One of Tommy's brothers took a snapshot of Tommy and I playing in his family's kitchen, and this photo is featured on the inside booklet of my first major label album *South of I-10*.

With dad's help, our first booking was for a pool party set up by my dad's coworkers and their families from State Farm Insurance. We only knew a total of six songs, so we just played them over and over until the grown-ups had had enough and said we'd done a fine job but the show was over. When we each received $5 for playing the gig, I was hooked. Besides, for the same pay, it sure beat mowing yards on the weekends.

By this time, I'd been hanging around Prof Erny's so much that they hired me to work during the summer to help out with a little bit of everything in the store. I loved it because it was exciting to be involved with anything related to music, including the buzz of activity with selling albums, sound systems of the day ("stereos"), tape recorders, sheet music, school band instruments, accessories, amplifiers and, of course, all those guitars. An older kid, Raymond Decou, also worked there and he turned me on to Chet Atkins and taught me how to fingerpick Chet-style. That was HUGE. It was the beginning of my embracing the concept of playing multiple parts — melody, rhythm and bass patterns — simultaneously. That inspired me to want find out who all else was "out there" that I needed to get hip to. With my worker discount at the store as a resource, I bought lots of albums and tapes and listened to Wes Montgomery, Johnny Smith, Howard Roberts, Carlos Montoya, Andrés Segovia, Carl Perkins, Stephen Stills and Neil Young in Buffalo Springfield, Michael Bloomfield, Eric Clapton in Cream and many others. I heard B.B. King live at Leo's Rendevous in New Iberia (they didn't even check my ID) and Jimi Hendrix in concert at Independence Hall in Baton Rouge. Then I discovered the sound of slide guitar on many of the old Delta blues albums including those by my favorite, Robert Johnson. As I got into the Delta players, I realized they sang story songs with two distinct voices. They had their singing voice and they had their guitar voice. Especially with the slide, they could create different sounds that would embellish the lyrics of the songs. I was totally blown away by this "new" sound I was just discovering from the ancient 1920s, '30s and '40s, so I began to tackle it head on. With a metal slide on the little finger of my left hand (I would later switch to glass), I got the idea to incorporate the Chet Atkins fingerpicking approach with my right hand. That really set me on the path that would eventually lead me to developing a sound and voice of my own.

In spite of the wear and tear of all these years of traveling, playing shows and dealing with the ups and downs of the music business, I admit that I am still enthralled with the magic I first felt with this instrument. For me, what I love most about the guitar is its unlimited potential for expressing emotion regardless of style or musical genre. And, especially amped up, the sky is the limit, too, for creating sounds that can capture the imagination, stir the soul and turn you into a kid all over again. For that and for my family's support and all who have helped me along the way, I am most grateful.

Lurrie Bell

Chicago blues guitarist Lurrie Bell, the son of renowned blues harmonica player Carey Bell, performed with Big Walter Horton, Eddie Taylor, Willie Dixon and Bell's cousin Eddy Clearwater before he joined Koko Taylor's Blues Machine. Lurrie, who has recorded over forty albums during the course of his career, has been honored as a top Chicago blues musician by the *Chicago Reader*.

I was about six or seven years old when I picked up the guitar for the first time and taught myself to play the blues during my father's rehearsals on the west side of Chicago. The first song I wanted to learn was a Jimmy Reed song that I played on a Fender guitar. I moved down South at that age to my dad's hometown in Macon, Mississippi, for two or three years and, after that, I moved to Alabama to live with my grandparents at the age of seven or eight. At that time, I started attending church as an active member, and they had guitars there, too, which I played, performed and jammed on. But the first guitar I can say I ever truly owned was one that my father sent me through the mail from Chicago to Alabama. It was an acoustic guitar that looked exactly like a Fender. It was not an original Fender but a guitar made out of plastic made to look just like a Fender. I learned how to play in church, and for this reason I played church music back in those days. I wish I had a photo of this guitar but I do not.

The only instrument I've ever played is the guitar. Ever since I could remember, I wanted to learn how to perform and play the guitar because, at an early age, I found out I had the ear for it, especially because I was surrounded by blues music and blues musicians. I grew up listening to guys like Eddie Taylor and Roy Lee Johnson, Joe Harper and, of course, my father, Carey Bell. I always loved the blues and what my dad did back in the day because he was a blues entertainer who played with people like Howlin' Wolf and Muddy Waters way back before I was even born. When I was around the blues cats, I wanted to be a blues musician also! When I was living down in Lisbon, Alabama, I was playing the blues back in those days, but the message was about gospel — about religion. I always was around the blues cats so that's what I do these days — perform and play blues for a living.

What I like best about the guitar is the sound you can get out it. I can play guitar and discover a particular tone that I am looking for that I enjoy listening to. I like the sound of guitar, period. Just playing gives me a certain feeling that I can't get anywhere else. I also play electric guitar and right now I own a Gibson ES-335, which is what I usually play when entertaining at the clubs. Performing and playing the guitar, period, is a challenge in itself. You learn the guitar by exploring it and experimenting with tone on the instrument, and it teaches you and explains itself to you as best it can. My first performance playing for a public audience was at church in Alabama because I was the musician who officially played an instrument. Any kind of music, when it comes down to gospel music, I basically liked it. Gospel, back in those days, and spirituals, were the choir music. I enjoyed playing the guitar behind choirs and quartets of four singers. The special feeling that I got by playing at one of those sanctified churches, as they used to call them and I imagine they still do, has stayed with me most of my life. When it comes down to blues, it's similar — gospel and blues are almost related.

Right now I am sitting down by my Dobro. I just got a new Dobro, and I've always admired the sound that comes out of them. The tone you can get out of Dobro is something else, amazing, and I am enjoying exploring it. I have played Dobros on tours, but I've never owned one until now. I own about seven or eight guitars because each one has the correct sound I am looking for. Every day I am learning something new whenever I pick up the guitar. To break the story down, they pay the bills!

One story I can tell you about is my Gibson ES-335 — I'd only had it for a couple years when I found myself onstage in the middle of a performance, jamming on a blues song onstage, when the pick guard fell off. Right in the middle of the performance! That is the first and only time that ever happened with a guitar when I was on tour. My guitar looked so good without the pick guard on it that I kept it like it was. I never went in to get it repaired because it made me love playing the guitar more this way. Every time I pick it up if feels so much better to me, and I am playing the guitar now in a way that nobody else has ever played it before. The guitar somehow must have known that I really needed to be playing it this way.

I've been in the music business for over forty years, and I've recorded more than forty albums, and I know tons of blues musicians. In other words, I've been in the blues world all my life and wouldn't want to do anything else. I see myself as carrying on the tradition.

Rory Block

Rory Block is a blues guitarist who grew up in Manhattan's Greenwich Village during the '60s and felt inspired by the folk music scene to learn classical guitar. She left home at fifteen to seek out blues giants Mississippi John Hurt, Skip James, Reverend Gary Davis and Son House in order to learn traditional Delta blues. She has won five Blues Music Awards, two for Traditional Blues Female Artist and three for Acoustic Blues Album of the Year.

I was eight years old when I started playing the recorder and ten years old when I received my first guitar. The guitar was a Galiano, a classical guitar, that my mother had found and purchased for me from a flea market for $4. I changed the strings to a combination of silk and steel. I played this guitar for a while and found that I could bend strings if they were steel, but I could not bend them if the strings were nylon. I did put a light gauge steel string on this guitar, but then the neck broke because the steel had too much tension.

I had learned recorder because it had been a part of school instruction. If you were eight years old, you had a choice of either flute or recorder. I learned to read music at this time, which I then later forgot. I remember some instructors saying I had talent. One teacher complained, saying, "She doesn't actually read music as much as she anticipates it, and we'd like her to focus on what the sheet music says, even if she is playing it by some other method." At some point, I discovered in choir that I do not need to know the song in order to sing harmony, but I do need to know the song in order to sing the melody. I know where the chord is going to go and I know what the harmony is — there's something odd there!

My mother played folk music and my dad played folk music as well, but his preferences leaned more toward old-timey Appalachian and American roots music whereas my mother preferred Burl Ives and Pete Seeger, which was more contemporary and less rough around the edges. My dad played clawhammer style, and I learned this technique from him and applied it to playing Robert Johnson's music. My family found my interest in the guitar pretty much annoying, so I always tried to find a far-off corner so I could practice. Right away, my mom, bless her heart, became a big fan of mine. But I'd say everyone had been driven crazy first by my millionth version of "Froggy Went A-Courtin'." When I started backing my dad on Carter family–style songs, then I was in the loop, and there was a reason for me to be playing the guitar and my dad appreciated it.

I think the guitar is a funky, gritty, earthy, hands-on instrument. Piano is hands-on as well but with the guitar, you're actually touching the strings. It's probably, other than drums, the most primal instrument. I like to sit when I play the guitar so I can stomp with my feet. It's a good feeling to hold the guitar and play it, and I'm sure that with any instrument, it allows you to release emotion. It's a vehicle of expression that is good for my health. I think, without it, I'd be in a whole other space — who knows where!

When I first started listening to Robert Johnson's music, I thought, "This is so clean, so beautiful — it can't be slide guitar!" My friends who were playing slide guitar at the time, in the 1960s, sounded quite different. Their playing had more of a rough sound, less precise and less clean sounding. But they were experimenting, too. I made a decision to try to play with a slide but found that I had a hard time finding a slide that would fit my finger because they were all made from bottles. You had to break a bottle. The perfect bottle with a long slim neck was not to be found anywhere by me, but my guy friends all found that if you break a wine bottle neck and sand it down, then a larger hand will have a perfectly good slide. So I decided to just do all the Robert Johnson stuff without the slide. Then, years later, John Hammond told me to get myself a socket and so I found one of those, tried it and couldn't figure out why it sounded so horrible. I was trying to be very stiff and get to the fret exactly and not vary, go under or beyond that fret. It was like the fiddle. So I was trying to be very rigid in the process of getting to the note and discovered it sounded bad. Then one day, it locked in and I hit the pocket, discovering that playing with a slide is a lot less rigid than I'd thought. This was my biggest challenge with the guitar, and it's all about rocking and doing this in a very relaxed way. I realized I could conquer this and started practicing intensely. It was annoying, hard work because I had reached a plateau and remained there for years, playing everything I already knew how to play without pushing the envelope. When the socket came along, I had an obligation to do this because people consider me to be a role model as a musician and eventually, my effort bore fruit. I do not think I am a great slide player, but I know how to have a really good time with it.

I remember playing at the Peace Church in Greenwich Village, where everything that was anything took place. If you had a play, you could put it on at the Peace Church. It was just a big old church sitting on West 4th Street in New York. Somehow, I was able to get a booking there to hold a concert. I got up onstage, looked out into the audience and was totally terrified. I saw all my friends there — everybody I had ever met my whole life. It was a surreal moment, like something out of a Fellini film. They were all there looking at me. I thought, "I'm going to die." I just started shaking. I played all the country blues songs I knew how to play and felt so humiliated. I got offstage thinking I had played horribly and that everyone hated me. But then I saw a long line of these friends who all wanted to hug me. I was shaking again, and later, John S. Wilson from the *New York Times* gave me a stunning review. That's when I knew it was going to be all right — that I could do this professionally, if I wanted to. He'd said good things, great things.

Martin had given me one of their guitars because I already endorsed their strings. I was out of my mind with excitement, planning to attend a convention in Los Angeles where I was going to represent Martin guitars. Every guitar builder and brand on earth was there, and I was going to play a concert. Five minutes before showtime, I was backstage, tuning up, and discovered a huge gash on the back of my guitar. It looked as if someone came over with a wood-cutting axe and had thrown it down, creating an 8-inch wide gap. I started screaming. No one had a clue what had happened. The guitar must have gotten knocked over. Someone went to get Dick Boak from Martin Guitars to send out the red alert that my guitar was cracked. Roy Rogers was backstage and everyone was offering to let me use their guitars, but I said, "No, no, no." Dick duct-taped the guitar back together. Artie Traum was there. Michael Dorian was there. All these guitar builders where there, watching him squeeze the guitar and tape it. After the show, Martin took this guitar back and gave me a new one because the crack had grown wider, all the way around to the neck. The action had shifted during the first two songs of my set and then settled. My thought at the time was "Well, many blues artists have played guitars with action this high, so why not?"

David Tronzo

David Tronzo is an American guitarist known for his innovative techniques with the electric slide guitar in bebop, modern jazz, rock and experimental music. His playing can be heard on the soundtrack of Robert Altman's film *Short Cuts*, and he is an associate professor at the Berklee College of Music. He has been voted Best Experimental Guitarist and also as one of the Dirty Thirty Pioneers and Trailblazers of Guitar by *Guitar Player Magazine*.

When I became aware of slide guitar, I wondered why there was not more of a vocabulary to it and different objects used for different sounds. I was thirteen years old at the time, and I studied guitar with a teacher but would adapt what I just learned to what it was I wanted to do with the slide. I was committed to what seemed like the impossible.

My first guitar was a baby blue Fender Mustang abandoned by my brother that was sitting in his bedroom closet. I grabbed it up and took it to a guitar store so that the action could be raised and I could play slide guitar with it. My dad sawed off the handles of a bicycle so I could use those for slides. I had some of those slides for years and actually wore the chrome off them. Most slide guitar music is in open tuning and tends to be country and blues music. I did

Dave Tronzo, age thirteen, wearing a slide cut from a bicycle handle bar on his third finger. (*Courtesy David Tronzo*)

not play anyone else's music but stayed in standard tuning, eventually developing this trait of dropping the high E string down to D, which is known as universal tuning. I was trying to develop musically what it was I could hear inside my head and, along the way, I started experimenting and discovering that this idea of playing a stringed instrument with a different object other than fingers alone is actually a part of many different cultures. Microtonalism is part of this concept — we know microtonalism from blues string bending. I was very smitten by microtonal, twentieth-century music like the gamelan, so I started to use various objects of different densities that I can hold in my hand to play the guitar. I used plastic cigar tubes, an old Smokehouse Almonds can, metal, plastic, paper, wood, ceramics. I've used pencils, tubes and containers, shampoo bottles, plastic and paper cups. The items change the frequency spectrum of the harmonics on the guitar, which creates a textural change. And sometimes it is reminiscent of another instrument like an African kalimba or a wood drum. Or, for example, one time I was playing a piece in Europe that almost sounded like a Lebanese oud and people in the audience had been wondering the entire time where the oud player had been! Often when I play slide on the guitar, though, it is for a texture that is unique and not reminiscent of another instrument.

My love for modern twentieth-century music includes John Cage, who created "prepared" piano pieces, and when you look at his scores, they are normal piano scores except for the very beginning, where he lists what object is placed under what specific string. I realized the guitar is like a drum with strings just like a piano, so I started experimenting with using alligator clips and wooden chicken skewers that make an alternate bridge if you put them all the way through the strings. If you put the skewers only partially through, then the guitar becomes a resonant thing. I use corks of various sizes floated between the strings and it creates gorgeous overtones. It's much more complex and I have ideas for pieces with these new sounds.

My musical inspirations other than John Cage include Led Zeppelin *II*, Taj Mahal, Lee Morgan, Miles Davis, Chris Smither or Bonnie Raitt and Ornette Coleman. This was in my teens. I wore out that silver live Cream album to dust. I loved all the slide players I'd heard of various Delta bluesmen, but I am a staunch non-imitator. I later lived in New York for twenty-two years, where I worked as a studio musician and I would be called in, never knowing what it was I was going to be doing in terms of playing styles, and often artists would not know until I suggested something. You have to have a huge playing range — but my commitment has primarily been to develop this world, I call it, a strange orchestration.

My dad had no idea about the music business or how it worked, other than it being a road to hell, but he said, "Go for it!" My mom was the complete opposite and felt I was going to die, that this was not going to go well. And they both were right! So I was kind of on my own and took lessons in my first year. Then I did not take lessons in a long time. I was underage at fifteen when I was hired to play in a band with guys who were twice my age. See, the thing is I've always had these ideas about how I wanted to play and what it was I wanted to do on the guitar from the very beginning, so I am fond of saying to my students, "It is better to be a bad version of yourself than a polished version of somebody else." I lived it. I was a bad version of myself for a long time. It was not like I fit comfortably in these groups. Generally, there were two reactions I would receive — dramatically enthusiastic approval or else, "I don't know WHAT that is. I don't want any more of it."

When I wound up in New York, I was twenty-two years old and I found everything I needed musically, along with the education I had been looking for. I started to understand more about how to bring something to the public that is not your dad's Oldsmobile. In America, unlike other places, people get no exposure outside of really commercial music. Even school programs do not explore the depth of it. I do not mean to be so general because it is not intended to be a statement about who is teaching those programs or the kids' ability to be creative, which is endless. It's about the systemic non-recognition about a certain truth regarding music, which is that it is an art form that has more power that you can comprehend. That power is largely healing. When you go to Europe, they perceive instrumental music as a non-verbal version of a story.

What I love about the guitar is that all guitar players pick up the instrument and begin to play it. I watch my wife, who has no intention of learning how to play the guitar, pick it up, force her fingers onto the fretboard and start making a sound. She recognizes it and then makes another sound and says to herself, "No, that wasn't it." She will try again and say, "There it is!" and memorize it. Guitar players go right to home plate — they start playing and it is really slow, and they realize, "Oh my god . . . this is going to take a long time to figure out." I was talking to Pat [Martino] recently about how much diversity there is in this instrument culture. Guitar players are customarily acclimated to lots of diversity. I do not see as much diversity in other musical instruments. The guitar from the hands of one artist to the next, can sound completely different. That's a marvel to me to this day.

It is the most cryptic instrument — it gives you nothing. You can play the same pitch on it in six different locations. Harmonically, the number of ways you can treat groups of notes together is more limited. We have to recycle more and hear notes that we're not playing, but the truth is we live within the framework of what the guitar can do, which is quite enormous. There are certain physical limits to it. I love the fact that the guitar says, "Stop!" and makes you really think and spend time slowly. Right now I get the expectation, which I see even with my students, that we're to move and learn at a pace that is much faster than the reality. The guitar cannot be acquired quickly. Literally, they turn pale if I say, "Oh, that's a five-year goal." I'm just trying to get them to think about what it is you have to do today to move closer to your goal. So god help me if I say that is a twenty-year goal! If a student says to me, "I want to be able to play anything I hear," and I say, "That's a forty-year goal," they say, "WHAT?!" See, I used to get really heartened whenever I heard something like this because my own progress had seemed so slow that I'd think, "I'm *never* going to get there." All things do even out after a while, with effort.

I have been inspired by the guitar for the music I have been able to imagine and hear inside my head and even feel, amazingly enough. But I knew the music I wanted to make could not be done in a flash. I loved and was just magnetized to hear slide guitar on the radio or on records — it would stop me in my tracks.

When I was fifteen, we had this regular gig in this little town about forty miles from where I lived and it was a hangout for the local Hell's Angels chapter. They liked us a lot because we played Hank Williams tunes and blues. I was really kicking the fence down — I knew five good notes. I was going for it and they were all smiling and winking. I did not have problems with anyone at that place because basically if anyone hassled me, all I had to do was go over to one of these guys and say, "He's bothering me!" It was a two-days-per-week job throughout the year as a house gig. The second gig that I did in my life was at a school for the deaf. They lay down on the floor with their hands on the floor and listened to a set of music. I knew this was going to be special and always felt like this is the purpose of the music.

I'd like to say that my first guitar was a cheetah struck by lightning but actually, I have a wonderful friend who is a very well-known guitar maker whose name is Flip Scipio. He lives on Long Island and also on Martha's Vineyard. Flip is an old, dear friend and a great player. When I was playing modernist music, I was an endorser of Steinberger and Fender and Gibson guitars, which I loved. But I was always looking for another sound, and Flip, on the side, would rebuild all these cheap, old, junky Silvertones and Kay guitars — vintage but not well-made instruments. The short version is I would hang out, work on some guitars, play some and go down to a bar and play at this club and then we would have dinner. I'd come home at six a.m. He was working on one of my guitars, doing a re-fit of this Silvertone I was playing. We were alone in this giant workshop and I plugged into two stereo amps loudly. I was standing in the middle of the room, running this guitar for over an hour non-stop, playing everything with it that I do. This is maybe a $70 Masonite-bodied guitar. It's like a piece of junk but is magical because the materials are really crude. It's an acoustic guitar that is giving you all this information and characteristics similar to a human voice. I told him that I wanted this guitar. Scipio had this look on his face as if I was asking him to kill his firstborn: "I-I-I don't know how to tell you this but that's my favorite guitar and it is not for sale." I insisted, "I do not care what you ask me for this guitar but I want this guitar."

We went and played at this club and then came back to his house at five a.m., where we had a single malt scotch. So I let him have a couple of drinks before I picked up this guitar and asked if he minded at all if I played it for a little bit. "Oh no, that'd be great!" I played this really sweet, mournful gospel blues music, which was the kind of music he loved. I played for about ten minutes and watched his head growing lower and lower until finally, he just said, "Okay. The guitar is yours."

I would say this guitar has about 100,000 road miles on it. I've owned it since 1994, and it was made some time in 1960, so it has held up pretty well. Scipio is a delight. He was in Amsterdam at the time my wife and I were living there in '97–'98 on a boat on the docks, which is very beautiful in the center of the city. Scipio was there to work on the first installment of what was going to be the Buena Vista Social Club film. Scipio was there to work on all the instruments because when the musicians took their guitars out of Cuba, they'd exploded from being accustomed to anything but that climate. So I was sitting on my boat, playing this Höfner archtop, and I hear this knock, "Captain, are you in there?" I had no idea who it was. I stepped out and saw Flip with the foreman and this young kid. Out in the shadows on the street, I hear this voice say, "God, that boat's a beauty!" Ry Cooder stepped out of the shadows and I invited him in for some tea. He came in and I made him this cup of tea, and we were all sitting in the living room with this Höfner archtop. Cooder, Flip and I are all staring at this guitar wearing the same expression, like, "Who's going to go for this guitar first?" So gradually, everybody picked up the guitar and played a little bit.

Thirty Minutes Inside a Guitar Shop

I had thirty minutes to kill on Ventura Boulevard and the only place that seemed like a feasible, air-conditioned escape was the Guitar Center. I made my way to the back of the store and discovered a classical guitar room, empty but for one bored salesman who listened to me as I played a guitar I'd selected from an array displayed upon the wall. He then insisted that I try one of the $10,000 Ramírezes locked up in the case behind me, though I told him I was not in the market to buy anything. This did not seem to discourage him. I warned him that I'd be unlikely to be able to discern the difference between a crap guitar and a nicer one because my hearing had disappeared in one ear after a summer cold. The salesman was still not scared away. "I have to confess my intention is purely selfish," he said. "I like listening to you play and I would much rather hear you on one of these guitars instead."

I exchanged guitars. To my surprise, when I started to play the Ramírez, the difference in tonal quality was distinct, immediate and obvious. I remain forever indebted to this man. I had lost my hearing about two years after graduating from college and perceived the loss as an excuse, just another nail in the coffin burying myself alive from what it was I'd loved most. I bought a factory-made Spanish classical guitar, not a Ramírez, but a guitar I knew would inspire me to spend hours with it for the ease of its left-hand action. The minute I came home, I dug through old moving boxes and found all of my sheet music and music books, many of which bore fastidious and ancient dates written in red ink by Sonia Michelson, whom I felt I had disappointed long ago for quitting, though I had never told her what had happened at home.

The theater people had attempted to intervene on my behalf back then but they found themselves sandwiched between a raging mother and the police department threatening to shut them down for harboring a minor. I spent the last two years of high school yo-yo-ing between social services and my home, with in-between moments of bunking out in the library and sleeping in front hallways. The evening after I was inducted into the National Honors Society I spent the night propped up against a tombstone in Calvary Cemetery. What I had learned at the theatre is that no situation is so grim nor sacred that you couldn't pry the humor from it and wring the rest for a story.

One rooming house tenant, a taxi driver from Peru, told me of the author Isabel Allende, whose books had not yet been published in English at the time. He believed I ought to write, and he purchased a Big Chief writing tablet for me from the pharmacy. I wrote long letters of my adventures and shoved them beneath the theater door. The collected letters became the basis of my application and acceptance into the University of Chicago, where I eventually graduated with a degree in English literature. I had the fortune to study with author Richard Stern, who told stories both of looking after Ezra Pound during his dying days in Venice and visiting Flannery O'Connor on her farm, Andalusia, teeming with her beloved yet nasty peacocks.

I did many things for a living after graduating, from working long hours at two Chicago newspapers to sewing bridal gowns. I moved to New York and worked on the independent film producer floor of Warner Bros., vetting books for film potential. Life kept coming full circle. I knew that no one had yet purchased rights to Allende's novel *El plan infinito,* though a rival film company had just spent a fortune to produce *The House of the Spirits (La casa de los espíritus)* that the taxi driver roomer had urged me to read long ago. I translated her new novel from its original Editorial Sudamerica edition and, though the film company did not option the title, I later had a chance to meet with Ms. Allende.

During this time, I had all but amputated music from my life. I had resigned myself to not playing guitar, though it itched like a phantom limb. Playing the guitar had always come easily, to the point where I took my ability for granted, yet I had also been punished severely for it and wanted to forget all of it. The sudden hearing loss felt like one more reason that suggested there was no point in picking up my guitar again.

I was wrong. I retain what I hear now to a far greater degree. I feel more, absorb more and respond to sound in a way I had never paid much attention to before. I can walk into any room and immediately assess the refraction of acoustics the same way a pool shark intuitively understands the geometry of the table.

I started work on relearning several favorite pieces and discovered that Sonia had relocated from Chicago to her hometown of Los Angeles, nine miles from my house. I arranged for a lesson that happened to fall on the same December date I had taken my very first lesson with her when I was eleven years old. She listened to me play some Villa-Lobos études and a small snippet of Britten's *Nocturne* as she arranged the dozen pink roses I had brought for her. She was not certain that she actually had much to teach me. I told her that I was considering graduate school but felt worried about my hearing loss. I had altered my approach to music — sound now came through my bones. It came through touch and varying frequencies. Before, I used to be lazy, skimming and floating along the surface like a lost afternoon spent aboard an inflatable pool raft, playing for the sheer enjoyment of listening to the sounds I could make. Now my music required actual focus so that what I played came from the inside and projected outward. Music had never left me, plus I still have all my hearing in one ear — I simply had to adjust from what I knew and cultivate a new relationship with how I now heard sound.

Sonia and I both agreed that if I was performing at this level, then my hearing loss was nobody's business. She offered to help me prepare for graduate school auditions by building my repertoire, and I worked on putting together concert programs for performances around Los Angeles. Yet I had to contend with one more bump in the road. Weeks before I was to perform for an assembly of inner-city public school students, I learned I would be blind in both eyes if I did not undergo surgery immediately for retinal detachment. The doctor's words had been, "Have surgery now or be blind by Monday." Great.

The news couldn't have been any more stupefying. That a busy eye surgeon in Santa Monica would push aside his other patients to see me immediately is never a sign of good things to come. I had come this far, conquering all these hurdles, for this?

I called the school where I was scheduled to perform and spoke with the teacher. She offered her best wishes and assumed that I wanted to cancel. I told her that I preferred to wait and just see how the recovery went. I'd already had the repertoire memorized. It was not a paid gig, but it meant a lot to me.

I underwent the surgery and spent a week at home in bed. With my eyes wrapped in bandages, I played my guitar when I felt well enough to sit upright and listened to Tom Stoppard radio plays when I was not. It is amazing how easy it is to play without the habitual crutch of looking at the keyboard. In fact, it was liberating. I knew I could do this concert whatever the final diagnosis turned out to be. Being unable to see while playing was not the end of the world at all, but a new one.

After a week in bed, I sat in my eye surgeon's examining room chair, listening to him rustle about in preparation to remove the bandages. When he asked, "What kind of guitar do you play?" I told him it was classical.

"I'm not really much of a fan of classical guitar, to tell you the truth."

I found this hard to believe. Who wouldn't like classical guitar?

"I find it, for the lack of a better word, boring," he told me. "Sorry. Not my cup of tea."

I grew more anxious as he unwrapped the bandages, fearful of what I would or would not see. I was also fuming at him inwardly, wondering what kind of cretin had operated on me. He peeled my eyelids back with what sounded like a Velcro-like rip, followed by a viciously bright penlight. It's strange how we can retreat and recede inside the body when faced with pain, even when it comes to our eyes, through which we normally takes in the world. He applied some drops and told me to sit up.

I heard him plop into his squeaky desk chair and click his pen to scribble out a prescription. "Let me tell you how lucky you are. I've been performing these kinds of surgeries for thirty years. Less than one percent of people who go through what you did ever have their vision fully restored. We do not catch it most the time. People do not register anything wrong until they start having problems reading, which means detachment has already hit the macular area. By then it's too late to fix, and you are left with some form of tunnel vision. You will see again in both eyes with a full range of periphery."

Had he not told me so with such unflinching bluntness a moment ago of his distaste for classical guitar, I probably would not have believed him. At this point, the world around me was a canvas of light and shadow colored with hope. He said it would take three months for my vision to stabilize.

"I like jazz guitar," he told me on the way out the door. "Jazz is where it's at."

I called the public school again to confirm the concert. I felt certain I could play. The teacher and I agreed that it was not necessary to have to explain anything other than the pieces I was going to perform —*Asturias (Leyenda)*, Tárrega's *Gran Jota* and *Recuerdos de la Alhambra*.

I arrived at the school early. The teacher had drawn the blinds to cut some of the direct light. My vision consisted of a pair of black and blotchy full moons in each eye that still obliterated the field of view. I set up my chair and footstool and waited in place with my guitar as I heard the students clamoring in the hallway before they lined up and entered the classroom. Chairs clattered, backpacks thudded against the floor, gym shoes squeaked. Chattering and fidgeting filled the room, which ceased the minute the teacher commanded attention with a series of hand movements, which represented musical notes in a system called *solfège*. The children responded immediately by singing the notes back to her and they came to order. She introduced them to me and allowed me to speak a little of the music that I was about to play.

I do not think I ever played better in my life. The students were attentive and enthralled, wanting to see afterward how I had made those sounds in the *Gran Jota* by drumming crossed bass strings and creating harmonics. Several students were thrilled to learn that the words used for many techniques were in the same language they spoke at home. One student thanked me later for playing the *Gran Jota* because it was one of the longest pieces of music he had ever heard, so long, in fact, that it got him out of part of math class. Someone else said that they had a guitar at home that they were going to go pick up tonight. When the room emptied out, I folded up my footstool and spoke to the teacher about my plans to return to New York.

Her attention was diverted by a small shadow lingering anxiously in the doorway. "Excuse me one moment," she said to me. "What is it, Matthew? Did you forget something?"

"I just wanted to thank Miss Crowe," he said. "I never heard the guitar sound like that before."

Melissa Etheridge

Melissa Etheridge is a Grammy-winning rock singer-songwriter from Leavenworth, Kansas, with two platinum-selling albums.

I was eight years old when I got my first guitar, and it was a steel-string acoustic Stella, made by Harmony. I was just insane about music, starting from the age of three. Before I had a guitar, I used to jump up and down, strumming my badminton rackets.

I'd started playing clarinet in school. My first choice had been the drums, but I was told girls couldn't play drums. My second choice was the trumpet, but I was told girls couldn't play the trumpet, either. So that left the guitar.

I used to tell this one story about how I got my first guitar — mainly, that I was jumping around so much with my badminton rackets that my dad finally brought home a guitar. But then my mother reminded me that's not exactly how it happened. My dad had brought the guitar home for my sister, who was twelve years old at the time, and I just begged and begged to play it but her teacher said my hands were too small. Finally, my sister gave it up and the guitar became mine.

I listened to a lot of folk music at the time — this was in Kansas, 1969. My parents had a great collection of music, like Simon & Garfunkel, and my mother had a few Neil Diamond records. My sister had The Beatles and some early, early Led Zeppelin. And of course, on the radio, I heard bubblegum stuff like the Jackson Five. I loved Motown.

My teacher at the time was a jazz guitarist named Don Raymond, and he'd had several of his fingers cut off at one time in a terrible accident. For this reason, he was very intimidating to me as an eight year old. Just look at his hands — and, oh my god! He was also very stern. Music was serious business to him. If I didn't practice, he'd let me know how disappointed he was. There was a little fear involved here but I really wanted to learn. I remember he used to tap his foot on a stool and say to me, "I don't care if you play the wrong note, just *never* lose the beat." Ask my drummer today and he'll tell you I keep the best time in my songs!

The guitar is an extension of me. It's the tool I use to express my soul. It is truly a part of my soul. If I've had any challenge with the guitar, it's that I have very small hands. I am about five feet, three inches tall, and when I went to Berklee to study guitar, I couldn't do many of the jazz chords with those stretches between the fourth finger and pinkie. I had to come up with different fingerings and eventually, with my own style.

My first gig was at a shopping mall in Leavenworth, Kansas. I was eleven years old and played a folksy song that I had written with my girlfriends in sixth grade.

One story I have is about a guitar I had from when I was about fourteen years old. It was a round-backed ovation, which is really a great guitar for women because the necks are smaller and it fits the body well. This guitar was a 12-string, and I had it until I was about twenty-one. It was stolen from me and it was my fault. I'd parked outside of a friend's house in Venice Beach, California, with the guitar in the back of my pickup and had left it there. (Hey, I'm from Kansas.) Someone must have grabbed it from my truck. I've learned since to stop becoming emotionally attached to my guitars. I have a whole bunch of them now so if I lose one, I'll play another.

Muriel Anderson

Award-winning fingerstyle and harp guitarist Muriel Anderson is the founder Muriel Anderson's All Star Guitar Night and the Music For Life Alliance, a charity that aids the efforts of individuals and organizations that foster music learning. Her music can be heard in the soundtrack for Woody Allen's film *Vicky Cristina Barcelona*.

A friend of my parents, Adele Knight, was throwing away a guitar, a half-size, possibly three-quarter-sized Decca nylon-string guitar. I picked the garbage out of the sound hole and tuned up the three strings that were remaining on it. When Adele saw this, she said, "Why don't you keep it?" So I took it into the backseat of the car with me on the way home and started figuring out melodies and making up tunes. My parents realized I had an affinity for it right away. I remember at that time, it seemed really big. I was eight years old. I eventually gave this guitar to my niece.

What I think really appealed to me is the way the guitar vibrates against you when it's played. When you touch the strings, you have direct contact with the sound coming out. As I found later, in studying classical guitar, you have direct *control* over what kind of sound and exactly what nuances come out and this is something you just don't have with piano. With piano, you are separated from the instrument by a hammer that comes up and hits the strings for you — you don't have direct contact with the strings. So I think that intimacy with the string and the instrument is part of my attraction with the guitar.

My parents asked my first guitar teacher, Anne Jones, what to get me for Christmas, so she recommended the album *Doc Watson in Nashville*. When I opened the present, my first thought was "What are my parents giving me an album for?" I put it on my record player to listen and it never left the turntable. I would run home from school to learn every song on that album and try to figure out what it was he was doing. In my lessons, I had started out learning folk guitar so it was mostly chords, accompanying songs and playing with other people. It was a release, a joy and a way to relate to other people.

The first time I ever played in class was in the third grade. I played "Blues My Naughty Sweetie Gives to Me" and "Nobody Knows You When You're Down and Out." I hadn't a clue this was kind of unusual material for a third-grader. Just not a *clue*. The class laughed. They thought it was really funny. Both songs had very adult lyrics, like, "There are blues you get from women when you see 'em goin' swimmin' and you haven't got a bathing suit yourself." And, "There are blues you get much quicker when you're drinking lots of liquor and somebody goes and takes it off the shelf." This is what I was singing. I don't recall what my teacher said. I don't think she even knew what to make of it.

My first professional gig was at the Two Way Street coffeehouse in Downers Grove, Illinois, and I return there every year, about the time of my annual concert, to do a workshop at that same venue. I was playing with a banjo player, Kim Koskella, and fiddle-player Cathy Jones, who was the daughter of my guitar teacher. That was our first gig where we actually got paid money. We were *so* excited. We got $20 to split three ways among us for the evening. We were so excited that someone would care enough to actually pay us for playing music.

In college, I realized the only way to study guitar was to study classical. I had no intention of staying with it. My thought was "I guess I have to do this now in order to keep studying guitar." After my first nylon-string guitar, my first good guitar was a three-quarter-size steel-string Guild. After that I played bluegrass on an old Martin D-35 and some jazz on an ES-335 Gibson semi-hollow body. So in returning to a nylon-string guitar for playing classical, I equated a nylon-string guitar with my beginner guitar — the one with no tone and the strings kind of flapped. I traded my Guild steel-string for a nylon-string guitar when I was in Spain for a summer. I came back to the States and, for the first time, heard the music of Christopher Parkening. I thought to myself, "Wow, how can anything be *so* beautiful?" It was *Capriccio Arabe*. I'd heard it on the radio and was just spellbound. Then I started listening to other pieces and Segovia. In college, I discovered the richness of the classical guitar and learned just how much you can shape the emotion, tone and phrasing. It was a new and exciting world for me.

You would think my family would have reacted in some way toward my obsession with the guitar because my mother's father was a musician, so she knew the pitfalls of the industry. He played saxophone with John Philip Sousa's band then went on to form his own dance band. He was living very high during the Depression, but when the musicians' union went on strike, right about the time cylinder records came out, the DJs realized they did not have to hire live bands anymore. They could just spin the cylinders. In one fell swoop, all the bands were fired and my grandfather lost all of his work and was never able to recover from that. Pretty soon after cylinder records came 78 records. What I gleaned from this is, the music industry changes very quickly. I think both my parents knew that if their children have a passion for something, to encourage it.

At first I didn't know why I loved playing the guitar. It had something to do with just picking it up and saying, "Ahhh, this feels right!" I think a lot of it has to do with the vibrations of the instrument and why music has such a connection to the spirit. The cells of our body are vibrating, and they are responding to vibrations around us. So when we play music, we are not only listening with our ears but with every cell in our body. Even within the cells, every part of the way life is arranged reacts not only with vibration but, oftentimes, in harmonic sequence. The body has the same properties as music, and so even down to the elementary particles, it's all vibration. So we are touching upon something very deep and essential to life in making music. We are using the same properties that god uses in creating life and matter.

Just before I entered junior high school, I had a dream that I was carrying my guitar to school for some reason. As I walked, the guitar became heavier and heavier with each step until finally, I just set the guitar down, sat on top of it and rode it to school. It lifted a couple inches off the ground and took off. I was having so much fun that when the schoolbell rang, I didn't get off. I just kept riding around on the playground with my guitar. So when I woke up from that dream, I realized the guitar was my vehicle.

Muriel Anderson (on the right) giving her big sister Marguerite a guitar lesson on how to play the Rumba strum on "Sloop John B." (*Courtesy Muriel Anderson*)

I have been playing a Paul McGill guitar for quite some time and finally, Paul said, "You've been playing this old guitar for so long, it's about time for you to get a new guitar because I am a much better builder than I was when you got that first one." He showed me some beautiful wood for the back and sides and started working on it. After a while, I realized it really was not a good time for me to be buying a new guitar, that I should hold off and wait maybe a year or so. I told him this. He finished up the guitar to sell to a dealer in New York instead.

Well, I happened to be in New York the day this guitar shipped in to sell. I stopped by my friend Nato Lima's house and found Paul McGill and a friend of his, a prospective client, visiting there also with this guitar. I got the chance to play it and just fell in love with it. It was beautiful. I played it for a couple hours and then he left to bring the guitar to the dealer. His friend, Greg, decided to buy the guitar with the stipulation that I would play it in for a few years. Greg is now loaning it to me long-term. He told me to take it on tour and said, "It's okay if it gets a few road bumps on it, that's normal." So I have been playing this guitar and enjoying it. It's amazing, this is the wood I had seen that was meant to be my guitar, and here I am, playing it.

Tommy Emmanuel

Australian fingerstyle guitarist Tommy Emmanuel's career has spanned five decades. He received his first Grammy nomination for his recording with Chet Atkins, *The Day the Finger Pickers Took Over the World*. Emmanuel is best known for his complex fingerpicking style, percussive effects on the guitar and his blazingly energetic performances.

If you look at the photograph, you'll see my first guitar was a full-sized, Australian-made Maton with 1950s writing on the headstock. My father bought it for me, and my mother put the guitar in my hands when I was five years old. She could play a bit so she really got me started to playing it, too. I remember being in kindergarten and as soon as I heard that bell ring, I remember jumping the fence and crossing the road to run home and pick up my guitar. I couldn't wait to get home from school — our whole family was obsessed with the guitar.

This Maton had a little amp that came with it and my mother would join me, playing a Hawaiian steel guitar. She helped teach me chords and tap out the time with my foot. My older brother, Phil, had the same guitar. Except mine had a sunburst on it and his was a blond maple top. We formed a little band and he

Tommy Emmanuel, age five.
(*Courtesy Tommy Emmanuel*)

played lead while I played rhythm. Accompaniment is in my blood. I used this guitar professionally throughout the '60s until I got a steel solid-body guitar later on in '68. But this is the guitar I used for our family band, called the Emmanuel Quartet, consisting of my brothers Chris and Phil on guitar, my sister on the Hawaiian lap steel and myself on drums. We changed our name in 1963 because everyone thought that with "quartet" in our name, we were classical.

Because I loved to play "Wipe Out" by The Surfaris, we called ourselves The Midget Safaries before deciding on The Trailblazers. I had that bass part covered. Our first gig was a local TV program where we each got paid a bag of chips and a Coke for playing "Apache." My father passed away in 1966, and I started teaching guitar at age twelve to help the family make ends meet. Winning a TV show talent contest gave us our first chance to produce an EP. I was a teenager when I left home and moved to Sydney to pursue a professional career as a guitarist, and I played clubs all over the city, which lead to my becoming a session player for Stevie Wonder and playing with John Denver, Ziggy Marley and Tina Turner.

When it comes to musical influences, my earliest memory is of hearing Marty Robbins singing "El Paso" and the guitar sounding so beautiful. Grady Martin was another hero. I'd wear the grooves out of my records from playing them over and over, trying to learn from them. To this day, I don't read notes. I am ear trained and I learned out of sheer determination. I didn't hear of Chet Atkins until I was seven and his music made such an impact on me. I'd listen closely, trying to figure out that scratch he had, but I think I figured it out by the way I set up the pickups.

As far as challenges go, I get challenged all the time to improve. I remember being sixteen and so hungry for knowledge. I listened to George Benson and Chet Atkins and wanted to break through the barrier to know what they knew. I wanted it *so* badly that I could barely sleep. All I did was listen and play. Then I had a breakthrough. Things I never thought I could do, I was doing. A light had come on. What I realized is, if I really tried hard and galvanized myself out of sheer determination and digging for that sound, I could reach it.

My love for the guitar is about making music first. It requires a lot of work but because of the time I am willing to put into it, it seems like it comes easy and the real joy is with sharing music. Think of how good it feels to make someone else feel great and to see them get lost in the music, too. We'd have no enemy in the world if we were all musicians. I have the greatest job and I think the guitar is a very expressive instrument. It speaks from the soul. When I'm teaching, I tell people, you cannot separate your soul's personality from the kind of music you play or listen to — it's all intertwined. You listen to B.B. King, Eric Clapton or George Benson and you'll hear they've all got their own voice. And I can say I've got my place here, too.

Ever hear that phrase, "This is Frank Sinatra's world and you're just living in it"? With music, I've got my place, so when I sit down to play, I like to pull my audience in close and say I'm not going to let you go till I'm finished with you. You're going to come take a trip with me. The best is getting a new audience that doesn't know what to expect and then finding that my playing disarms and releases them.

My guitar story: last year I was playing in the Netherlands — in Amsterdam — to a huge crowd. And at the end of the night, my favorite small guitar, again, a Maton, was stolen. What got me is how upset other people became over this news, weeping. They'd become attached to that guitar, too. Just as one realizes a shattered glass can't be glued back together, I had to accept the guitar was gone. I had to move on. I filed a report at the police station and they told me I had a snowball's chance in hell of getting it back because Amsterdam is the kind of town a lot of people pass through. The next day I tried combing through the city to look for pawnshops but I discovered that pawnshops are not really a part of their culture. I was completely lost.

I had a luncheon that I couldn't get out of, so I went to the restaurant, which was a beautiful place. The waiter came over and said to me, "Mr. Emmanuel?

You have a phone call." It was my friend Dim, telling me they'd found my guitar. I was given an address to an Irish pub and the name of a woman, Linda. I couldn't believe it. I had tears in my eyes and we just bolted into town. This place was in the Red Light District and my heart was beating hard when we stepped into that pub. Linda was this Irish lady and she handed me my guitar in its zip bag. The guitar hadn't even been touched.

What had happened was Linda had gone to my concert the night before and then had a party at her apartment where a lot of people showed up, played and then promptly fell asleep on her floor. She was on her way into work when she spotted the guitar standing upright in a corner, and she thought it looked a little too nice to belong to anyone there. So she opened one of the pockets and found my name on the business card along with my U.K. agent. She was in shock. Someone must have picked up the guitar from backstage. My U.K. agent called my manager, Gina, who was on her way to Sydney, and all these calls finally bounced their way to me at that restaurant.

That guitar is now in lockup in Germany. I've named it "The Mouse that Roars," because it's a little guitar, a BG808 Maton, and I've played it for audiences of over 100,000. The Maton Company has since built me a replica. Wherever I go, I keep a few guitars. I have some stashed in England and Melbourne. I have favorites stored in different places as backup and for recording.

Martin Taylor

British jazz guitarist and composer Martin Taylor is a self-taught musician who has won numerous awards for his contributions to jazz music. He has collaborated with Stéphane Grappelli, Jeff Beck, Chet Atkins, Bill Wyman, George Harrison, Dionne Warwick and Jamie Cullum, and his solo album *Artistry* was produced by Steve Howe. He received an honorary doctorate in music from the Royal Scottish Academy of Music & Drama and was appointed Member of the British Empire "For Services to Jazz Music" in the Queen's Birthday Honours List in 2002.

I received my first guitar when I was five years old — I'd been given a red little ukulele first with a palm tree painted on it, when I was four years old. The three-quarter-size guitar my dad bought for me had originally been made in Russia. He bought it from a market in the east end of London, and it was like a classical guitar but it had steel-strings and the action had been very high. I couldn't stop playing it — I was obsessed by it to the point where it made my fingers bleed. It was bad to have this *bad* guitar but, the fact that it did not put me off meant that I was dedicated to it. If I'd had a good guitar, who knows? I think I still would have become a guitar player.

My dad did not start playing music until he was thirty years old, and he had sent away for a catalog guitar, a Höfner President. I can remember it arriving. As soon as I saw it inside its open case, I thought it was the most magical thing I'd ever seen. The case had a red velvet lining and the guitar, for being new, was fragrant. I used to play it when my dad was at work. My mum let me play it, though I never told him this. Then finally, my mum asked my dad if he would get me a guitar, and that was really the start of it.

I did not really have any great ambitions with playing the guitar. I played it for fun, as a hobby. My dad had a band, and the guitar player did not show up one day. I think I was about eleven years old at the time. My dad came back from the gig and told me to put on a jacket and bowtie and accompany him. I had played one gig before this, my first real gig, when I was about eight years old. It had been inside a music store shop window, playing jazz. I basically replaced the guitar player in my dad's band that day and was in the band officially from that point forward for a couple of years. When I was fourteen, I realized playing is what I wanted to do professionally, so I left school at age fifteen. I've been on the road ever since.

My dad knew this is what I wanted to do for a living, so he was very supportive. I don't think my mother was as enthusiastic, particularly because I left home when I was sixteen and was touring all over England and playing on cruise ships. I think she thought I was a bit young to be doing this, especially in the bad company of musicians who drank and smoked cigarettes. The musicians I worked with were encouraging because they were all in their thirties and forties and older but they could see there was something in what I was doing, and they liked my playing. I was very lucky to have their encouragement.

I find that the guitar allows me to express myself. I can express myself far better through music than through words, as most musicians probably do — it is one aspect of music that attracts us. I also love to perform for people. I've never been great about sitting in a room, just practicing. I like to get out and play, and I love to play in bands.

There have been many times when I've wondered about playing. When I first started playing, I'd found myself in jobs that I did not enjoy doing. I always made a point of getting out of that because when I started playing the guitar, it was because I enjoyed it. I found myself in a few jobs where I was only doing it to pay the rent, and I thought this is not good — I'd be better off getting a job and then just playing for fun. People seem to enjoy my music and I enjoy playing it, so it seems to be my destiny, really. That's what I have to do, so I make the point of enjoying myself.

I started playing when I was so young that I can't really remember *learning* to play it. Probably, playing the guitar is the only thing in my life that has actually come easily to me. I suppose I did work hard at learning to play the guitar, but it never felt like work.

There was an Irish singer on TV in the '60s called Val Doonican, and he was comparable to Perry Como or Bing Crosby. He had a real cozy kind of sound and used to sit in a rocking chair, wearing a sweater. His television show gave the impression of extending an invitation into his comfy house. Chet Atkins used to appear as a guest on his show and I appeared on there many years later. I used to look at this guitar on the cover of a Val Doonican album that my parents had bought for me, a beautiful Clifford Essex guitar, made in England. Because I had this terrible first guitar that made my fingers bleed, I used to ask my mum and dad, "Why can't I have a guitar like that?" They said, "Well, we cannot afford a guitar like that." I used to sit and stare at this album cover, just wishing I had a guitar like that. When Christmas arrived, and my mum said, "We've got a present for you," I thought it would be this guitar. But she had knit me a sweater exactly like the one Val was wearing on the album cover. She thought the *sweater* was what I'd been staring at.

I came to know Val many years later and, when I told him this story, he did not know whether to laugh or cry. A couple weeks later I was playing a concert and his daughter came backstage and told me, "My dad couldn't come this evening because he's got a cold, but he sent this in his place." And she gave me the guitar that was on that album cover.

Dave Alvin

Grammy-winning guitarist and songwriter Dave Alvin is renowned for forming the '80s American roots rock band The Blasters with his older brother Phil, and then joining Exene Cervenka of X as lead guitarist. I was supposed to phone Dave for an interview an hour after speaking to Dick Dale, but that interview had stretched unexpectedly into the three-hour mark. When I apologized for the delay, Dave assuaged my anxiety, telling me that, of all coincidences, he grew up hearing Dale's surf guitar music outside his bedroom window and, later on in life, he had the opportunity to meet Dale backstage at a gig. Dave noted, "He *is* a loquacious fellow."

My first guitar was a 1964 Fender Mustang. I was twenty-two when James Harman, the great blues harmonica player, bought it for me at a pawnshop in Santa Ana, California. He paid seventy-five bucks and I still owe him the money. My Mustang had a slightly longer neck than usual for a Mustang, and someone had taken out the Fender pickups and replaced them with Schecters. It was a bit of a mongrel guitar. There were always guitars lying around our family house: a cheap but loud 12-string, my brother Phil's 1941 Epiphone and Gary Massey's old Silvertone, but the Mustang was the first guitar that I could call my own.

You see, I never thought I could be a guitar player because when I was a kid my neighborhood had a lot of great guitar players who should have gone on to fame and fortune but never did. Guys like Mike Roach, Tom deMott and Gary Massey. They were a few years older than me, and I was extremely intimidated by them and never thought I could be as good as them. I still don't. Anyway, in order to get to hang out jam sessions, I figured I had to play something other than guitar, so I got pretty good on the flute and reasonably bad on the tenor sax but all the while I'd watch the guitarist's fingers and then, when no one was around, I'd grab a guitar and try to play like them. My brother, Phil, taught himself to play in the fingerpicking styles of Blind Blake and Blind Boy, Fuller and I'd do the same routine with him: watch him play and then as soon as he'd leave the room, I'd grab the guitar and try to figure out what he'd been doing. It really wasn't until years later when we started The Blasters, and I had my Mustang, that my brother and I even played guitar together, that's how intimidated I was.

When I was real little kid growing up in Downey, California, surf music was real popular, and I remember waking up on Saturday mornings to the sounds of different wannabe surf bands practicing in their parents garages'. It was great!

There was a surf record label/recording studio in town called, appropriately, Downey Records, and they released the original version of "Pipeline" by The Chantays as well as my favorite surf instrumental, "Boss" by The Rumblers. I guess that stuff was my first guitar influence. Off the top of my head, I'd say my biggest influences, though, were blues and early rock and roll guys like Johnny "Guitar" Watson, Big Bill Broonzy, Magic Sam, Chuck Berry, Carl Perkins, Lonnie Johnson — I could go on with a million names, most of whom you've never heard of. When I was older, around twelve or thirteen, my brother and I would go to blues bars like The Ash Grove and see Albert and Freddie King and Lightnin' Hopkins. Just a few notes from those guys hit me on such a deep emotional level. They still do.

Despite my blues and R&B background, the main reason I'm a professional guitarist today is the influence of punk rock. You see whenever you pick up a guitar, you're going up against everyone that ever played the instrument — Django, T-Bone Walker, Michael Bloomfield, Richard Thompson, Segovia, the guys in your neighborhood, whomever.

It can be quite scary. There are always going to be guys who are better than you. In my case, it's a very long line of guys. But when I started hearing the early Ramones, Clash and Sex Pistols records around 1976, I realized that on a certain level, technique didn't matter. Just plug in, turn up and beat the hell out of the guitar. It didn't matter whether you were playing a $10,000 '58 Les Paul or a $75 Mustang. Knowing this gave me the courage to get onstage and make a damn racket.

In the early days of The Blasters, I took some lumps from guys who'd say, "That guy sucks! If only they had a better guitarist." I can't say stuff like that didn't hurt, but all in all I didn't care. Punk rock changed the rules for a while and guys like me who were working as fry cooks could become rock and rollers. Over the years I've practiced hard to be a better guitarist, whether acoustic or electric, but part of me will always be a loud punk rock basher.

What I love about the guitar is its dexterity. Guitars can make and imitate any kind of sound or texture. For example, Adrian Belew can make a guitar sound like a herd of elephants. Blind Willie Johnson can make the guitar sound like a mournful choir. Jimi Hendrix can make the guitar sound like an erupting volcano or a flock of beautiful birds. I think that's the reason the guitar became, and has stayed, the number one instrument in pop and rock 'n' roll. Another reason is that no two great guitar players sound alike. Pat Martino plays differently than Ralph Towner who plays differently than Bob Margolin who plays differently than Johnny Ramone and yet, to me, all approaches are valid. The guitar is a good democratic, egalitarian instrument.

My Mustang still has glass imbedded in it from flying beer bottles that were hurled at us in the early days of The Blasters. There's a dent and a slice down the upper cutaway horn from a particularly strong beer bottle thrower. Some of the audiences we played for in those days had very direct ways of letting you know if they liked you or not, and sometimes the Mustang was my only defense.

More recently I ran over my gig bag, with both my beloved '64 Stratocaster and my '61 reissue Strat inside it, with my van. I was leaving a sound check at the Beachland Ballroom in Cleveland, my mind on a million other things (motel rooms, ticket sales, salaries to pay, where to eat, interviews, etc.), when I leaned the double guitar gig bag against the side of van, got on the cell phone about something, jumped into the van, threw it into reverse and ran over the guitars. When I felt the bump beneath the tires, I stopped the van and had a minor nervous breakdown. The '61 reissue is a nice guitar, but the '64 Strat is irreplaceable. I ran into the club like a lunatic, shaking, sweating and cussing, and got Chris Miller, who plays guitar in my band, to come out, open the bag and inspect the damage. I sat down on a curb about thirty feet away, lit a cigarette and prayed to whatever deity looks out for dumbbell guitar players. I asked Chris to tell me what the damage was then I said, "No, don't tell me. No, tell me. No, don't tell me. No, tell me." He opened the bag and, unbelievably, there was no major damage to the '61 and absolutely no damage to the '64 Strat. Whoever is the god of guitar players was looking favorably on me that day.

I retired my Mustang from touring when I bought the '64 Strat in 1982. Just this year I retired the '64 from touring also. It's just become too difficult to travel anywhere these days with vintage guitars, and I don't just mean the threat of someone stealing the guitars or me running them over. Last year I was flying home from Europe and I had a document from the Musicians Union that says the airlines, by law, have to permit me to bring a guitar in a gig bag onboard a plane, but all it takes is one power-drunk flight attendant to tell you no. Then they'll just throw the guitar on top of the checked baggage while you can only hope for the best. I travel now with my '61 reissue that I hot-rodded to approximate my '64. If something happens to it, at least I can get another. My dear old Mustang and my beloved old Strat, I'm glad to say, get to stay safely at home and swap old barroom gig stories with each other.

Bob Taylor

Bob Taylor is the cofounder and president of the California-based Taylor Guitar company.

I was ten years old when I received my first guitar, and it had no brand name that I recall. No artists had inspired me to play — it really had been the kids who lived on my street who had persuaded me to get a guitar because they all played one, too. I did not play any other instrument back then, though I can play a banjo and a ukulele now. My family saw my guitar playing as a kid's hobby. It wasn't regarded any differently from a kid who would like to play piano, like my sister did, or someone who would like to play football. They never saw me as being obsessed with it, not at that age! When I started building guitars they started taking notice that I was intimately obsessed with it.

I wanted to buy a guitar in high school that I could not afford, so I just made one, and this seemed like a normal approach for me. I was in auto shop and told my teacher that I wanted to get into wood shop class so I could build a guitar. He let me transfer classes in tenth grade, and I used the wood shop to build my guitars. I had already been building stuff in industrial arts class from seventh grade onward and had won state fairs in metalwork, so I knew I was good at making things.

I found a little book on how to make classical guitars, and though I did not make a classical guitar, I used some of these construction methods. I also looked at other guitars, dissected them in my mind and simply went at it and created a 12-string guitar. It had the body of a Yamaha guitar (traced from a friend's Yamaha) and the peghead of a Japanese guitar that was actually a copy of a Gibson, though I had never seen a Gibson at that time to know this. I had never seen any good guitars at that time like a Martin, Gibson or Fender.

During my junior and senior years in high school I ended up making three acoustic guitars and a banjo. I spent a lot of time in wood shop, and had a teacher who left me on my own to do my thing. He did not know how to make a guitar, but he gave me the room to experiment and work on these projects. As a result, I started to learn how to do some inlay work. This was in the days when you could go snorkeling off the coast of San Diego and catch abalone for your dinner, so I would catch abalone and grind the shells down to do inlay work. The guitars I made were crude by today's standards, but I still have one of them today.

I like guitar music and I'm not a great guitar player. When I graduated from high school in '73, you were either listening to Cream or Iron Butterfly or Jefferson Airplane or Grateful Dead — or else you were listening to Peter, Paul & Mary; John Denver; Gordon Lightfoot and the more folky musicians. Then bands like The Eagles came along and created folk rock. The first time I heard The Eagles play, I was a junior in high school. I heard their song "Take It Easy" on the radio and thought, "Oooh, I'm home now!" Up to that point, I'd tended to listen to John Denver and Gordon Lightfoot and The Kingston Trio. Sparked by the film *Deliverance*, there was also a bunch of bluegrass music that you could listen to that had been and, as a result, the banjo received a huge shot in the arm in terms of resurgence in popularity.

If you gave me the choice of playing music or giving me the tools to build things, I would choose tools and building things. If I had to give up one, I would give up the music. In reality, building guitars is the perfect pursuit for me because it combines two of my favorite things in life. I could live without playing the guitar, but I would not have a very satisfying life if I was not making something all the time.

I'm a better player than most people, but once you leave the "most people"

Bob Taylor as a teenager. (*Courtesy Bob Taylor*)

circle, then anyone accomplished on the guitar is a better player than I am. I can pick out things by ear and play along with people — it's not hard and I enjoy doing that sort of thing for my own entertainment, but I'm not a performer and do not want to be a performer. The challenge with guitar playing for me is to become a better player, as I do not have the natural gift for it. If I work at it, I do become pretty good but then, by the next week, I'll have forgotten it all. However, when I work at building something, I never forget anything. I just get better and better and better at it. I have not forgotten one thing about building something, but I've forgotten everything about playing the guitar.

You can spend twenty years figuring out how to build a guitar that is easy to play. Taylor is a major guitar supplier to the music industry — we've been the number one seller in the U.S. for acoustic guitars for a couple of years now.

However, if you randomly selected 100 guitar players, placed them in a room and asked them to raise their hand if they felt Taylor Guitars makes the *greatest sounding* guitar there is — I would say maybe thirty to forty percent of them would agree. Preference in sound is a very subjective choice. That's like putting everybody in a room and saying, "Raise your hand if you think Breyer's vanilla ice cream is *the best* vanilla ice cream you've ever tasted." For some people it is and to others, it's not. That's the way it is.

However, if I asked, "Raise your hand if you think Taylor makes guitars that are the easiest to play," all those hands would fly up in a heartbeat. Learning how to build a guitar that is easy to play? I have a Ph.D. in that! I've spent my lifetime learning how to do that, and I've figured it out better than anybody else, really. Other things you cannot win so easily but this, well, it took me about twenty-five years to learn how to do it. Taylor guitars allow players to push the strings down easily on the fretboard and not have to struggle so much to make it easy to play — it's like a car that is easy to drive.

We started getting good at this early on, but it has been continuously perfected. Over time, this process became streamlined because we've refined our factory methods to produce a great-playing guitar, each and every time. We almost cannot make a bad one for how well developed our design and manufacturing process is. Along the way, other makers started looking at our guitars and because of our efforts, many guitars became easier to play. Other makers do not do it quite as well as we do but, boy, they sure make their guitars better than they did thirty years ago.

I'm not a big saver of things. It gives me great pleasure to throw stuff out and, every once in a while, I'll decide that I want to collect something like say, watches. I'll have a bunch of watches, and then it will occur to me that I cannot handle having all these watches, so I'll decide to get rid of some. I built those three guitars in high school, and when I reached the point where I started having a little career going, I began looking at these three guitars like they were the enemy. "What if somebody sees them," I asked myself. "I'm out there trying to tell people I'm a good guitar maker and the last thing I need is for those beginner guitars to be floating out there." You know how it is whenever a famous actor simply hates it when an old video or film audition happens to turn up on YouTube from the days when they happened to be a total dork. I felt the same way toward these guitars. One of the guitars was in my brother-in-law's possession (I actually still have that one, thank god), but the other two guitars I managed to get a hold of. I blew one of them up with a cherry bomb

— it blew up spectacularly. I bought one of those firecrackers from Tijuana, lit that thing and it went ka-boom. The other I ran over with a motorcycle. I got rid of the evidence, but now I sort of regret it. Sixteen years later I asked myself, "Why did I *do* that?" I didn't know there was going to be a *museum*.

Graham Parker

British rock singer and songwriter Graham Parker released several critically acclaimed albums in the '70s as Graham Parker & the Rumour. He has continued his career with various collaborations that produced hit albums like *The Mona Lisa's Sister, Struck by Lightning* and *Acid Bubblegum.*

I guess I was twelve or thirteen when I got my first guitar. It would have been in 1963, when The Beatles emerged. They made music accessible to my age group.

My cousin, who was a couple of years older, gave me an acoustic guitar, which may or may not have had a brand name. All I remember about it is the frayed, thick, colored cord that served as a strap. When I saw either Brian Jones or Mick Jagger playing the harmonica on TV, I immediately took that up and found that stringing together a few blues riffs was a lot easier than playing the guitar.

After The Beatles and the Rolling Stones, all the beat groups started appearing as if by magic. This was followed by soul, ska, blues: the stuff that influenced the beat groups in the first place. But I'd say that both Otis Redding and Levi Stubbs were the greatest influences on my singing.

I was actually never that obsessed with the guitar, and I still had many

Graham Parker (far left), age twelve, in the Black Rockers. (*Courtesy Graham Parker*)

other interests. I was a poor learner and never really got any good until a couple of years ago! But my parents were always supportive of whatever I did, apart from hanging around cafés smoking cigarettes and playing pinball.

I love playing lead guitar, which I do now on my records. However, I'm an awfully clunky guitarist, and it's only in recent years that I figured out how you do it. I discovered by accident that if you turn the amp up really loud, you can't go wrong! Really, you can just flail around and good stuff will come out. I guess the challenge is finding an amp that goes up to eleven and not being afraid to use it. Going "rocka rocka rocka rocka" on a Fender Telecaster is as close to sex as you can get with your trousers on. My career didn't start until I was twenty-five, so I went from being totally unknown and unschooled to leading a crack band in front of hip London audiences. It wasn't playing live that made me think I could make a career out of it, it was writing the songs that became my first album, in the two years before those first performances. I was convinced that I was writing the best songs that could possibly be written by anybody, at least at that period of time, when quite frankly, the competition wasn't up to much.

Wolf Marshall

Acclaimed guitarist and educator Wolf Marshall is known for his transcription books and for serving as editor-in-chief of *GuitarOne* magazine. He has been on faculty of the UCLA Jazz Department since 2007.

I was fourteen years old and I wanted a guitar because I was really into the guitar-driven music of the day, like British Invasion, early surf music. In Southern California, surf music was a big deal. I had already taken music lessons on the violin, piano and cello, and finally after three instruments where my mom, who was a classical pianist, had been pushing me into classical music — it didn't take —I asked her for an electric guitar and she rented one for a month. It was a stupid little guitar called a Kay — solid-body with one pickup and it was just a piece of junk. I didn't even rent an amp with it — that's how bad it was. I could play it but I just did not enjoy it. You have to find an instrument that you love and stick with it all your life. When I had to return this guitar at the end of the month , my mom took me to a store and got me my first real guitar, a Les Paul Junior. I had that guitar for a year and a half. I do not have it any longer and have been through so many guitars, but I look back on all of them fondly.

Wolf Marshall at age fourteen in Los Angeles, California, with his first guitar, a 1950s Gibson Les Paul Junior. (*Courtesy Wolf Marshall*)

The first real guitar that I played with professionally was a Fender Telecaster. What I love about the guitar is that it was part of the scene and part of one's peer group. The cello was not for me — the business of sitting down — but I did love the strings. There's something about a kid being taught by a parent, it's too loose and lacks the formality and structure compared to taking lessons with someone who is not your parent. With the piano, cello and violin, I found myself saying, "Mom, I've got homework — I cannot practice"; "Mom, I'm going out to see a movie with my friends" — and that's not going to work in terms of learning. With the guitar, I was self-motivated and wanted to learn stuff by The Beatles and Rolling Stones. Those bands and surf music were the first to make an impression on my mind in the mid-'60s, along with early rock 'n' roll coming out of England.

I had always loved music from the time I was seven and wanted to be holding an instrument, being creative with it and communicating through it. Kids always want to be in bands, have camaraderie and learn the songs of the day, impress their friends and then impress themselves. You realize if you impress your friends first, then you might as well go back to impressing yourself while you are struggling with chords and licks and trying to make music somehow. My grand plan did not take shape until I started formally studying guitar. Then I realized that there was a real career ahead because I had been through a number of bands as a kid. My mom let me drop out of school then, which might seem surprising for someone who had been so strict — saying, "You've got to finish up when you're eighteen." School was impossible when I was sixteen years old and out playing till one a.m., then coming home and trying to get up and get to class by eight a.m. It just never happened and I kept getting sick. She said, "Go ahead and play this out." So I played around the Southland, and she let me go do this, finish high school and go to college.

While my mom was encouraging me in music, my father, an engineer, was scared half to death, thinking it wasn't possible to make a career in music. Later on he was very happy about my success, however in those early stages, he kept thinking playing guitar meant a lifetime of being that guy out there with a hat on a street corner. It was a case of the classic two images: my mother looking at me, thinking, "Concert. Stage. Carnegie Hall," and my dad thinking, "Street corner. Hat. A few coins." It's like the old joke of the two-career paths of the guitarist: one picture shows this guy giving a concert and entering a limo afterward, and the other picture shows a guy asking, "Would you like fries with that, ma'am?"

I had a few mentors along the way. My first mentors were great theory professors in college. Two of them were not really big names but they were big in Los Angeles City College, and they both really helped me develop my ear, which is what ultimately helped my career more than just being able to play an instrument. I learned to transcribe and write music. Professionally, I would say George Van Eps, Howard Roberts and Pat Martino were my mentors who kept encouraging me to pursue music. On the rock side, members of this old psychedelic San Francisco group called Moby Grape, which probably few people remember, were mentors of mine who came down to L.A. and helped me pick out my second professional guitar at a place called Wallichs Music City at the corner of Sunset and Vine, a very famous music store that no longer exists — there is a strip mall there now — but this was a Hollywood place where everyone bought their instruments. It used to be a big record store, kind of like a Barnes

& Noble of records that also had a self-contained music store and repair department. You could buy some really nice guitars or basses, and you would have the possibility of shopping for music. Everybody used to go look at the instruments in the window, and this was back in the day when you could have nice instruments on display without having a big security chain attached to it. This band Moby Grape hung around at this place, and I met them when I was a kid. They told me, "You've got to get rid of that Telecaster and get a Les Paul!"

One thing I've really enjoyed about the guitar is learning something that I didn't know before, especially when picking up something from a recording. If you listen to something that was improvised, it hadn't been written out because that was the nature of the music — it was made up and improvised on the spot. A big breakthrough for me was a song by Eric Clapton called "Hideaway," an instrumental that I eventually figured out, note for note, simply by trial and error. Then I discovered my joy in being able to teach the song to others in my group and arranging it with them.

Sometimes I can get too tunnel-visioned about playing guitar, such as when I was totally devoted to classical to the point of getting rid of all my electric guitars. A friend of mine who had been in the band Steppenwolf came over and asked if I had an electric guitar and was wondering what happened to them. A lot of friends disowned me when I was in this period. I had gone from playing guitar in rock clubs at night to being a diligent student of classical guitar with books of theory in one hand and guitar in the other. I'd gone to school at UCLA and had been a composition major. Really, I need to be playing lots of different musical styles because that is what brings me joy. The constant is that nothing has been constant — which is the nature of music itself because every time you think there is only one form of music that you're involved in, you'll hear something like a blues song that really excites you and must become a part of your consciousness.

Daniel Lanois

Grammy-winning Canadian guitarist, songwriter and record producer Daniel Lanois has worked with Bob Dylan, Neil Young, Peter Gabriel, Emmylou Harris and Willie Nelson. He is also renowned for his work with Brian Eno and with U2 on their album *The Joshua Tree*.

I got my first guitar when I was ten years old, and I was not interested in the guitar. I was in fact, playing a little plastic recorder at the time. The year before I received the guitar, I had bought a little white plastic recorder for $1 that I saw in a shop window. It had a little bit of purple around the finger holes and I loved that. Then I wanted to take up the clarinet. One day a man knocked on my mother's door and asked my mother, "Do you have any kid who like music?" She said, "Yes," because there were four of us. The man said, "Let's try them out on an aptitude test," and I'd passed. He'd offered me a choice of either accordion or slide guitar. I said I would take the slide guitar. I had no idea what slide guitar involved.

I attended my first lesson at the Ontario Conservatory of Music, which was downtown from where we lived. I was presented with a guitar that was generally lent to students for their first eighteen lessons. They lent me an acoustic guitar, which was a no-name brand with raised action — they'd put a big metal riser at the nut and then a similar contraption at the bridge so that you would play this by putting it on your lap. That was the beginning of my playing slide guitar.

At this time, I was really just listening to my teacher and felt it was funny that I had to play this guitar on my lap. I asked my teacher at one point, "When do I get to hold this guitar like Elvis?" He said, "Well, you could switch to the Spanish guitar after eighteen lessons." That is when I switched to playing the Spanish guitar and bought a little guitar from the conservatory. That guitar again, was a no-name brand.

I learned to play old American classics like "Little Brown Jug," "Red River Valley" and "Oh! Susanna." I was in a class of people with maybe six other students. We would play melody in unison, and the teacher would strum an accompaniment. That was it. I kept up with the guitar and became better at it, eventually ordering a guitar from the Eaton's catalog, the Canadian equivalent of the Sears catalog. I picked a Beltone guitar and a strawberry-colored naugahyde-vinyl-covered Beltone amp. It was a pretty nice little amp.

My mother was very happy about my interest in the guitar. My parents had split up by this time, so really, it was just my mom. I had found something that I loved. I found that I just got better and better at the guitar. I became so good at the guitar that I started teaching other students by the time I was thirteen. I started playing with friends, forming a neighborhood band that would play on the rooftops of houses.

What I love about the guitar is that it is my friend and it never talks back. The pedal steel guitar especially is a place that I go to in order to secretly escape to a magic place. Everything is a challenge and I experienced a few hurdles along the way. I was ready to be a fingerpicker and that was difficult for me at first until it became systematic and then rolling — and then I eventually found a freedom in it, which is called independence, which is a nice thing. Athletes obviously experience this when they catch a ball and run. Independence is an incredible drug to get, and I do not think everyone reaches independence. I think there is probably academic independence for people who read one thing and start thinking about another. I think it is part of exercising our incredible brain. The more you do it, the better you get. It's a process of building one's intelligence. To this day I exercise my independence.

My first gig was playing in the church hall. I'm French-Canadian so my family would attend this French-Canadian church where they held bazaars.

People would bring in baked goods and have a little festival. I remember playing popular songs with my friends in the basement like "The House of the Rising Sun" and some English rock hits at the time that were making airwaves in Canada. We also played "Wipe Out" and a few other surf songs. I'd graduated to an Ampeg Reverberocket amplifier, which really helped on the surf music, and I bought a used white Stratocaster. There were lots of beautiful Stratocasters around then because they were common instruments at that time in the early '60s.

I went through many guitars when I was starting out. I had a baby Rickenbacker that I liked a lot; in fact, it was a 12-string that I could add six strings on. Later, when I went traveling on my motorcycle, I had a Fender Esquire, which is like a Telecaster with just a back pickup, and I would dismantle the neck and remove it so that I could fit it into my pack and travel with it. I do remember buying a brand new Rickenbacker 12-string. The first one I'd told you about was a solid-body guitar, but this one was semi-hollow and beautiful because we were fascinated with The Byrds and their song, "Turn, Turn, Turn." I didn't play Gibsons at all until the '80s, when I played my first Goldtop Les Paul and got hooked on it. I kind of had a major turning point when I went to work with U2 in '83. I had a chance to try The Edge's rig, which was a black Stratocaster through a Vox, with quite a few effects, and this really opened my eyes to new sounds.

Sharon Isbin

Grammy-winning classical guitarist Sharon Isbin is the author of *Classical Guitar Answer Book* and the founder the guitar department at the Juilliard School of Music in Manhattan. Her career took off after she won the 1975 Toronto guitar competition at age twenty. She has a catalog of over twenty-five recordings and has commissioned many new concertos for the guitar by world famous composers. Her playing is also featured on the soundtrack of Martin Scorsese's 2006 film *The Departed*.

Our family moved to Italy from Minneapolis when I was nine years old because my father was on sabbatical to consult for a scientific project. When we settled in Varese, located about an hour outside of Milan, it was time then for my parents to figure out who was going to continue with their music lessons. I was resigned to taking up the piano again — I'd already given it up at the ripe old age of eight. My older brother, Ira, said he wanted guitar lessons. Elvis Presley and The Beatles were in vogue then, this being the late '60s.

My parents, not knowing what he had in mind, took him more seriously. They found a wonderful teacher named Aldo Minella, who commuted from Milan to Varese. At this time, he was playing concerts all over Italy. He had studied with Segovia and was a friend and colleague of Oscar Ghiglia's. So my parents took Ira in for an interview. My brother realized immediately this was not the right instrument for him when he learned he had to have long nails on his right hand and practice at least an hour a day. My parents said, "Who's going to take advantage of this? *Somebody's* got to study with this wonderful guy." I volunteered out of family duty because I *was* the only viable candidate, though I didn't know what classical guitar was.

Because I was only nine years old, I couldn't play a full size instrument. Aldo suggested we see Mario Pabé. "If you go to Mario, he'll figure out what size instrument you need and he'll make you one. You'll have it in a month and in the meantime, you can study *solfeggio*." I'd thought, oh great, *solfeggio,* sight-singing, just what I wanted!

I remember we went out to the countryside. This guy lived on a chicken farm, and we had to mount these rickety old wooden stairs with chickens gawking at us amidst a sea of white feathers flying all around. We reached the top, and there was Mario's studio. He measured my hands to see how long my fingers were and said, "Come back in a month, and I'll have your guitar for you." Then the next torment started, which was this *solfeggio* business. Being a shy kid, I really wasn't primed for having to do something like this and I was ready to bail after the second lesson. But I couldn't, because we had already ordered the guitar from Mario Pabé. I was stuck. I couldn't make my parents go through having ordered this instrument and then renege. I survived the month of *solfeggio,* the guitar came and I fell in love with it. It had the fresh smell of new wood.

What I remember about being attracted to it was the very personal, intimate nature of one's relationship with the instrument. The reason I gave up piano was because I just felt it was too mechanical of a process. You touch the keys and then something else happens with hammers and by the time the sound comes out, there is a lot of distance. It was not something unusual, because twenty other kids would fall into their lessons after me. But the guitar — this was *exotic*. This was something truly special. And in the late '60s, in the United States, you could count on less then one hand the number of universities or conservatories that even had a guitar department. It was unheard of.

And most kids who studied classical guitar at that time, were, very often, young boys who played rock guitar, heard a Segovia album, thought that was cool and switched gears in midstream at the age of fourteen or fifteen. Not many girls were studying classical guitar because they weren't playing rock guitar. But in Italy, there was a whole different tradition. It was not unusual for young women to play the guitar, but it was definitely something out of the ordinary, and this is what attracted me. It's the direct contact with the instrument. There are no keys, no hammers. You're touching the instrument with your fingernails, your flesh. You're caressing it, you feel the vibration against your body. It's a *part* of you. It became an extension of myself, really. And it allowed me to express myself. I was a shy kid and this was another means of being able to let out my feelings.

I went back to Varese, Italy, after thirty-five years. I made a little pilgrimage because I was playing in a town nearby. I just had to go back and see this school where I first studied and where I played on my first guitar. I remembered, at the end of the year, there had been a little recital where all the students of Aldo and his father performed, and I had played a little Carulli study.

I found the music school and of course, I had to find this little recital room where I had once played. I was looking around and couldn't find it. It had to be there, somewhere. Finally, I opened a door and there it was, this little room, exactly as I had remembered it. The studio where I had the lessons had been backstage and sure enough, there was a hallway with four rooms. I couldn't remember which room I had studied in, but I peeked through each door and said, "Well, it's one of these. This is where it happened."

The recital hall was empty so I took a chair and put it right in the middle of the stage. And I said to myself, "Thirty-five years ago, I sat on this very same spot with my first instrument and played my first concert. And here I am. The space is exactly the same. Time has vanished, as if it were yesterday." It was an *amazing* feeling. It was so powerful, a remarkable experience. Almost like stepping into another dimension. It's almost like turning on the radio and listening to something from California: you don't have to travel by plane or how many days by car. It's instantaneous. And this is what that felt like, an instant shift in time. Except that it was thirty-five years later, and I thought, "My god, what have I done in all this time? Who would have imagined?" I imagined myself as that child, nervously performing in front of these people on an instrument I was still new to playing. Who would have predicted the path that my life would take from that moment on?

I had approached it as a hobby, practicing only twenty minutes a day at the start. What was really kind of funny was when Aldo came too busy to teach, he had to turn all his students over to his father, Papá Minella. His father was a wonderful, ebullient type of guy who made you feel great about everything

Sharon Isbin, age nine, in Varese, Italy, with her first guitar made by Mario Pabé. (*Courtesy Sharon Isbin*)

you did, even if it wasn't great. He kept telling my mother, "It's amazing — when I put Sharon's hands on the guitar, it's like putting Aldo's hands on it when he was a little boy. She's such a natural." So my mother had this prophetic dream one night there in Italy that that headlines read, "Papá does it again." Of course, this was as foreign to me as you can imagine. It was just a hobby. I had no interest in classical music. I thought classical music was a very stuffy kind of thing, and I used to fall asleep at symphony concerts and get fidgety whenever my parents dragged me there. It was just not on my radar. But I did find this a very *intriguing* kind of hobby and I liked it.

The night I returned to Varese, I invited Aldo to my concert. He sat in the front row. And when I finished playing, I told the audience about my pilgrimage that day to the music school where I had played my first instrument. I said, "In fact, my first teacher is sitting right here," and I introduced him. At that point, it struck me that Aldo looked exactly like his father did when I had started lessons, thirty-five years before. It was a powerful, emotional moment, because I never saw his father again. Since that time, Aldo has come to give classes with my students at Juilliard. I remember looking at him, teaching and thinking, "This is the man I owe my whole life to, the one who determined my future."

When my family returned home from Varese, I started to study with Jeff Van in Minneapolis. He left on sabbatical when I was sixteen. I had already had a few lessons with Sophocles Papas in Washington, D.C. My father had arranged for me to meet Pappas because it was on the way to my father's work. Papas introduced me to Segovia, and I had my first lesson with Segovia when I was fourteen. This is something I was able to do for several years. Papas was the first to tell me I should be practicing scales. He said, "If you don't learn all the Segovia major and minor diatonic scales by your next lesson, we're going to spend the whole lesson doing that." Well, I didn't like that threat, so I learned those damn scales. That really made a big difference, to start to get some discipline into my life. And then I discovered, the more time I put in, the better I got and the more I enjoyed it. By the time I was in high school, I was able to practice five hours a day.

What really made that happen is that when I was fourteen, I entered a competition with the Minnesota Orchestra and won. The reward was to perform two concerts with the orchestra in front of five thousand people, each day. I played the Vivaldi *Concerto in D Major* and I thought, "This is even more fun than what I was doing before," which had been spending hours building and launching model rockets and dissecting worms, bugs and caterpillars under the microscope. So I decided it was time to switch gears from science to making music my profession because I figured this is where I wanted to go.

I remember working shortly with Alirio Díaz and Van in the summer and being exposed to the whole world of Latin and South American music, which was exciting. Diaz had been talking about some tours he had done and said to me, "You, too, will do that." I said, "You think so?" and he said yes. Sure enough, when I was sixteen, I played a concert at Rice University, where my brother was going to school. It was a full house at Hammond Hall, my first real professional performance that was given a wonderful review, which started off, "They *say* she is only sixteen . . ." The reviewer clearly didn't believe it.

In those days, I was using a Mark Leaf case. I had just gotten into the elevator in Toronto to go to the hall where my competition was taking place. I stepped onto the elevator with a case that was shut but not locked, and someone noticed, bless their heart. At any moment that guitar could have fallen out and that would have been the end of that. My life would have taken a very different trajectory.

When my family had come back to Minneapolis after living in Italy, one of the recordings that really inspired me, one that I would listen to every night before falling asleep was Julian Bream playing Rodrigo's *Concierto de Aranjuez* and on the other side, Britten's *Gloriana*. It doesn't sound like any Britten you've ever heard. They're Renaissance-style court dances. It's absolutely delightful. My dream was to play the *Concierto de Aranjuez*. That was my goal. I've had more than my fill of that work now, after hundreds of performances!

Minnesota was a great place to grow up because there were a number of music organizations that catered to young people and their growth, such as the Schubert Club, Thursday Musical and the Minnesota Young Artist Competition. They also had the performance forums, such as hospitals and schools. There was a chance to really groom yourself for the profession. In each of the competitions I entered, I was always the first guitarist to have ever entered. I had to petition them.

There was one situation where it was a different competition, affiliated with the Minnesota Orchestra and geared more toward college students. I applied to enter this competition two years after I'd won the Minnesota Young Artist Competition. They accepted my application and, a week before the competition, they phoned to tell me I would not be able to participate because the guitar was not an orchestral instrument. I said, "Well, then how could you have let a saxophonist win last year?" They said, "Once in a while, a saxophone does play with an orchestra." I said, "Once in a while the guitar plays with an orchestra, too." I compiled my sources and drew up a list of all the symphonic works for guitar and matched them against symphonic works for saxophone. The list was at least comparable, if not longer for guitar than it was for saxophone. I presented this material and they said, "I'm sorry but that still won't work." When Lee Foley, the head of the competition, found out about this, he threatened to resign if they did not let me enter. He was concertmaster and head of the jury. They were forced to let me enter. It turned out all this was going on because the donor of the $1,000 grand prize was a big supporter of the Minnesota Orchestra and she had it in her mind the guitar was a gutter instrument that was only useful to accompany pop singers. Apparently there were telegrams flying back and forth to her in Europe, where she was vacationing, and Lee Foley's threat forced them to at least allow me to enter. However, they told me I would not be eligible to win the prize, whereupon Lee Foley again said he would resign. I ended up winning. The prize included performing with the Minnesota Orchestra, and that's when I did my first concerto premiere. I commissioned the Israeli composer Ami Maayani to write a concerto.

This experience taught me several things right away: "No" means just put up a better fight. Stand up for what you believe in and never back down. Stick to your principles because that's the only way there's ever going to be growth and change. And don't let anybody ever tell you what to do if they're wrong. It's usually just ignorance that causes the barrier. You've got to forge a path. Don't take no for an answer if it's just a matter of changing someone's way of thinking. This was something that proved very useful later on. It's given me the philosophy that somewhere there is always a solution. It may not be the one you'd planned on, but there is always a solution.

Once I happened to be traveling and I caught a story on CNN about this fellow, Roscoe Wright, showing this unique travel guitar that is basically a wooden guitar neck with three removable aluminum tubes that attach to make the body shape of the guitar. A nine-volt battery along with earphones allows you, and no one else, to hear. It can also plug into a sound system to be heard by others or in concert. I thought this was great for portability and ease — this is *exactly* what I had been looking for to go on vacation with and not feel like I have to give up practice. I tracked him down in Eugene, Oregon and spoke with him. It took me a while because I'd thought he'd be so busy making these guitars but it turned out he was about to go out of business. I said, "You're kidding me!" He told me no one knew about his guitar. So I wrote about his SoloEtte travel guitar for my very last column in *Acoustic Guitar* magazine. It worked. He started to get orders and was soon able to expand his shop. This was just over ten years ago. He sent me an instrument, and it's everything that I dreamed of. What's wonderful about it is that nothing is changed about how you hold the guitar — it's as if you are holding a three-dimensional instrument. This is so important, because otherwise you'll mess around with some aspect of your playing and ruin your technique. The other part is the sound is great. I've used it in concerts, when I did the Guitar Summit Tour with Stanley Jordan and Michael Hedges and played duets with Steve Vai.

One day in 1995, I got a call from an astronaut named Chris Hadfield. He was living in Houston and working at the Johnson Space Center for his training, and he'd seen someone playing one of these travel guitars in a park in Houston. This person told him where to get it so he ordered one to give as a gift to the Russian cosmonauts on the Mir space station. One of the other cosmonauts was a classical guitarist.

The only change he needed Roscoe to make was to install a hinge on the middle of neck so it could bend and fit through the tunnel that connects the Atlanta Space Shuttle with Mir. He came back with tons of photographs, including one of my CDs floating in the shuttle. They had an astronaut band, in fact. Several months later, when I was in Houston for a concert, he gave me a four-hour tour of the Johnson Space Center. If you'll remember, rockets were once my passion. So the two parts of my life were reunited: I got to sit in the space shuttle simulator used for training and use the controls to see the stars flying by.

The Music Conservatory of Life

Within months of landing in New York, I started writing a monthly column for *Classical Guitar* magazine in the U.K., along with cover stories, features and reviews for other U.S. guitar publications. Speaking to working guitarists in their milieu became its own education, particularly as we strayed from interview questions to consider such relevant topics as whether to fill up the spare suitcase intended for effects gear with the entire hospitality stash of Red Bull.

While my fellow classical guitarists studiously applied Schenkerian analysis to Bach cello suites, the Music Conservatory of Life had my cell phone vibrating in my back pocket. Gary Lucas called from Prague to check our interview time. The hilarity was not lost on me that a rock star was calling from Prague, right in the middle of my gig at a Turkish grocery, where I had been playing in their outdoor café, seated beside the trash bin buzzing with yellowjackets. I apologized for the distracting noise of someone smashing their crunchy plastic salad tray into the bin. He understood.

Between the café gig and performing at nursing homes, I was learning to vary my repertoire at a tiny restaurant in Hell's Kitchen as a way of not becoming a bore to the wait staff, who could easily sway the owner into hiring a belly dancer instead of a guitarist. If I succeeded in capturing the attention of someone who did not come to hear me play but to eat, I considered that its own sweet reward. A Croatian composer and conductor who gave me weekly lessons in Inwood expressed his disappointment that I was wasting my talent and concert material in such a common setting. But audience members at Carnegie Hall are not likely to break bread with you or send you a drink. Nor do they tip or tell you afterward what the music you played reminded them of and what it means to them.

I imagine that if I had been playing at Carnegie Hall, I would not have to share the restroom with the needle junkie who had just left the walls splattered with blood. (Growing up in a rooming house allows you to recognize what sometimes happens in bathrooms.) I am uncertain if anyone else in my shoes would have had the composure to keep the staff of three together after the waitress, who had succumbed to her curiosity and taken a peek, turned ashen and ran through the kitchen to retch out in the back alley. I played a requested *malagueña* for our hungry dope fiends, underscoring the madness of this moment. They got up and departed when they saw the busboy rolling by with an ancient, squeaky mop bucket.

If I'd played at Carnegie Hall that evening, I would not have a story that causes everyone to lean in when I tell it. I have nothing against Carnegie Hall. It's just that when you play at a place like a restaurant in Hell's Kitchen, there is no established Apollonian scrim of formality separating life from the music and the audience from the performer. We closed the restaurant doors for an hour following that incident. The waitress pulled a bottle of red from under the counter and poured a round for the staff, who huddled together in grim silence until someone piped up and asked if I could play some Debussy to calm everyone down.

Not long after this, I traveled to Towson University in Maryland to attend the first and only World Guitar Congress, which featured a melee of guitar classes and concerts ranging from classical to flamenco, rock and jazz. The entire campus shimmered in the summer heat with the maddening drone of a seventeen-year cicada cycle thrumming endlessly. Dogs and people alike swatted at these ungainly bugs zinging lazily through the air, and I tried my best to avoid stepping on the sea of their fallen carcasses. I started pouncing on artists for interviews for this book, including a comical moment in a crowded, chaotic classroom where I'd tried handing Dick Dale my business card.

He scribbled on the back and handed it back to me. He'd given me his autograph. I tried handing the card back to him, telling him I needed his email address. Seeing the confused look on his face, I explained that I was requesting an interview. Before I knew it, he had inexplicably dipped me backwards and off-balance and planted one squarely on my cheek.

I watched Marty Friedman acknowledge a bashful, awestruck fan who had approached him to ask for help in learning a Megadeth lick. Marty stood with this kid in the far corner of the room, one leg propped up against the wall to support the guitar, and patiently took the time to demonstrate and break down the passage for him.

At an evening ceremony, Les Paul received a lifetime achievement award and I had gathered with other photographers at the foot of the stage to capture the moment. Someone tapped me from behind and I saw it was a man who had been seated in the front row. He told me that he and his brother wanted to ask if I wouldn't mind stepping to the side because I was blocking their view. I apologized and complied. After the ceremony, as Les Paul from the stage the crowd surged forward. There was no way I could even hope to speak with him. People held out guitars for him to autograph and the vibe of the crowd felt unpleasantly hungry, turning into a multi-footed, multi-headed beast breathing hot desperation.

Les Paul seemed gracious, even when one proud owner of a newly autographed Gibson guitar doffed his cowboy hat and whooped that though his guitar may no longer be playable, it was now worth at least ninety grand, guar-an-teed. I slipped away from this crush and left a message for the event's publicist, asking if she could communicate my interview request for this book.

All I could do was wait and hope for the best. When she phoned me back, her response was that Les Paul's two sons, who had been seated in the front row in the theater, told her they remembered me as the only photographer who had listened to their request to clear the foot of the stage. I was granted a private interview with Les Paul at his hotel room, which his sons videotaped.

Les Paul was a charismatic genius whose voice carried a distinctive Midwestern lilt. His genius revealed itself in his curiosity and eagerness, as well as his penchant for undaunted experiments and endless cheer. As laughter filled the room, I remember thinking, "If I should be so lucky to live into to my nineties, he'll set the bar for being young in spirit."

That same day, I found myself standing in a buffet line with Andy Summers, the guitarist from The Police. I took one look at the food selection on his plate and said, "Aha! You're on the Blood Type Diet." He denied it. I said I'd bet his blood type was O Negative. He expressed surprise, affirming that he was O Negative, the ancient caveman blood type, but he insisted that he was not any diet. He spent the rest of that meal giving me a suspicious squint. I sat sandwiched awkwardly at the dinner between him and Maurice Summerfield, the publisher of *Classical Guitar Magazine,* who announced to everyone at the table I was writing this book.

"I cannot give you my story because I am writing a book of my own," Andy responded.

Later on that evening, at a concert, I found myself sitting alone in a row of seats, stewing about getting rebuffed for the interview. What's another interview to a rock superstar who has been interviewed thousands of times? To hell with that, I thought. If I did not believe in this book enough to convince others to believe in it then I had no business being here. I got up and brazenly found my way backstage and recognized Andy by his fawn-colored suede jacket. He flinched when he saw me coming, The Blood Type Diet Girl. I clamped my hand on his shoulder and leaned in.

"You've played many, many concerts in your career, no?" He gave me a look somewhere between patience and pity but then his gaze broke away.

"Oh my god, is that Ralph Towner?" Andy asked distractedly, in awe. The jazz guitarist walked by, looking professorial in his corduroy jacket with elbow patches on the sleeves. I continued.

"I'll bet you would rather move on and do something new, musically," I said, "But at each of these concerts, the audience insists you play some old song that you're probably sick to death of, like 'Message in a Bottle.' They beg you to play these songs. And you oblige them, don't you?" I could see he was curious where I was going with this.

"If you give me this one story about your first guitar, it will not detract from your own project because it doesn't matter how many times an audience or reader has heard it before — if it is coming from you, they will want to read it again."

Later, I told Andy that I felt bad about cornering him like this because I could sense how important his own book was to him. I suggested a compromise. How about keeping his own story for his book and maybe writing the foreword for mine? He said he would think about it.

For the remaining days of the event, I bunkered out in the front lobby of Marriott Hotel beside the Starbucks cart, waiting to catch guitarists as they wandered groggily into the hotel's brunch room. After I had interviewed classical guitarists Eli Kassner and David Russell, an elderly couple eating pancakes at a table nearby leaned in, raised the back of their forks toward me and cheerfully said, "We've been watching you every morning, my dear. In fact, we have a nickname for you — 'The Huntress!'"

Not every interview fell into my lap so easily. Some had to be ferreted out and pried with *Green Eggs and Ham*–style persistence due to the reluctance of those who dreaded the unpalatable prospect of doing another interview with yet another punk journalist who presumes to know one's entire career better than the artist themself. Often, after the interview I would hear, "This was fun. This was actually fun. Have you spoken to Artist X?"

My mobile phone soon took on a charmed aura, emitting the kind of voicemail stream that must be commonplace for a record executive or music mogul. One of these calls came in as I was teaching my weekly after-school guitar class at a public school in downtown Manhattan. A male British accent on the other end said, "Julia. Do you know who this is?"

I was frazzled, just having defended the classroom teacher's stash of personal snacks from being decimated by one famished child and having admonished another for looking up an anatomical body part in the pictorial encyclopedia that was not relevant to the guitar. Now I had a British guitarist on the phone, attempting to stump me. I hoped that he had a sense of humor as the words flew out of my mouth.

"Well, I know it's not John Lennon," I answered.

"Ooooh! You've forgotten me already, then? It's Andy. Andy Summers. I've just emailed you the foreword for your book." Small faces gathered around me, abruptly silent. I'd forgotten my cell phone had been set to speaker.

One boy leaned in, "Andy Summers?! From The Police? My mother has their albums."

Andy invited me to dinner at La Trattoria to ask my advice on selecting a literary agent for his memoir. I recommended my own agent, whom he signed with. He later invited me to attend his photography exhibit on the top floor of the Hermés store on Madison Avenue one autumn evening, an event that attracted many celebrities. One of the Hermés shop clerks ventured to ask me, with great politeness, if the necklace I was wearing was estate jewelry. I hated to break the news that it was an $11 rhinestone necklace I had purchased from a thrift shop in Skokie, Illinois, when I was sixteen years old. This sadly left one more person in the room squinting at me, trying to make out just who the hell I was in the scheme of things.

Male models in white waiter jackets and black bowties served up tiny hors d'oeuvres and glasses of wine. I backed up against the wall, terrified that I might spill a drop of wine on a set of $500 silk scarves. Manhattan's ubiquitous society photographer Patrick McMullan was on hand with his flash-pan camera. I am not practiced in the art of the female celebrity three-quarter-swirl-and-pose-with-hand-on-hip, so the only record of me at this event is a photo of me huddled over the pages of Andy Summers and Ralph Gibson's book collaboration, looking like Cousin Itt with a champagne flute clutched tightly in hand.

If it felt strange to be in the big-top company of Page Six boldface names, but I soon realized how much scarier it was if you were up on the tightrope trying to balance public and private personas. Andy invited me to attend his jazz trio set at Birdland, where I was accosted by a beefy middle-aged man who possessed the wattles of an amiable St. Bernard. He asked if I was Andy's wife or girlfriend, and I replied neither, that I was a music journalist. He slipped me a handwritten note with the request that I give it to Andy. One brief scan of its contents prompted me to seek Andy's body-guard, who took the note and sat beside me for safety.

After the show, when this fan approached to request an autograph, Andy handled the encounter with a tough finesse, establishing a defined boundary and defusing the situation. The crush of people seeking autographs also helped to propel this fan along and on his way. I was still feeling shaky about the note, but Andy brushed off the incident, telling me it comes with the territory and that handling these things was a skill he had learned early on in his career. I recalled Dave Alvin's story of discovering his guitar came in handy for walloping an aggressive, disgruntled audience member who tried to storm his stage. Different ways to get the same thing done.

At another event that I was covering for several guitar magazines, I ran into Andy again. We sat in on a concert by Vernon Reid's Living Colour and loped out into the theater lobby afterward to check out the array of CDs and books for sale. Andy noticed the woman before I did — she was wearing that stupefied expression that veered from recognition to disbelief to incredulousness upon spotting him. She wandered toward us, wide-eyed. I saw Andy's body tighten a little. He turned toward me and grimaced. This was an inescapable facet of his life — the guitar has turned him forever into an instantly recognizable curiosity to strangers wherever he goes. This is the trade-off that comes with writing guitar riffs that more or less define a generation.

He composed himself when she approached and asked if he was indeed Andy Summers of The Police. When he said yes, she gushed that she'd been a huge Police fan since high school. Andy murmured his thanks. A few awkward seconds of silence hung tensely in the air. She wanted to say something more but looked overwhelmed. This woman was accompanied by her preschool-aged daughter dressed in a long tutu and pink gym shoes, with glittery barrettes affixed to her long, curled brunette hair. The little girl wore a pair of long tube socks on her arms, an obvious intent to be elegant, elbow-length opera gloves. She looked at her mother questioningly.

Andy crouched down and spoke to the daughter at eye-level. "Are you a ballerina? May I spin you around?" He took ahold of her little sock-encased hand and held it high as she obliged, inching her way around in a full-circle pirouette with a bright smile on her face.

David Russell

Grammy-winning classical guitarist David Russell was born in Glasgow, Scotland, and at the age of five moved to Minorca, Spain, where he started studying the guitar and where a street is now named in his honor, "Avinguda David Russell." In 2005, the Music Conservatory of Vigo, Spain, christened their new auditorium in his honor as well, naming it "Auditorio David Russell."

My first guitar belonged to my mother. My father had given my mother a guitar when they got married. It was a really pretty, old French guitar from the nineteenth century that he had discovered in a junk store. That was my guitar from the age of zero till about eight and then I got my real first one, a Spanish one that my brother still has in Minorca, Spain. It cost about a thousand *pesetas*, which is about $6. It was a normal, cheap Spanish guitar. Even the rosette design was just a couple circles — very basic. It was actually quite nice, though now it is fairly beat up. I keep asking my brother for it back but he tells me, "Eh, I have got nothing else." So he's got it.

My mother tells the story — I don't quite remember this — but she learned to play while she was pregnant with me. She insists I was learning along with her while still inside the womb. My father had all these old 78s of Segovia,

David Russell, eighteen years old, with his younger brother Vincent. (*Courtesy David Russell*)

so that is the music we heard all the time. I learned how to play "Recuerdos de la Alhambra" by ear. With my father, that's the way we did it. When I started to become proficient at playing, he switched from classical to flamenco. I never studied flamenco because that was special to him. I remember getting together and playing with him, but then he moved on to learn flamenco — it was not because things got competitive, but more of a personal preference. He loved jazz. He would have loved Les Paul.

What I loved about playing the guitar as a kid was the satisfaction of hearing myself get better, almost by the week or by the month when I practiced a lot. It's great. You learn a new piece and arrive at another level. Then there is also something nice about doing something nobody else does, doing it well or better than everyone else. I was a very, very shy little boy — painfully shy. Papa would say, "Give him a guitar. He may not be talking to anyone yet but give him the guitar." And I would sit down and play my "Recuerdos." So there was that little mix of show-off between the shyness. Socially, the guitar really helped me get used to being with people.

When I just finished my degree, I realized I had felt protected from the world during the time I was in school. I had made my own world within the

Royal Academy and was not aware, till the moment I got out of school, that there is this really huge world I knew absolutely nothing about, such as how to make a living and how to pay the rent. This is not easy for anyone coming out of college, not unless you are really lucky and things go smoothly. It was a horrible moment when I thought I would have to give up guitar and get a job. I was kind of lucky in that a few months after graduation I won an Andrés Segovia competition. I was not ready to give up. I had to look for a way to make this work. I won a Ramírez guitar for it, and up till then, I did not have a nice guitar because they are too expensive. So that was my first really nice guitar.

I have no one defining moment of an early performance simply because I played so often with my dad or about our small town in Minorca. I do remember my New York debut at Carnegie Hall, particularly how obsessed I became. You hope that reviewers will come, you hope to play perfectly and cleanly and all that.

About three weeks after this concert, I went to play in the Philippines. I was taken to a Vietnamese refugee camp with about four thousand people there and I performed in an open square. There was a full moon, and because we were located right on the equator, the moon was shining directly from above. It was an unbelievable sight, surrounded by a big, glowing halo. There were thousands of people in front of me, all standing. Things were really rough for these people. It was a very difficult time, about 1980. I played piece after piece, every single piece I knew and it was really such a contrast from my New York concert because all the things I had been worried and concerned about really did not matter. It really did not matter how it came out. I just played and played and played. Also, when I look into an audience people will often look away, but all these Vietnamese, if you looked at them, they would all smile back. It was a fantastic night, just fantastic. I meant, things were really difficult for these people but afterward I got to hang out with them.

Some years later, I was on a bus in Australia when an Asian-looking guy said to me, "Mr. Russell?" He was one of the other guitarists at this festival. He said, "Do you remember playing at Palawan on this island?"

I said, "Yes, sure, of course I remember."

"Do you remember going into the water with a group of children? I was one of them," he said.

And he'd grown up to play guitar.

Roland Dyens

Tunisian-French classical guitarist, arranger and composer Roland Dyens is a unique artist, known for his extraordinary improvisatory skills and his brilliantly colorful and evocative compositions that incorporate elements of jazz and folk music. He was the only classical guitarist invited to participate in the concert honoring the great Django Reinhardt at the Théâtre du Châtelet in Paris. Dyens teaches at the Conservatoire national supérieur de musique et de danse de Paris.

I was nine, maybe ten years old when I received my first guitar. It was a very rudimentary, classical nylon-string guitar — not the worst, mind you but it had been made from some kind of imitation wood. Of course, I was not very demanding at the time. I still have this guitar and it is very close to my heart. I played a bit of piano when I was a music composition student later on, but I play just enough piano as I need — my focus has always been on the guitar.

In terms of musicians who inspired me, I cannot answer that it was classical players like Segovia. My musical influences were much simpler — mostly French pop singers from when I was very little, about three years old. It was not classical guitar that influenced me but all other kinds of music — jazz,

South American, American and French pop songs. I would name the artists but they are not even known by French people as they have all disappeared completely. Harry Belafonte's music I loved. More than anything, I fell in love with the sound of the guitar at that time.

I come from a family of artists, so my interest in the guitar did not come as a shock to them. My father is a painter and my uncle is a sculptor in Montreal and nearly everyone in the family was doing something in the arts, so what I was doing with the guitar was not considered at all weird. They supported me and it was great. When I received my first guitar, my intention was to improvise music and find chords and learn it all on my own before I attempted lessons. I was always improvising, just as I do now. And when I start recitals, often it is with an improvisation.

I was always looking for new sounds and I was a composer already at ten years old. The very first music I wrote was a piece in the style of a *barcarolle*. I played it to my first teacher, Robert Maison, who was a great man. Teachers like him no longer exist in this world — he seems to have belonged to the nineteenth century rather than the twentieth century. He was my master of music. I was not certain what kind of music it was that I was playing for him, and he informed me it was a *barcarolle*. It sounded so nice to my ears, and that I was able to write a *barcarolle* on my own by ear seemed great to me. After two years Maison informed my parents he no longer had anything more to teach me, that I needed to find a new teacher.

Unfortunately, my second teacher turned out to be very bad for me. At that time, in France during the mid-'60s, the musical landscape was barren. There was nobody who taught guitar. My second teacher was actually a violin teacher who never played the guitar. But she was given the position of teaching guitar because at this time violin and the guitar were considered the same. Only my third teacher, Ernesto Ponce, was a real guitar maestro. I studied with him for seven years. It was very rare to find someone who taught guitar in the big cities in France, and there were no guitar teachers in the conservatories at this time either — you had to go to Spain to find a guitar teacher! I had real support from my parents at this time because they helped me find the right teacher.

I think the guitar surprises me every day. I have a reverence for the instrument — while it is the most rudimentary instrument, it is also the most complex. I'm always amazed by its possibilities. The piano seems a bit more clear as an instrument, yet the guitar has so many elements to it, such as harmonics and the fact that you can have the same note positioned elsewhere along

the fretboard positions — it offers an incredible number of possibilities.

My first performance took place when I was studying with my bad teacher, unfortunately. She took advantage of my skills to tell the audience that I was her student, yet she had not taught me much of anything, and really had no right to take the credit. The piece I played was a *bourée* by Robert de Visée and people loved it. And on that day, during that particular performance, I had the very first feeling that maybe I could be a professional musician.

Roland Dyens holding his first guitar, which he still owns. (*Courtesy Roland Dyens*)

In 1986, I was scheduled to perform in one of the most important concerts of my career at Salle Gaveau, which is one of the three biggest concert halls in all of Paris. As usual, I performed an improvisation as my introduction. Roughly thirty seconds into the piece, I heard somebody's watch alarm ringing. This watch was playing, "Oh! Susanna" in a sharp, loud, high pitch. I thought it would stop after the first few seconds but it didn't. It continued to play the entire song. I'd thought it would stop then. But it started over at the very beginning. The owner of this watch had ruined my improvisation. This came as a complete shock. I had to surrender. I had to give up. In my brain, I had been fighting it, wondering if I should continue to play the improvisation or whether I should stop playing. What do I do? What I did in that very moment was play "Oh! Susanna" in duet along with the watch alarm. This became the best thing I ever did in my life. People in the audience were amazed and gave me a big standing ovation. Many people told me after the concert that this particular moment had been great and they wanted to know how I had rehearsed it, but I had to tell them the truth — that this had not been prepared or anticipated at all. I did not know whose watch that had been. It had just happened.

Years later, I came to learn the identity of that watch owner. He was my uncle. He was ashamed of it and waited to tell me, saying, "I wanted to die because I could not stop it." To this day I remember how I easily could have stopped playing but something in me had said, "No, go on, take it. Go play 'Oh! Susanna'" because the improvisation I had been doing was ruined now and there was nothing else left to lose. It was the best I had to offer and I did it.

When it comes to the word challenge and the guitar — I think it is the key word of my life as a musician because I am a real challenger. I am always seeking difficult musical situations — I hate comfortable musical situations. I am always putting myself under great pressure. When faced with almost impossible challenges, I love that. The fact that I am both a soloist and a composer, not to mention the fact that I am a teacher, makes my life more complicated and trickier but much more fun. I have a lot of fun because, in the classical world, we have a few people who are both soloists and composers. There are many composers but they do not play their own music and do not play well, or we have good players who do not compose. That I am doing both is challenging and extremely important. In the past, it was more common to have composers who were players, especially during the Baroque era. But in this century, there seems to have been a gradual divorce between the two functions.

To me, a composer must be a whole musician. This is something I wanted to point out because it is what I love in my life, because it allows me to be both the cook and the eater. I find much in common between the profession of cooks and composers. When I see cooks interviewed, I always feel they say the same things I do, like, "ok, next time, I will try this and I will change my recipe." When I compose, I think to myself, "I shall change the recipe to make it a little more like this or that." I love when other people play my music, but I am proud to say I'm both the cook and the first eater of my musical food, and it is a privilege to be the first ambassador of my own music.

Los Angeles Guitar Quartet

The original Los Angeles Guitar Quartet, featuring guitarists Andrew York, William Kanengiser, John Dearman and Scott Tennant, won a Grammy in 2005 for Best Classical Crossover for their CD *Guitar Heroes*. Andrew York, who played with the quartet for sixteen years, has departed for a solo career. William Kanengiser is currently faculty at the guitar department at USC. John Dearman plays the 7-string guitar in the quartet and currently teaches at the University of California, Santa Barbara. Scott Tennant is the author of the bestselling classical guitar method book series *Pumping Nylon*. Matthew Greif, not interviewed here, replaced Andrew York in 2006 and is a former student of both Kanengiser and Tennant.

Andrew York

My first guitar was actually my father's guitar. He plays and so does my uncle. I think it was a 1957 Martin. Getting it was huge because I had started playing when I was about seven or eight years old. We're not sure because even before I really began to play, I was faking it because the guitar was always there. When

Teenaged Andrew York. (*Courtesy Andrew York*)

my dad showed me certain things, I picked it up quickly, so he found a teacher for me. My own guitar, which is lost in the mists of history, was a small cheap guitar with very high action and that quickly gave way to a nylon-string classical guitar. My real first guitar would have to be my dad's Martin '57.

We had a piano in the house. My mom sings and my dad was always listening to classical music and playing folk music, so the guitar was just there. It is a great instrument because it is self-sufficient. I did start playing trombone early in fifth grade and actually majored in flute in college but the guitar was always present and available within the house, and I've resonated with it as both a harmony and solo instrument. Being such a lover of music, I found it to be such a gas to learn and have a musical idea and then be able to realize it or else learn a picking pattern for a new folk song. It was a deep thrill to begin to play and I started writing music right away. I think I knew at a young age that I was going to be a musician my whole life. It was clear and nothing else struck me as quite so interesting.

I was very young when I played my first professional gig, probably eight or nine years old. One of my sisters, who is ten years older than me, had me join her to play in a big auditorium that could have been an old folks' retirement home. She sang a song called "The Green Leaves of Summer," and I accompanied her as she sang. I also played a Sor piece with a bit of tremolo that came out of one of Aaron Shearer's books. It was Giuliani or Sor.

I really loved pop music — The Beatles and anything that came out on the radio, I'd follow. Some of it liked, some of it did not but I was aware of what was happening. And I loved classical music. I used to listen to Leonard Bernstein conducting Beethoven's Ninth Symphony. I listened to that over and over until I wore out the LP, and then my sister bought me another and I bought Beethoven's Seventh as well. I was really into Beethoven. My uncle had a record of Sousa marches that astounded me. So I was really open, in terms of what I listened to and when I found something I liked, I became obsessed with it. I would listen to music over and over and listen deeply, hearing harmonies though I did not know what to call anything. Now that I've studied music, I can hear a song and know the chords and know what to call them. My dad found a really great teacher for me in Richmond, Virginia, named Greta Dollitz, who had been a student of Aaron Shearer. She is still teaching and has one of the longest running classical guitar radio shows in the country.

What I like about the guitar is that it is a self-sufficient instrument. You can play it by yourself and have harmony and melody and everything there. You can also play with others, and it is a portable instrument. The trombone is not like that — it's made to be played with an orchestra or jazz band. I like the guitar because it is complete. Music is a life journey, and if you are in it seriously, your life issues will begin to emerge with the music and you will begin to question everything. If you approach music as a life and art, then you are forced to confront yourself in various stages along the way.

William Kanengiser

I was eight years old when I started playing my first guitar, which had actually been my brother's guitar that he got by collecting S&H Green Stamps in the '60s. These stamps were collected at the grocery store checkout counter, they would give you sheets and sheets of these incredibly sticky stamps. It took about twenty of these books, just thousands of these ridiculous stamps. We turned them in for a guitar, which today, would be described more as a GSO or Guitar-Shaped Object because it was not a high-end instrument.

It was my brother's guitar because he is the one who had wanted the guitar.

William Kanengiser, age fifteen, at music summer camp. "I was going for the Jimi Hendrix look!" he says. (*Courtesy William Kanengiser*)

He is three years older than me and he was working with a book to learn how to play. At first he would not let me try to play his guitar. He had it for about three months and worked his way through a few pages of the book. Then he relented and let me try it. I went through the first five pages of the book in a week and this left him pretty much demoralized, to the point where he said, "You know what? Why don't you keep the guitar?" I've never played another instrument outside of the college requirement of piano, which I just stunk horribly at. I have no keyboard skills whatsoever. I did always want to be a drummer but the guitar is my instrument.

I have a very clear recollection of sitting with my guitar, though I did not know any notes yet, performing what I called an "open string concert." I was just playing patterns on open strings, fingerstyle. I was already thinking of myself, at the age of eight, as playing for an audience and, possibly, in a way, this carried me through. My feeling about playing is that it is not complete until you ultimately give it to the audience.

The artists who interested me included James Taylor — I remember being ecstatic when I figured out on my own the little lick to the beginning of his song, "Fire and Rain." It was a eureka moment and my brother was going to kill me because I played just that opening little slide of a G chord to an A chord so many times. The Beatles' "Blackbird" was the first complicated song I learned, one that traveled up and down the neck. Someone wrote it out for me in a sort of rudimentary tablature and I figured it out. I heard a little bit of Segovia back then and tried to emulate it, not knowing what I was doing. When I was in high school, I was really into the group Yes — Steve Howe was my idol. I figured out his "Mood for a Day" off the album *Fragile* in a day. I also played it in my junior high talent show. For the LAGQ *Guitar Heroes* album, I had to include this piece so it was fun for me to revisit it.

I have to say my family was great about my interest in the guitar. There are no musicians in my immediate family. I had two cousins who were professional pianists — one was classical and the other was a Broadway showtunes kind of guy. No one else in my family had musical talent but they loved music, especially jazz. My dad was a huge jazz aficionado. My parents encouraged me — they were never pushy and they were not stage parents. Basically, I practiced because I wanted to.

I remember there was one seminal moment when I was maybe a junior in high school. I was starting to get pretty good on the guitar and I was also a good student. I think my parents thought, hey, compared to the less desirable things most teenagers could be doing with their free time, demonstrating an interest in music was not so bad. I wondered if I should go into medicine and get a real job. I had a discussion with my parents. They asked, "Are you really serious about music as what it is you want to study, as opposed to it being a hobby?" Ultimately, they did not put up any roadblocks. They said, "Bill's going to give this a chance and see how he does with it." And it worked out pretty well. I'm just as surprised as anybody!

Like many kids at that age, when I started playing, I thought, "If I can learn to play the guitar, then I'll be really cool. Girls will find me interesting." Of course, what happened was I became so focused on practicing that I sort of just locked myself inside my room for a couple years — so much for the social aspect. A friend of mine went to a high school reunion and found out there were a bunch of girls who had thought I was kind of cute, but I'd been oblivious because all I was doing at the time was practicing my guitar.

I was entranced by the instrument and found that it felt like a natural extension of myself. It did not feel *easy*, but natural, and I could not imagine doing anything else. I had a few crucial moments of questioning what I was doing playing. I was on my way to becoming a professional guitarist when I heard David Russell perform for the first time, and I remember calling up my mom and saying, "I just saw this guy play and I'm *never* going to play like that. I can't do that." I had this crisis because he had rocked my world so much. And I love David. My mom was cool about it, saying, "Well, just do your best." I thought that I would give it a try for a couple more years and if it did not work out, I would learn something about computers. As it turned out, David Russell was a huge inspiration and model and forced me to reevaluate my playing. I practiced my ass off.

Believe it or not, one of my first professional gigs as a student in Los Angeles was also the moment when I met my wife. I was a student at USC at the time, and a friend of mine who is a jazz player received a call that a cigar store was having a party and they wanted a classical guitarist to play. He passed along the gig to me. I did not have a car. In Los Angeles, it's kind of hard to get around without a car. I said, "Look, I'll take the bus there, but someone has got to give me a ride home." So I went to this party and played my guitar. And there was this girl there. She was a friend of the owner's sister and had been enlisted to make sure that no one stole any of the high-end pipes in the shop. The shop owner was supposed to give me the ride home, but he had won the pipe-smoking contest and became sick as a result. She wound up giving me a ride home and we went out for Chinese food. The embarrassing part was when the bill came. I realized that I had a check inside my wallet for playing the gig but not enough cash to pay for dinner. So we went Dutch on our first date. And the very next day was Valentine's Day, in 1979. We just celebrated our twenty-ninth wedding anniversary. I'd have to say that was a pretty good gig.

One memorable guitar I owned was really gorgeous instrument that I'd bought from Pepe Romero's brother, Celin, when I first started to study with the Romeros. It was a Miguel Rodriguez church door spruce top, very unusual. And it had a pedigree because Celin had played it on their recording of the *Concierto Andaluz*. I played this guitar for ten years in several competitions and, toward the end of those ten years, I'd found that this guitar was becoming very temperamental and did not like traveling. I bought another instrument that I'd fallen in love with and did not touch the Rodriguez for two years. When I did, I just felt that this instrument no longer did anything for me. This was about the time my daughter was about to be born and we were kind of low on money, so I sold it. I sold the Rodriguez to a guy who was a real Romero devotee and collector, but I sold it for a song, bottom of the market.

Twelve years later, I received tax advice from my accountant, who said, "You know, Bill, you haven't bought a guitar in five years and you need to buy a guitar as a tax write-off." I called a friend who happens to be a guitar trader in town and told him that I needed to buy a guitar. He said to me, "I cannot believe you are calling me right now because two days ago your old Rodriguez arrived in my shop."

I hadn't played this guitar in twelve years. It turned out that the guy I had sold it to later traded it for Julian Bream's lute, and then somebody else sold it to somebody else and so on until it ended up in Los Angeles. I drove over to the shop, played about three notes on this guitar and I couldn't believe that I'd ever sold it. I fell madly in love with it and I remembered every single nook and cranny of this guitar.

There is a tradition with Rodriguez guitars that Pepe Romero started, where you give them a name and christen them. Pepe calls his guitar "La Wonderful." I called mine "L'Enamorada," and I had put this little piece of masking tape with that name on it inside next to the label. And my little piece of tape with that name was still there. And for the love of this guitar, I paid about five times more for it than what I had sold it for.

John Dearman

I saw The Beatles play on *Ed Sullivan* when I was seven years old, and after that, I started carrying on constantly to my parents about how I wanted to play drums. When my birthday came around I received my present with great anticipation. And it was not a drum set. I think my parents realized that would be a little painful for a few years. What they'd bought me instead was a baritone ukulele. I guess they had spoken to someone at a music store who told them, for a kid my age, this would be a good instrument. It's tuned like a ukulele but it is bigger and you play it with felt pick. From there, I took a couple months' worth of lessons — learning to read from a Mel Bay book and playing songs like "Aura Lea."

Then we moved to Orange County, California, from Minneapolis. My little stint with the ukulele bombed but this time around, I wanted a guitar. They got me a nylon-string called an Avila. It was unusual — the whole thing was painted chocolate brown, front and back. Again, they took me in for lessons and I had the greatest teacher. He showed me how to play "Secret Agent Man" and "Wipe Out." I think he might have showed me a little *malagueña*. He was showing me stuff directly — there were no books. I just went nuts with that.

I did not come from a musical family but my dad liked listening to jazz. He liked guitar, what a lot of people had at that time, like Charlie Byrd, Chet Atkins and Luiz Bonfá. I really remember the Bonfá album. My dad was a pharmacist, with no other particular interest in music. I was not particularly into music as a kid, either. It was just that the whole Beatles thing had gotten me excited. The ukulele lessons did not interest me to the extent that my teacher had when he showed me how to play the guitar licks. That's what excited me again.

There was a long period after this where I did not take lessons. My parents split up. When I was a teenager, I got back into playing again by just picking stuff up off records. I remember learning songs by The Doors and by Chet Atkins and all the fingerstyle guitarists. Above all, my earliest influence was Chet Atkins. When I went to live with my dad at thirteen, he took me in for lessons.

He said, "You have that old guitar still. Why aren't you playing it?" I said, "Well, you know, I'm not that interested." "Let's take some lessons" was his response. I agreed and took lessons for six months. They put me on the Mel Bay methods again. I could not get past page three because I found it to be the most boring stuff. Again I ignored the guitar until a year later when I started picking up stuff off records. Then I just went nuts all through high school. I spent all my time next to the record player, learning everything by Chet Atkins. I learned a lot of folk stuff, too. I was into Neil Young. I transcribed some Wes Montgomery albums, Segovia and Parkening records. Everything I learned was by ear. If you put a piece of sheet music in front of me, it would take me a year to read it. So I picked up a wide range of stuff, including classical.

My dad was happy to see me playing the guitar, given whatever else I could have been doing in high school in the '70s. I became known as the guitar guy at school. It was not until I was out of high school that I started to study classical guitar, because that is when I met the Romeros.

At this point, I was a fairly accomplished fingerstyle player who knew a wide range of stuff. I had studied some Brazilian music, basic *bossa nova*. I knew a few classical pieces — and I was teaching at a music store. I met a guy there who was studying classical and he was very good. We became best friends and he said, "You should see my teacher, Celin Romero." I had heard of the Romeros, that they were a famous guitar family, but I didn't know much about them. So my friend took me over to Celin's house in San Diego one day and we chatted a little bit, then my friend said, "Why don't you play something for me?" Celin asked what I was going to play and I told him I knew this piece called "Yellowbird," a Chet Atkins arrangement. He said, "Oh, Shet Atkeens! I love heeem — he's a good friend of mine." I might have also played a Bach piece and one of the Venezuelan waltzes that I'd taken off a record. He took me on for lessons. At that point I had a steel-string acoustic, a couple of electric guitars, a slide guitar, a banjo — but within a month I sold all of them to buy a Contreras guitar from the Romeros. After studying with the Romeros, I started to attend USC to study music.

I find the guitar fascinating. It just becomes part of your identity in a way, even if it's just playing for your friends. For me, it took over my whole life. The guitar is all I've ever wanted to do. I never questioned playing the guitar or whether or not it should be a career. I just followed the next step that was in front of me, and I've met with great fortune doing that because if I hadn't met that guy who introduced me to Celin, I would probably still be sitting a that music store, teaching to this day and playing at restaurants. I had no intention to go to college or anything because I was going to be a musician.

Learning by symbols never agreed with me. I learned full classical and fingerstyle pieces from a record in one long day, memorizing as I went. Recently, I thought that perhaps I should go back and try to relearn theses pieces from the sheet music. I try to encourage my students to learn that way, too. It's very interesting to me that it takes people a long time to memorize pieces from sight. But when learning from hearing, it seems to go faster. There are no symbols involved. It's a direct process of the finger motion and your awareness of the fingerboard.

I once had a Reyes flamenco guitar, a nice guitar when I was gigging a lot out of college. I had to take two guitars to this gig in my Volvo station wagon, an old beat-up thing. I was in a big rush one day — I ran out to the car, put everything in the back, got in and started backing up. As I was backing up, I heard this BANG! I got out and realized I had left the Reyes tilted against the back bumper so when I backed up, it flipped backwards and the car ran over it. It wasn't totaled but it was smashed up pretty good in one place. I managed to get it repaired and it plays well — I think it helped that the damage was confined to a localized area, just one part of the guitar. The grain on the top of the guitar had been compressed, but Yuris Zeltins, who is legendary for guitar repair in San Diego, managed to fix it. He has restored, modified and repaired every one of the Romeros' guitars since the '70s.

It's all a process of evolution when you're starting to perform. Your first departmental recital turns into your junior recital and turns into your senior recital and your masters degree recital, and then you've got some crummy little gig and it keeps creeping upward. I first thought, "Wow, this quartet is really going somewhere" at one gig at a big hall for a classical guitar congress in either Baltimore or Washington, D.C. I remember walking out onstage and seeing the place packed. People were screaming. It was weird. We had played some pretty big concerts up to that date, like one or two GFA (Guitar Foundation of America) conventions, but it was still early in our career. It was the first time we became aware that people really liked us, that we were reaching some kind of critical mass. All of us had a little chill go down our spines.

All kinds of weird things happen, too. We had only been together for about a year when someone from the Ministry of Mexican culture visited USC in search of talent to hire for a tour throughout rural areas of Mexico at schools and small towns in Mexico. This was in May or June of 1981. It was going to be forty-eight concerts in six weeks, so we were doing two concerts a day. In the afternoon, we would pile into our little Volkswagen with our guitars and drive into the next town to play in schools, movie theaters and museums. The movie theater was a strange experience because they did not have lighting for the stage. The audience was lit up but our stage was dark and we could not see our music.

When we landed in Mexico City, we unloaded into the hotel, slept for a little and then wanted to look for a place to eat. Anisa Angarola, who was in the group originally, did not like being in hotels because she was worried about theft. She said, "We can't leave our guitars in our room." She decided to leave her guitar at the front desk. We figured she might be right so we all did the same.

We went to lunch, walked around the city and had a great time. Then we returned to the hotel. As we were walking up the steps to the hotel, we heard people playing our guitars! We walked in and there were the bellboys and the front desk people — all our guitar cases were wide open and people were playing them, just jamming away.

I find that a lot of students are worried about their future in terms of job security and career. My advice is if you aren't really sure that you *love* playing the guitar and making music, you should move on. If you *are* sure, the best thing to do is just excel. If you have a good teacher and mentor and devote yourself to practicing with intelligence and discipline, you will become a good, or maybe a great, player. And when you're done with school, even if it looks like you may not be able to make a go of it as a professional, you will have at least developed confidence and a capacity for creative problem-solving that will allow you to excel in other fields.

Scott Tennant

I got my first guitar when I was six after bugging my parents for it. Apparently — and I don't have much memory of this — but my brother and I were bugging them for a guitar since I was four. To stop us from complaining, they got us both a tiny guitar for Christmas. It was a just a little acoustic steel-string guitar. I was thrilled. I thought I could play it right away so I started strumming it, but they insisted on lessons, which I didn't like.

My first *real* guitar was a little three-quarter-sized Sears steel-string. I can't exactly tell you why I was fascinated by the guitar — a past life maybe? I don't know. I always knew that I just wanted to be a guitar player. There was no real reason I chose it — it just came out of my deep subconscious somewhere. Throughout the years, though, I have had to study other instruments, like violin, piano.

When you're six years old, your grand plans, basically, are trying to get through your fifteen-minute practice session. My mom had to sit down beside me for fifteen minutes to make sure I got those fifteen minutes' practice though it was very painful. My grand plans when I was six were to become a really great guitar player, a famous hockey player and an archeologist. I figured I'd cover my bases.

My family was always supportive. Especially my mother, who had been a musician in her youth — she'd played clarinet. She thought it was great that I was becoming more serious about this instrument. Eventually, she did not have to watch me to make sure I practiced. I actually practiced on my own. Both my parents were very supportive, the whole way. And sometimes they were a little embarrassing about it, too. My mom did the stage mom thing by introducing me to people, writing letters to TV shows and of course, never got any response. I remember seeing once a letter she had written to *The Mike Douglas Show* and thinking, "Oh, you're not going to send that. Don't embarrass me, please." She would say, "You just never know."

My father managed a hotel in Detroit, Michigan, the Yorba Hotel. In fact, the White Stripes wrote a song about it, and I guess they lived there for a while. I grew up in that hotel. When I was able to play enough tunes for people, my father started organizing recitals for me. They had a big lounge area with sofas and we'd fill the place up. I was about ten years old, and that was my first real sense of performing. It was a real thrill. I never got nervous, either. That came later on when I had a teacher, a real European maestro type, who noticed I was not nervous. So he announced to the audience, "This child may not be nervous now but he *will* be later." It sunk in or something. He shouldn't have said that!

There is just something about the plucked sound of a guitar. In the beginning I was not even really good at playing, but I enjoyed that sound. Later, of course, I enjoyed the ease that comes with practicing and being able to play a few tunes. That is very rewarding. I've never questioned what I was doing playing the guitar. I did, however, have to question whether or not I would be a good hockey player, which I was not. And the archeologist dream? I'd thought, well, no. The idea of digging of Egypt for years on end was not really my cup of tea. So, I never questioned playing the guitar for an instant.

I started out on plectrum guitar, a big old red Gibson electric guitar, which was my second guitar. That's the guitar I actually started learning to play classical guitar on. The hard part I remember was having a classical piece in my method book, a Tchaikovsky melody or something, and for some reason this seemed a little harder than the usual folk melodies in the book. This just stands out to me, that it was a difficulty in my mind, not an actual difficulty. Somehow, it demanded more attention. That's what made me want to play classical guitar.

My guitars have gotten lost a couple of times. A couple years ago, I got on a plane in Belgium to come back home to Los Angeles and my guitar did not make the flight for some reason. It was not a full flight, either. Of course, when I reached Los Angeles, I complained to the baggage people. This was before 9/11 when you didn't get arrested for yelling at flight attendants and baggage people. They said they'd do what could and took my address and everything. They gave me the number to call the baggage handling the next day. They said, "It will go out on the next flight." I waited. I had to leave again in the next few days for Europe so I waited and called several times a day. No sign of my guitar. Not even in the computer. They said, "As best we know, it got onto a SwissAir flight and it was supposed to come to Los Angeles the next day."

I had to go back on tour, so every day I was calling from Europe to check up on my guitar. I was talking to the head of the airline at this point. Still there was no sign of the guitar. By now, they were becoming very apologetic about it. The guitar that was lost was my David Bailey guitar, which was the guitar I was playing most those days. Also, it was in a good luggage case. Luckily I had a substitute guitar to take on the next tour.

I continued to call every day for three weeks, though at this point, I had pretty much written it off. I was about to get a lawyer because I was so mad. On the way back from *that* tour, I was in the Atlanta airport waiting for my flight and checking my phone messages. There was a message from customs at the LAX airport, telling me they've had this guitar-shaped thing sitting here for three weeks and if I didn't pick it up by tomorrow, it was going to go to government holding. Nobody had notified me about this before. I was *absolutely* incensed — I called that number right away and told them I was heading to Los Angeles right now and if anything happened to that guitar at all, I was going to just go insane.

When I got to LAX, we went to the warehouse and they went way, way back and used a forklift to lift it down from some shelf. Apparently, it had arrived in Los Angeles that next flight, as promised. But no one ever logged it into the computer. There was a tire track over the case and signs of it having been bumped around for three weeks. A forklift had run over it. It was a good case, luckily. I look back on it now and it's kind of funny, though it was definitely *not* funny at the time.

Alex Lifeson

Canadian guitarist Alex Lifeson is best known as the guitarist of the rock band Rush. He and his bandmates, Neil Peart and Geddy Lee, are the first rock band to be made Officers of the Order of Canada.

I was twelve years old when I received my first guitar from my parents for Christmas in 1965. It was a Kent Classic — a classical guitar that I put steel strings on. It cost $10 and was manufactured in Japan. My first electric guitar, which I received the following Christmas, had been a $59 red Canora, which was also a Japanese-made guitar. It looked like a smaller version of a double-cutaway Gretsch. I actually still have this guitar. My mom had it sitting inside a closet for years and just brought it over a couple weeks ago. This guitar had been stripped down. Geddy and I painted those first guitars of ours the same way Eric Clapton and Jack Bruce had their guitars painted, all psychedelic and groovy-looking in the '60s. We had painted our own version, so you can imagine what they look like! So this guitar has all its beautiful artwork stripped from the body, but it still has some green fluorescent paint on the neck. There were no machine heads, no hardware or anything. I might try to put it back together at some point.

I'd started playing viola in seventh and eighth grade, but that was the only other instrument I had played besides the guitar. Just about any kind of music inspired me at the time. Before I took up the guitar, anything I listened to, whether it was Serbian folk music or classical music, moved me deeply. When I started listening to rock music, I enjoyed The Beach Boys to mid-'60s pop music — The Who, Jimi Hendrix, Cream and, of course, Led Zeppelin and blues primarily from Britain at that time, like John Mayall and Jeff Beck. Jimmy Page was a huge influence. My parents were rather worried about all this, hoping I might become a plastic surgeon instead or that I would at least enter a profession they did not have to worry about. I, along with Geddy, am so passionate about playing music. I do not think my parents really stopped worrying until we were on a local TV show, and then they realized, "Oh, we get it now. There is hope."

To this day, after forty-five years of playing, I still get completely lost in the joy of playing the guitar. I am sitting here in my office, surrounded by guitars. I have mostly guitars in my office. I have two Les Paul guitars here, a PRS 12-string guitar, a J-55 Gibson acoustic, a Geddy Lee Fender bass and a *cümbüş* (a 12-stringed Turkish instrument that looks like a banjo with a pot on the body, but it is a very evocative-sounding instrument).

I have a routine that, often in the evening after my wife and I have dinner, we will maybe watch some TV and eventually I drift into my office, sit down and play for a couple hours because it is so enjoyable simply to play. I'm not practicing or trying to work something out — I'm just playing. It's an escape and a wonderful place to go.

I do recall in the early days that it seemed as if you never got any better. The plateaus were very far apart. I would come home from school and the first thing I would do is come home and play until dinner. I would have dinner then I would go back to my bedroom and play before I went to bed, and I never did my homework. All I wanted to do was play guitar. I recall playing and playing and playing and working so hard to learn parts but it seemed that it would take forever before you felt as if you'd finally made that next major step in improvement. I found that challenging, in terms of not getting frustrated or losing interest. But once you hit that next step up, boy, it was life changing. I guess it is like this with any pursuit. Sometimes it can be difficult physically, in terms of playing, because I've had psoriasis since I was a kid, and it is primarily on my hands. It is a bit more under control these days, but in the early days, I used to endure these very inflammatory cycles where my hands would become very swollen, split and bleed, especially during a sweaty, hot night in some

Alex Lifeson with his first guitar, a Canora. (*Courtesy Melanija Zivojinovich*)

little arena. The salt from the sweat would get into the open cuts, and it was a significant challenge on a few nights, very difficult.

My first performance was in the basement of a church drop-in center called The Coffin on September 18, 1968. We were paid $10. We knew seven or eight songs that we just played over and over. We really did not have any equipment. We used Geddy's amp with both of us plugged into it. John [Rutsey, the band's original drummer] had his drums and we had a floor lamp stand we taped a mic to, and that was our first gig.

I have an ES-335 that I adore that I've had for years. We were playing a gig with Blue Öyster Cult in the late '70s at the Nassau Veterans Memorial Coliseum out on Long Island. On the side of the stage, I had that guitar and my double-necked Gibson, an EDS-1275, I believe it was, just sitting in place on their guitar stands. Someone in the crew had not tied down the horns on the PA, so this horn vibrated and fell off the back of the PA stack. Fortunately, the stack was on the side of the stage and not out over the house. It fell back and then fell over and landed on both guitars, taking a big gouge out of the 335's neck. I retired that guitar after that happened. The 12-string fared worse — it broke the headstock, and I had to replace that guitar entirely. Not a happy guitar story, I know, but I still have that 335 and it is a joy to play. It survived a couple new little scars on it — to go with all the hundreds of other scars on it! As far as the 12-string went, what had happened gave me the perfect excuse not to play it for a while — it weighed a ton.

Steve Lukather

Grammy-winner Steve Lukather is the guitarist for the band Toto, which formed in Los Angeles in 1977, when Lukather was nineteen years old. He is also renowned as a songwriter, composer, arranger and producer as well as for his efficient and prolific session work. He played the rhythm guitar and bass on "Beat It," "Human Nature" and the duet with Paul McCartney "The Girl is Mine" on Michael Jackson's *Thriller* album, one of the bestselling records of all time. Jeff Beck and Carlos Santana number among the many artists he has toured with.

My first guitar was a Kay acoustic and I still have it. It is now a lamp at my dad's house. We thought it would be a cool thing to do with it, because it was just sitting there at his house anyway. I was seven years old and wanted a guitar after seeing The Beatles on TV in 1964, so we bought the Kay from the Thrifty drugstore. We bought my first electric guitar, an Astro Tone with four pickups, from that drugstore as well. A friend of mine accidentally broke the neck on it and my dad was so mad he made me play it broken for the next four years.

I never played any other instrument. To me, the sound of the guitar goes deep inside — it's a powerful sound. When I heard George Harrison and

Paul McCartney playing, my first thought was "I want to be *that* guy." The funny thing is, during the course of my career, I actually did get the chance to play with my two guitar heroes. I met George Harrison while playing at a Jeff Porcaro tribute concert in Los Angeles, and we hit it off. He was a really sweet guy. I met Paul McCartney while working on Michael Jackson's *Thriller* album, and he asked me to be a part of his movie *Give My Regards to Broad Street*.

Later, I got a fake Les Paul, a Vox Les Paul. Then when my dad saw how serious I was about the guitar, he took me to the original Guitar Center in Hollywood. At first, he was planning to buy a car, but he wound up getting me a Les Paul Deluxe — a '71 or '72 sunburst, when I was about fourteen years old. I practically made love to this guitar. I was so happy to have it that I'd fall asleep in bed with it.

Jimmy Wyble was my first teacher. He was also the teacher to the Porcaro brothers, Steve and Mike. I learned how to read music from him. He used to yell at me for relying on my ears too much.

My family was very supportive about my playing. My mother and sister can't sing "Happy Birthday" if they tried, but my mother was patient and dedicated about driving me to rehearsals and gigs. One time when my dad picked me up after a rehearsal, he saw a trumpet standing in a corner and surprised the hell out of me by picking it up and playing bebop on it. I never knew this about him but he was modest about it and said, "Ah, well, I used to play a little." But I was like, "*Damn*, my old man can play!"

I've never really thought about anything else other than playing guitar. The guitar has been it. When I was eleven years old, I played my first gig in grammar school on a Jazzmaster Bosstone that I'd borrowed from my teacher, Mark, and the girls were just screaming, when we played "Foxy Lady" and "Back in the USSR" I got a taste of that and thought that was *it*. Basically, I went overnight from being the guy who had his underwear pulled up his butt crack to being a cool guy. Soon afterward, I was playing in Battle of the Bands with kids twice my age.

Another great local player Mike Landau and I played in about one hundred bands together and we kept each other honest in our playing. Jeff Porcaro and I like to think outside of the box of rock by listening to everything, and that includes players like Larry Carlton, the Mahavishnu Orchestra and Dr. Albert Harris, to name a few. Of course, we were still digging The Beatles. Jeff and I put in hours of doing studio sessions, and when I was nineteen, I got hired to play with Boz Scaggs.

I've been pretty careful with my guitars except for what has gotten stolen from storage, and that's always tough to track down because you never know exactly when it happened. I had a '51 Esquire and '51 Burst stolen, along with old boogie amps, C12 mics and a handmade guitar with guts strings. One really great guitar that I have I'd picked up with drummer Paul Jackson in '79 from a pawnshop in Arizona. It is a '59 Les Paul sunburst that I paid about $6,000 for.

I can tell you stories about PA systems flying out the back of the truck and the look on people's faces when they see this big puffy column in mid-air. Jeff Porcaro had his dad's prized drum cymbals rolling out onto the road one time.

What I love about the guitar is that I feel it is the most powerfully expressive instrument out there, and you can get the most amazing variety of sounds. You can take ten guys and put them in a room with the same guitar and the same amp and get entirely different readings. The guitar has a very soulful sound. And guitar players get the most beautiful women.

Joe Satriani

Joe Satriani studied music with jazz guitarist Billy Bauer and pianist Lennie Tristano and then later taught guitar himself for ten years to artists like David Bryson (Counting Crows), Kirk Hammett (Metallica) and Steve Vai. Two years after releasing his first solo instrumental CD, he toured with Mick Jagger as lead guitarist for Jagger's first solo tour. When he phoned to do this interview, I felt very un–rock 'n' roll and embarrassingly domestic, having to excuse myself for a moment so I could remove a freshly baked baguette from the oven with an unceremonious clatter. Joe, I owe you a guitar-shaped baguette.

I was fourteen years old when my older sister, Carol, bought a guitar for me with her first paycheck as an art teacher. It was a Hagström III, a Swedish guitar that we picked up for about $120. I had started taking lessons on drums when I was about nine, but in 1970, when Hendrix died, something clicked in me — I was going to be a guitarist instead. My parents, of course, were mystified, but my sisters were into it. Another sister of mine, Marian, had a nylon-string folk guitar that I started to pick up and practice on when I came home from high school. That's when Carol said, "How about this? If you promise to practice, I will get you your own guitar."

I grew up in Long Island, one mile from Roosevelt Field, where pilot Charles Lindbergh took off on his first transatlantic flight. It's now a shopping mall, and at the time, it had a small music store called Matthew's Music. I saw this Hagström III guitar there and thought it looked like the guitar Hendrix played — what did I know? I was a kid. And the price was right.

I was the youngest of five kids in my family, with a nine year spread between siblings. So, I'd gotten exposed to all the older music of the '60s plus rock 'n' roll, the British Invasion, Chuck Berry, The Temptations, The Supremes, The Beatles, The Rolling Stones, Led Zeppelin, Cream, The Who, plus blues records from my brother and jazz from my mom's records. It was not unusual at my house to hear Johnny Lee Hooker coming from one room, Cream from another and then Wes Montgomery from downstairs. Being the youngest, as everyone started leaving the house, I inherited a great, eclectic record collection.

I did not have a guitar teacher, but I did have a drum instructor, Mr. Patrikos. He was a swinging jazz drummer who taught me how to play and read music. I'd grown up singing with my family and goofing around with music because it was always in our house. Taking lessons was not a big step from what I was learning — it was more of an addition to what I was doing. Quitting lessons was not a big step, either, for the same reason. In high school, I had a gifted music teacher who taught us how to read choral music and taught us music theory and all the ear-training concepts while we were in eleventh and twelfth grade. He was a great teacher. Bill Wescott was his name. He was a concert pianist who wound up teaching at Carle Place High School. But, to this day, I still use all the concepts he taught us in those classes. A few years behind me, Steve Vai also studied with Bill.

A few other musically minded guys and I graduated a half year early because the principal wanted to get rid of us, so I remember we were cramming advanced music theory for the first half of that last year — modes, keys, quartets, cantatas, mini-symphonies. And of course I was listening to Led Zeppelin, The Doors and Black Sabbath. On the weekends, we were doing mini tours since age sixteen out in the Hamptons. This was when the drinking age was eighteen and it was okay to be in a bar at sixteen, as long as it had a practical application, like playing in the band.

I love all instruments equally. I could tell, though, when I was eleven years old, that there was a limit to what I could play and what I could not play. I have been playing guitar now for thirty-four years, and it's still a lot of hard work,

Joe Satriani, age fifteen, in bassist Steve Mueller's basement. (*Courtesy Joe Satriani*)

mostly in technique. But back then I felt like I had a future with it. With the drums, I felt like I was eighty-five percent good but I couldn't quite nail that last fifteen percent, which meant everything. Same with the piano; I could see it and hear it, but my hands would not cooperate. The guitar was difficult; it hurt yet I always felt like I was moving ahead. It's the one instrument that provided the least resistance.

The other thing is that I came of age during a time of great, virtuosic guitarists, when it was acceptable to be great with impunity. (During the '90s, I'd say a lot of bands shunned showing any technical prowess.) My era celebrated guitarists for this — Jimmy Page, Jeff Beck, Eric Clapton — whether they were playing rhythms, solos or improvising. It was a great time to be excited about playing guitar and be inspired. Hendrix was completely open about his influences, mentioning Wes Montgomery, Buddy Guy. And The Rolling Stones were openly into old American blues as their stock.

I have so many guitar stories through the years. One that comes to mind, because it just happened recently, is that my wife, son and I were watching the Conan O'Brien ten-year anniversary special DVD filmed at the Beacon Theater, in New York City, and I remembered that about three years ago, at that very same venue, Steve Vai, John Petrucci and I did a G3 show. The gig fell on my birthday and I didn't know this at the time, but Steve had secretly coached the audience beforehand to sing "Happy Birthday" after I finished playing and wished them good night. I thought it was sweet. What I was totally unprepared for was an ambush with hidden cans of silly string. They completely covered me right onstage!

What's important to me — and probably best illustrates the strange soul of the musician — is focusing on that three-second moment of playing. Like when you hit that F-sharp and it's the most beautiful sound you've made. It's these moments I carry with me, and they become part of my musical makeup. That is what I draw from — all these moments put together.

For fans, it's records and videos. For me, that is all a byproduct of what I'm doing. Each note and moment is both cathartic and a catalyst to me.

Steve Vai

Multiple Grammy-winning guitarist Steve Vai launched his solo career after touring with Frank Zappa for two years. Vai has recorded with David Lee Roth and Whitesnake and is a regular touring member of G3, a concert tour organized by Joe Satriani.

I was thirteen years old when I got my first guitar, a red Teisco del Rey that I'd bought from a friend for $5. It seemed like a small guitar and because it had all these buttons and pickups, I thought it was the bomb! It was difficult to play, but that didn't matter. When I first got it, I just stared at it for a few days. It was the most beautiful thing I had ever seen, and it was mine. It also had a whammy bar and *that* would get me out of bed in the morning. My second guitar was a Univox Les Paul, which is the guitar in the photos. I'd gotten it because Jimmy Page played a Les Paul and so did Satriani — he had a black one. Mine was a real clunker, though.

Like most good Italian boys from Long Island, I also played the accordion, and when I was about nine to twelve years old "Arrivederci, Roma" and "In-a-Gadda-Da-Vida" were favorites. I also used to play the tuba in the high school band. I was composing music and the tuba helped me to understand and read the bass clef. Plus, it made a great bong for me and my teenage buddies.

For the first two years of my musical guitar awakening, my inspirations had been Jimmy Page and Joe Satriani. When I heard the solo to "Heartbreaker," that's when I decided to play the guitar. Nothing else was comparable to Led Zeppelin. I was taking lessons from Satriani when I was thirteen to fifteen years old and this had a huge impact on me.

Steve Vai, age thirteen, playing in his band called Circus. (*Courtesy Steve Vai*)

John Sergio, a friend who lived on my street, was a real music lover, and he had turned me onto Queen, Jethro Tull, Deep Purple and all those great progressive rock bands of the '70s — but Zeppelin still holds a special place for me. My folks were always tremendously supportive, even when I would play "The Star-Spangled Banner" with my teeth. Perhaps they thought I was a musical idiot, but I think they became a little worried when they realized that all I wanted to do was play. Nothing else mattered. The guitar is expressive liberation. It's freedom itself. For me, playing the guitar is a blessed relief. Everyone should play an instrument of sorts, but the guitar is the best.

I think we all have an inherent attraction to music because it resonates in our soul. When I was a child I distinctly remember thinking, while swooning in my mother's arms as she whispered lullabies into my soul, "Hmmm, I could make a living out of this."

I don't get bored playing the guitar, ever. When I'm not playing the guitar my heart is crying for it. Every time I play a song that I have played many times before, I focus on going deeper and deeper into the notes. When I can hold my focus in the emotional awareness of the moment, the melodies continue to reveal layers of deeper intimacy and truth. It's a lifelong process. It's like climbing a ladder that reaches into infinity from the abyss. Sometimes the air gets very thin as a result of my shallow breathing, and I fall helplessly, but there are those around me who have wings, and they inspire me to keep climbing.

All aspects of evolving on an instrument are a challenge, but when you love the instrument there is never any discipline involved because it is a joy. When you cannot do something that you would like to do, then you work on it and until you can do it — this is one of the truly delicious things in life. We thrive on the gratification we feel when we achieve something and, for me, the guitar has always been about discovering new things, everyday. Playing an instrument is a cathartic experience of self-discovery.

My challenges have never been with the guitar or the music business in general. But if I had to point out the biggest caveat it would be time. Finding enough time to explore, develop and record the way that I would like is the real challenge.

The photographs are from my first gig. I was so nervous for a week before that I could not sleep and kept throwing up. I loved playing the guitar more than anything but I felt as though this whole live thing, playing in front of people, was just not the thing for me. All I could think about was what could go wrong. But the moment I got on the stage and hit the first chord all that anxiety went away and I felt lifted up. I felt like a wizard and savored every moment. I realized I had found my comfort zone and that was on the stage. And it felt like home.

Twenty-five years or so ago I designed a guitar for Ibanez around the idiosyncrasies of my playing style. It's called the Jem. It has become wildly successful, along with its sister model, the RG. We will occasionally come out with a unique aesthetic for the guitar for special occasions such as a tenth or twentieth anniversary. For the tenth anniversary Jem, the idea of mixing my blood in the swirling paint job presented itself, and I went to a hospital to have blood drawn — a *lot* of blood. The guitar was dubbed the "DNA guitar," and we did a limited run of 300 guitars, and you can see my blood in the paint swirls. I figure that, in a hundred years or so, if they ever get cloning down to a science, they'll be able to clone me from the DNA in one of those guitars — and perhaps that guy could figure out a way to get his music on the radio.

Gary Lucas

Guitarist and songwriter Gary Lucas has been cited by David Fricke of *Rolling Stone* as "one of the best and most original guitarist in America." Lucas has toured with Captain Beefheart and cowrote Joan Osborne's Grammy-nominated song "Spider Web" from her album *Relish* and he also cowrote "Grace" and "Mojo Pin" from Jeff Buckley's album *Grace*.

I was nine years old when I got my first guitar, and I couldn't tell you what the make was because it was such a bad guitar. My father had the whole notion I'd play the guitar — I was clueless. One day, he said to me, "How'd you like to play the guitar?" I said, "*Gee*, Dad, great idea." So he arranged for me to take lessons with a teacher in Syracuse, New York, where I grew up. This guitar was a cheap rental guitar with strings that were about an inch off the fretboard.

Right away, I hated this thing. It produced terrible calluses and painful blisters on my fingers. So I only lasted about a month because I hated practicing and I hated this guitar. I was learning out of your basic Mel Bay instructional book about the rudiments of guitar — I don't remember the title. I just remember hating disciplining myself to practice. Then, luckily, or my career would have ended shortly after this, my parents came back from a trip to

Mexico with a cheap but decent Spanish guitar with nylon strings. This made a world of difference to my development as a guitar player. I found this guitar so easy to play.

I was listening to lots of folk music, or what the purists would call "fake" music, like Peter, Paul & Mary — hootenanny-type pop music. I could play it really well. I did want to rock out but, for the time being, this thing was completely adequate. This was 1961. Within a week of starting guitar lessons, I'd also started attempting the French horn, if only by coincidence. My local elementary school teachers had administered a test for musical aptitude where they played various pitches and rhythms to test your ear. I'd scored one hundred percent on this test. The school's band director then approached me about playing the most difficult instrument in the entire band — the French horn. I was a good sport. I told him this sounded good, whatever. So I rented a French horn and found this equally daunting because, to this day, I do not have a significant upper lip. I never really had a good embouchure but I stuck it out for eight years, playing in school bands and orchestras with the horn. The guitar was something I vastly preferred. My junior year, I got thrown out of the band for wearing sandals.

The truth is, I had guitar lessons for only a month and the rest is self-taught. My parents had a lot of pop Broadway music like *South Pacific, The Pajama Game, West Side Story* and movie music, like the soundtrack to *A Man and a Woman*. I loved *My Fair Lady* and wrote Julie Andrews a love letter when I was about four or five years old. I also liked classical music like Ravel. I *loved* AM radio, and I remember before I could read or write, I used to sit in a rocking chair in the basement of our house and listen to what was top-forty radio of the day, in the late 1950s. I listened to Chubby Checker's "The Twist," "Little Bitty Pretty One" — the original, not the one the Jacksons covered later. I loved R&B, but they didn't play a lot of it in Syracuse. Basically it was Dick Clark American Bandstand music, like Bobby Vinton, Bobby Rydell, Bobby Vee — all the Bobbys. Then JFK died, closing '63 with everyone in mourning and then in February of 1964 The Beatles showed up on *Ed Sullivan*, and it was like morning in America again. Fortuitously, I played the guitar and this was a band based around the guitar. With the whole British Invasion, I was right there and in like Flynn.

Even before The Beatles, though, in '62, I can remember playing with a borrowed electric guitar from my teacher going through the back of an FM radio. You used to be able to plug into it with the external speaker jack and use it as an amplifier. What was called a combo back then later became a *band*. The Beatles, you know, were a *band*. When I was in a combo with my best friend, Walter Horn (we composed a soundtrack to a German silent horror film called *The Golem*), I had a trombone player and clarinet player and we used to play things at the school assembly like "Java" by Al Hirt or "Midnight in Moscow" by Acker Bilk, "A Swingin' Safari" by Burt Kaempfert and the *Peter Gunn* theme. These were light pop instrumentals of the day. We had fake books. We probably were not very good but this was my earliest experience in making music *en masse*.

Also with Walter I had a duo where he would sing and play maracas and I would play the 12-string guitar. It was a Swedish guitar, a Klira. When I got bar mitzvahed, I asked for an electric guitar. My parents had produced first a cheap one-pickup Epiphone to see if I could play that, and then, for the bar mitzvah, I was given a Fender Stratocaster, which I attempted to play for a year but failed because I couldn't get a good tone out of it. I had a Gibson Starfire amplifier. I tried to do a band at the Jewish Community Center with this gear, doing Rolling Stones and Beatles covers and failing miserably. Then my father said, "I'm going to trade in this guitar and get you a 12-string." He knew I liked folk music. This thing was so great. I gradually broke a lot of strings on it, so it became more like an 8-string guitar. The more strings I broke, the easier it became to play. I was bending the strings a lot, playing rock 'n' roll.

In the mid-'60s, I started to hear all this incredible stuff and wanted to get back into playing electric guitar. My earliest hero was Duane Eddy. "Dance with the Guitar Man" was the song I really wanted to play. Also, the theme from *Exodus*, which I did cover on an album called *Street of Lost Brothers*. I loved Eddy's twangy guitar sound. I was a big Anglophile fetishist when it came to guitarists.

My family laughed sometimes watching me play. My sisters used to accuse me, "You're making faces while you play. Why are you making that face when you play?" I was not aware that I was doing it. I probably felt like, "Yeah, I wanna make these faces because I feel cool." Guitar strings are like an extension of the nervous system. You hit that string and your whole face reacts. My family liked my playing. They tolerated it. It wasn't noisy or threatening. Then, years later, when I had a steady job and called my mother to tell her I'd joined Captain Beefheart and was planning on taking a leave-of-absence to make a record, my mother said, in horror, "The guitar? Murray, he's talking about the guitar again!" Like that was an episode or phase that had been safely relegated

Gary Lucas, ten years old, in Auburn, New York. (*Courtesy Gary Lucas*)

to the past. I had been working as a copywriter at CBS Records, writing copy for all their new artists. I'm most proud of the stuff I came up with for the new punk and new wave bands like The Clash, who I gave the slogan "The only group that matters."

About two years into this day job, I finally landed my dream of working with Beefheart. I'd seen his debut in New York when I was in my freshman year in college. He'd played in a little club on the Upper West Side called Ungano's. I was a fan and he'd already been on the cover of *Rolling Stone*. My buddies and I drove down to check him out and it changed my life. I'd never heard a band that was so intense and great. That night, I said if I ever do anything with guitar, I want to play with this guy. They were using guitars in a way I'd never heard. He once said, "A guitar is merely a stand-up piano."

They used a lot of open tunings and bottleneck guitar playing. Their fingerpicking was amazing, simply because he wrote a lot of tunes on piano, just improvising, and then the guitarist would work for months to figure out their own transcription, which was sort of impossible. I secretly woodshedded, listening to his records, wondering how he was doing it and working it out in private.

Don Van Vliet [Beefheart] came to play at Yale eight months after I saw him play at Ungano's and, as I was his biggest fan and proselytizer, the program director of WYBC Radio at Yale asked me, the music director, to interview him over the phone before his gig to help promote it. I still have the tape somewhere. My voice is shaking at the beginning, as I am about to meet my idol, but he was really warm and put me at ease. When he showed up to play, I hung out with him all night and we became friends. Subsequently I visited him backstage at many New York–based shows for a few years afterward. I met him in 1971, but I didn't tell him I played until 1975 when he was touring with Zappa on the *Bongo Fury* tour and they came to Syracuse to play. I'd thought, "He's got a band. I'll just keep working and someday I might get my chance." Sure enough, one version of his band eventually walked out on him after different trials and tribulations and my big chance came in '76.

I saw in the paper that he was going to play with Frank Zappa, who was his patron, associate and nemesis, according to him. But I think overall Zappa was very supportive of Don Van Vliet. I thought, "I've got to see him." I hadn't seen him in years, but we were close and on friendly terms. I met him backstage after the concert and he remembered me. I asked if I could audition and he said, "*What?* You play the guitar? Why didn't you tell me?" I told him I didn't think I was good enough. I took the Greyhound bus up to their next concert in Boston and auditioned in his hotel. He was enthusiastic, but nothing happened. So I went off to Taipei and came back with my first wife. I called him up and he said, "Gary, great — you're back." Don was living in the Mojave Desert and working on a new album. He had a music piece he wanted me to learn for it called "Flavor Bud Living." He sent me a copy. It was an angular, bizarre little instrumental piece and I worked my ass off to master it, modify it and sculpt it. I went out to the desert. He said, "You have to use my exploding note theory," which is to play every note like it has no relation to the previous one or subsequent one. Like bombs bursting, *pop-ba-ba-pa-bop!* A very staccato phraseology and attack.

While I was at Yale, I'd played in Leonard Bernstein's *Mass* project. He was a big hero of mine, growing up. He'd written a Catholic Mass — a Jewish guy writing a Mass — and the Yale Symphony Orchestra, with about seventy singers and dancers and auxiliary people like me on guitar, went to Vienna for the premiere of this in '73. I had a great evening with him telling me how to play my guitar in this piece.

I like the guitar because you can get the sound of a human struggling through the sound of the bent strings. To me, you can get to the voice of god, which comes through a bent note. The physical act of bending a note, whether on brass, strings or whatever, it's the closest thing to wailing. It's a melismatic raising and lowering of pitch. The sitar or santur does this, too. It just feels right. And I can make a good guitar face, unlike with the French horn. The guitar is very sexual to me, honestly. Not in the phallic aspect of its shape but in hugging its body close and feeling this cavity resonating. I can see why Jimi Hendrix would do *Electric Ladyland*.

I love the guitar. It's my life and my living. I was a late starter in that respect. I didn't get the impetus or nerve to do it full time until I was at the advanced age of thirty-six. Beefheart stopped making music to concentrate on painting in '82, and his group had been my whole life for five years. I floundered for a few years, kept my day job and fielded offers to play with other lesser bands downtown but I thought, "Why, after having been in the best band ever?" I played on Matthew Sweet's *Earth* album and with The Woodentops. I played with Adrian Sherwood, an English reggae mixer.

Once at a session, I was playing on a session with Vin Diesel, who used to work in this very store when it used to be Minter's Ice Cream Store. Vin Diesel's real name is Mark Sinclair, and he was this skinny little kid who used to stand on the other side of the counter selling ice cream, and I got him a deal to make a rap record. I was helping out on the session with him, which was being produced by my friend, the great Arthur Russell. Arthur was an incredible cellist, dance music writer and songwriter, minimalist composer and an influence on Philip Glass. It was Arthur who gave me the impetus to return to playing on that session, saying to me, "You know, Gary, you're always happiest with the guitar in your hand." I was really scared because I knew how hard it would be, and I had this cushy security day job and the prospect of leaving it was really scary. But I'm glad I did. It took a few years.

The Knitting Factory opened up and it was a nice little space. This girl dared me to perform there and I thought, hmm, well I'll show *her*. So I got busy and put together a program. Then I arranged for my debut and they gave me the worst possible night, a Tuesday. The day of the show, the newspapers didn't even list my gig. They left me out by mistake or whatever. I put up signs around the Village and the show sold out. They turned people away. I was so thrilled with the reception. I got many encores and they handed me a fistful of money. I said, "*This* is what I should be doing." A friend told me it was like my life had changed overnight. I was determined to hit music about as hard as I could, and this time, when I did another show there, the *New York Times* came and wrote me up as " guitarist of a thousand ideas." I started my band Gods & Monsters after this.

I had a guitar that I got for $200, a Fender Strat, in '64 or thereabouts. It might have been a hot guitar, but there were some kids at Yale that ran a little company called Guitars Unlimited, and I got a couple very good '60s guitars from them worth more than what I paid for them. The '64 the guitar I used when playing with Beefheart. It was my workhorse guitar. A couple years ago I was on a train leaving New Haven after visiting a friend that night. Right before the train departed, smoke started welling up in the compartment and the conductor came running in, ordering everybody off. Stupidly, I left my guitar up on the rack overhead and ran out with my other bag onto another train across the platform. And when the doors were closing, I'd realized I left my guitar on the other train. I made frantic calls, spoke with the conductor, filed police reports and never saw this guitar again. I lost this beautiful guitar — well, it wasn't that beautiful — it had a warped neck. But it was *my* guitar. I had it insured and managed to collect $10,000 so I bought another '66 Strat for about $3,000. I'm pretty sure someone found my guitar and said, "Hey, look, let's give this to Johnny!" and it's sitting in someone's rec room in the middle of suburbia.

One more thing I have to say is that when you move from amateur status to professional, there are some paradoxically frustrating and interesting things that happen. For me, before I even contemplated going professional, I liked to play for fun. That is the root of amateur, *ama*, or love. I was open to other people's music, collecting it and going out to see it in a much more expansive way. When I decided to do this for a living, one of the unfortunate fallouts of that decision was I found it increasingly painful sometimes to sit in a concert that wasn't my own because I'd sit there, torturing myself, thinking, "How does this relate to what I do?" Or, "I should be home, practicing." I think I've loosened up a little bit. But I was more driven to want to shun new music once I turned pro. I always thought the trick was to make a pop artifact that could function as an avant-garde object of art. I was trying to develop my own voice in an original, singular way.

Michael McKean

New York–born actor, comedian, composer and musician Michael McKean appeared in parody metal band Spinal Tap as David St. Hubbins. He is also known for playing the character Leonard "Lenny" Kosnowski on the sitcom *Laverne & Shirley*, releasing an album as Lenny and the Squigtones. The album also featured guitarist Christopher Guest credited as "Nigel Tufnel," the name Guest used again for the rockumentary spoof *This Is Spinal Tap*.

I was fourteen years old when I got my first guitar, which was a nylon-string off-brand guitar from Mexico that my dad had picked up for a song. I think it needed work, but at the time I thought a guitar was like furniture, that is, that you just accepted it for how it was. The action was ridiculous — the strings were like a block away from the frets. Playing this guitar made it easier for me later on to play a steel-string because it made my hands strong.

My first steel-string was a Harmony Sovereign. This is the guitar I began writing songs on and playing when I was sixteen years old. Before that, I had borrowed a friend's Gibson and learned to flatpick a little. Then I started playing a Gibson J-something. I can't remember the models, but it was a cheap Gibson electric. Gibson sort of became my guitar for a while.

My era of rock music was inspired by The Beatles, The Who, The Kinks and The Yardbirds. One of my favorite folk guitarists was Jimmy Driftwood, from Arkansas. He was a musicologist and social studies history teacher who wrote the "The Battle of New Orleans," which was a big hit in '56. Driftwood loved to collect great old songs that were catchy and fun. He also wrote "Tennessee Stud," which was a big hit for Eddy Arnold. He had a way for coming up with these wacky, obscure American folk ballads. And I liked listening to show tunes at the time, too, because I was into theater. I liked acts that had humor. The Limelighters is another group that came up with a great range of stuff, and I also liked Paul Butterfield's blues band, Michael Bloomfield and Electric Play. I lived in New York City in my teens, and we used to be able to go up onto the rooftops on summer nights to hear the concerts in the Fillmore East. They used to keep their upstairs doors open, and one night, we listened in on three sets of a Who concert. If you mention guitar to my dad, the first player he'll think of is Charlie Christian and Kenny Burrell. He was into jazz and blues but not completely sold on folk or rock. My mom was fine with my playing because at least it wasn't the trumpet.

Playing is a pacifying state to be in. If you've got a lot of concerns and things are not going easy, you can always put everything at an arm's length long enough to play a song. For me, that song is "Bye, Bye, Blackbird," a slow song that's somehow cheerful. I also like a Hoagy Carmichael song that Johnny Mercer wrote called "Down to Uncle Bill's." It's just complex enough to make you feel like a great guitar player but, of course, you're all alone when you're playing anyway. Also, learning to play a little leads to songwriting, which is a lot of fun. My wife and I are a cottage industry for writing songs. If there's any challenge I've had with the guitar, it's barre chords! It's comparable to watching someone change water into wine and then say to you, "Don't worry, you'll be able to do this, too, no problem." I can't handle the idea of barre chords, and do not play them to this day if I don't have to.

The first time I ever got paid to play was for the groundbreaking of a church. I also played in a jug band called Cold Fish when I was in college. Arthur Sellers got us a gig to play at the apartment of the Dean of the Drama department at NYU, and I think we were paid $25. I saw him recently and he has completely forgiven me for that night, mainly because I put a lot of it on Arthur Sellers. In my twenties, I also got paid to do parodies for radio commercials.

For the most part, I'm vague about what happened to my first guitars. That

Harmony Sovereign evaporated. I think I left it at some guy's house and forgot to pick it up. I lost my 1970 Gibson in '92 during a house move, and my old white sg that I played in Spinal Tap was stolen, along with two Les Pauls and a Fender Telecaster Deluxe. I don't recommend moving with guitars because these things can happen.

These days, I'm playing a Martin guitar that was a gift from Christopher Guest after making *A Mighty Wind*. I also have a Gibson acoustic with pickups, a Music Man guitar, a Paul Reed Smith guitar and an Ibanez that was a gift from Joe Satriani, who I met when Christopher and I needed an escalating guitar jam for a recording of *Break Like the Wind*. We had Jeff Beck, Steve Lukather of Toto, Slash and we needed one more monster guitarist, but we didn't know Joe Satriani personally. We asked him and not only did he pay his way to fly in from San Francisco, but he did it in one take and was on the plane back home. And just for us *asking him* to do this gig, he had his designer make a guitar for me, Chris and Harry Shearer. We were stunned. To say thanks we sent an autoharp off to Joe's designer in secret to have him make one just for Joe, incorporating all the exotic designs from the guitars he'd given us, that is, inlays of skulls and Stonehenge. They're just amazing designs, very fancy guitars. This designer then made a truly psychedelic autoharp and we sent it off to Joe.

Christopher Guest

New York–born Christopher Haden-Guest is an American screenwriter, composer, musician, director, actor and comedian who cowrote the improvisational mockumentary *This Is Spinal Tap*, in which he played the character Nigel Tufnel, the lead guitarist of an English heavy metal band that embarks on a disastrous tour of America.

My first guitar was a Gibson LG-1, and I played clarinet at the school of Music and Art when it was in Harlem. I first started listening to folk music, then rock. I was mostly self-taught and learned to play guitar by ear — opposite of my experience with the clarinet, which was *all* about sight-reading. I'd found this Gibson guitar from somewhere — could have been a pawnshop. It was used, cheap and crappy.

My first musical influence was Doc Watson, then bluegrass. Jazz came later. Now, it's a collection of stuff, but Doc Watson and bluegrass are the first to come to mind. I also taught myself to play the mandolin.

My family didn't really have any reaction toward the guitar, not until I started playing electric guitar, which was loud. Acoustic guitar, they didn't mind. I got into playing my guitar eight hours a day. The reason for this is

Chris at age fourteen. (*Courtesy Christopher Guest*)

I couldn't sing and play the clarinet at the same time. I mean, I tried every conceivable way, but it just didn't work out. I like playing harmonics, especially on an acoustic guitar, and holding the instrument against my body and feeling it. I like playing all kinds of music and stuff that I've written from a comedic slant. Lately I've been playing mandolin more than the guitar.

You can always tell a beginner, especially on steel-string, because they'll say, "I want to play . . . *ouch, it hurts!*" Either you love it enough that you don't mind and you keep going or else you go home, stash the guitar in your grandmother's attic and get yourself a cat instead.

My first professional gig was playing the autoharp, the same instrument you see Catherine O'Hara playing in *A Mighty Wind*. This gig was in 1963, the day after John F. Kennedy was shot. We showed up at a New York hotel to do this band thing for someone's birthday, and we were paid a couple bucks to go home. Film composer Michael Kamen was in that band.

I've been collecting guitars since the late '60s. I've got an old Martin D-28 from 1946 that is very valuable. I bought it from Matt Umanov Guitars in New York, and it has a stencil on it of a band's name, "The Melody Kings." It also has a stain that looks like someone spilled beer inside the guitar. I've always fantasized that The Melody Kings was an older band that played outside of Nashville. But I never found out if this is true.

I have a Les Paul electric guitar that I had Les sign, but now I feel imprisoned by this because now I don't feel free to take it out anywhere. Though his autograph makes the guitar more valuable, I almost regret asking him to sign it. This is the guitar I played in *This Is Spinal Tap*.

I was visiting Jeff Beck at one of his sessions in Hollywood and gave him the leather jacket I'd worn in *Spinal Tap*. Later, he gave me one of his guitars. He called and told me to pick it up from the recording studio. When I spoke with him again, he asked, "Did you get them?"

I said, "*Them?* You mean, guitars, plural?" There had been two guitars. Someone had apparently lifted one of them. But at least I have the one. It's a Jeff Beck model Stratocaster in a color called sea foam.

A Sheepdog Raised by Ducks

The brick walls of Loho Studios are lined with a gallery of memorabilia signed by musicians who have recorded there — Joan Jett, Ryan Adams, Joey Ramone, Willie Nelson and Patti Smith. I was there sitting in on a recording session of Gary Lucas and his Gods & Monsters crew, which included Ernie Brooks of The Modern Lovers and Billy Ficca from Television. Gary and I took a break at a Chinese bakery and spent a few minutes debating the merits of steamed barbeque pork buns versus saffron yellow, sugar-crusted sweet red bean. We returned to the studio where saxophonist Jason Candler was experimenting with reverb effects on David Johansen's recorded vocals on the song "One Man's Meat."

"You play guitar, don't you?" Ernie asked.

"Classical guitar," I said. "I don't rock like you guys. But I could play you a picture of how Sid Vicious might have strolled down the street."

A few weeks later, Gary had been fighting a wicked head cold when he announced to the band that I was officially in charge of "logistics and general repping" for Gods & Monsters, moments before a charity benefit gig for God's Love We Deliver, which delivers meals to AIDS patents. I had struck up a friendship with Gary and his wife Caroline not long after the house concert where I'd found him sitting in the girl's frilly bedroom tuning his guitar. He and I spent one late afternoon into early evening of migrating from the White Horse Tavern to an ice cream shop where he told me the actor Vin Diesel used to work before his film career took off. After spotting mice racing across the floor during his book interview, we relocated to yet another restaurant and split a slice of key lime pie as we learned that we had both worked in Black Rock a few floors and years apart. Gary told me about his old ad-man days at CBS Records. The venue for this benefit concert was in an upstairs room at the Pussycat Lounge, a dive strip club that had somehow escaped Rudy Giuliani's purge of all things sleazy, perhaps due to its obscure location, a few blocks south of Ground Zero.

Having lived in New York long enough, any Little Miss Muffett propriety and skittishness I might have felt toward strangers and spiders had evolved, long ago, into a basic nonchalance. Yet I have to admit I felt squeamish about entering the Pussycat Lounge.

Someone must have shelled out real money in the 1960s for its marquee, which depicts a masked Catwoman extending a long cigarette holder elegantly beneath her chin with a look of inscrutable insouciance. But the rest of the lounge's facade — from its battered front door with the mirrored porthole windows to the slack velvet rope on the cracked sidewalk outside — spelled one word: dump. The lounge abutted a sex shop, Thunder Lingerie. A headless mannequin perched in the front window and its scanty costume changed by season and holiday — a red lace teddy with sequined heart-shaped pasties for St. Valentine's Day, a sexy leprechaun outfit with pot-of-gold panties for those looking to get lucky on St. Paddy's Day and a slutty elfin look with candy cane hosiery for the Christmas season.

Leave it to a Yale Music School graduate classical guitarist to advise me to not to touch the walls or sit on the furniture inside the lounge. Past denizens showed some wit by taping a pair of Hogarth posters between the strings of Christmas lights. Alison Gordy, who once sang with Johnny Thunders, opened the show with her beautifully raw voice accompanied by acoustic guitar and violin. All seven members of Gods & Monsters then took to the tiny stage like angels dancing atop the head of pin. Billy's wife, Ami, sang a few songs and endured the occasional belt in the back from the neck of Ernie's bass, causing her to pitch forward onto her tippy-toes and regain her balance while she kept singing. The crowd's faces looked tough, worn and thuggish, but they were clearly transported and enthralled by the raucous reverie of the band and Gary's guitar playing, shimmering forth leis of sonic wizardry.

I had not encountered anything overtly lurid at the Pussycat Lounge up to this point, but then I made the error of following Gary and the band downstairs, where I was welcomed with an eyeful of topless dancers in identical platinum pageboy wigs moving, more wearily that sultrily, through the haze of cigarette smoke. The intention may have differed but the display of nudity was nothing more than what you'd see inside the women's dressing rooms at Century 21 on any average weekend. Nevertheless, I beat it out onto the sidewalk, inhaled the cold air and felt relieved when the band gathered outside to say their goodbyes.

I booked the band to play at Austin's South by Southwest convention, an annual, sprawling, cacophonous spree, where nearly every musician in the universe steps over random puddles of vomit with the hope of seeing and being seen by music industry professionals. When we assembled at the airport, I panicked seeing Billy had no suitcase in tow. "Aren't you missing something?" I asked. He grinned and held up a small Duane Reade bag that flapped in the wind. It held his toothbrush, toothpaste and one change of underwear. He was not smiling later in the TSA line, however, because I'd screwed up the name on his airport ticket. "It's WILLIAM Ficca. It says WILLIAM Ficca on my driver's license." I had put him down as Billy Ficca and we now had to convince the TSA that he was the same person. "Billy is short for William — like some people say Holland when they actually mean The Netherlands," I tried.

The bane of any guitarist is getting his or her guitar onboard the plane. It is up to the whim of the gate attendants, even if you've perfected the art of lowering your guitar case to fit in neatly into the small of your back and shuffling penguin-like to escape notice. Gary wrangled the Fender on board, affecting a "don't mess with me" squint beneath his fedora. Jason Candler was the perfect picture of calm, with his enviably, easily disassembled sax squared away inside a case seemingly no larger than a shoebox. Billy tapped out rhythms on everything along the way. Once we'd landed and unloaded our stuff at a tiny motel on the outskirts of Austin, Jason drove us into downtown so we could case out the club.

I was in charge of stalking Tony Wilson to extend a personal invitation to him to attend our show. I had seen the film *24 Hour Party People*, so I knew his history of being the manager of Joy Division and the force behind the whole, trippy Manchester sound of the late '80s and early '90s. So it took some time to reconcile that the Tony Wilson in front of me looked like a friendly British grandfather who would more likely be reading you

Paddington Bear books beside a cozy, warm fireplace. When I approached him, he assessed me over the rim of his wireframe glasses. "That scene in the film in back of the van with the girls never happened, you know — pure fiction." I did not remember the scene. He wrote down the venue and time of the gig on his hand. That he had been willing to deface his own palm in black ink for Gods & Monsters gave me a bright spark of hope. When I asked him if he had any managing advice to impart, he replied, "Never, ever let your band do smack."

A wicked thunderstorm and bouncing hail crashed over Austin in the late afternoon as Michael Schoen, the singer with Gods & Monsters, and I were handing out flyers downtown. The remaining few flyers provided cover over our heads as we ran and took refuge on the stone front porch of the Driscoll Hotel. The rain swept in silvery arcs along the street and ended as abruptly as it started, leaving steadily streaming eddies swirling into the gutters. A rainbow appeared, luminous against the sky. I called Gary from my cell phone. He saw it, too. The rainbow brightened everyone's mood.

The bars in downtown Austin are ghost towns by day. And then, in the space of one magical hour, they flicker to life with thumping subwoofers and glowing neon. The bartenders stocked the bottles in front of the mirror with dizzying speed and we matched the pace, loading in. Gary drew up the set list to accommodate the rigid time schedule that needed to cram 6,000 bands into six nights within a three square block radius.

The band killed it onstage. If Tony Wilson had turned up, I did not see him in the packed crowd, which seemed to take on its own amorphous, cell-like shape. I could have throttled the guitar tech for bailing on his duty to stand guard over the instruments, leaving me tethered to them until someone finally showed up with a car. We stumbled through Austin in the dark, following the music. We said hello to Jesse Harris, who wrote Norah Jones' hit "Don't Know Why," and watched Sabina Sciubba croon as chanteuse with Brazilian Girls. We skipped past the bands that sounded like other bands and went hunting to hear something new.

Longhorn cattle horns and lone stars festooned almost every Austin pub and restaurant. Ernie noted that every restaurant we visited seemed to be members in good standing of the "Central Dispensary of Refried Beans." Billy and Ami went off the grid, going for some strip-mall Chinese, which they paid for dearly the next morning. The rest of us found a favorite in Hoover's BBQ. Gary raved about the smoked pork ribs, made sure I ordered enough to eat and then happily devoured my leftovers.

Even as I was settling into my duties for Gods & Monsters, I still felt weird for being wedged between the rock world and the more decorous classical guitar world. When I pitched rock promoters, I received responses right away, usually salted with colorful invective that would scald the fur off a dog. Classical guitar promoters tend to politely hem and officially haw, neither saying yes nor no but ensuring that you knew that any future decision made would come down from on high to you, your lowly self. Frankly, I was starting to prefer the "Are you outta your fuckin' mind," opening gambit of the rock promoters to the "We shall see, perhaps," of their classical brethren.

Working on this book left me confused, feeling that I had far more in common with the rock guitarists than I did with classical players. The rock guitarists, who played mostly electric guitar, struck me as deeply self-motivated, independent-minded and heavily ear-oriented, whereas classical guitarists, in order to establish a respectable career, are required to be sanctioned by conservatory guitar department degrees and competition prizes. Had I been playing the wrong kind of guitar all along? Could I have been a sheepdog raised by ducks? I *loved* ducks. All I had ever known musically had been how to waddle, flap and fly in formation — yet listening to these other players speak gave me a disconcerting, unexpected glimpse in the mirror at my own musically shaggy countenance. I couldn't fully wrap my mind around it because most classical guitarists who dabbled on an electric make sure to let the world know they are merely slumming or perhaps nobly elevating this Eliza Doolittle of an instrument into classical society by performing an "electric guitar concerto" — avowed classical guitarists would never actually marry themselves to an electric guitar. Unthinkable.

My friend Peter Van Wagner had been encouraging and nagging me since I was fifteen years old to go electric. I was on the verge, teetering, not fully convinced it was for me. "But you've met Jimmy Page, for god's sake! You have to play electric now!" he insisted. Peter, or The Riffmaster, as he was known at the Practical Theatre Company, is a rock 'n' roll electric guitar guru disguised as a professional actor. One summer I asked him to help me with notating music from a cover story with John Hammond for *Acoustic Guitar* magazine. Peter listened for a moment, and then stared at me like I was crazy. "Write it *down*? He's been playing the blues longer than you've been alive! You can't write that down!"

I told Peter what my dream guitar would be. I wanted a solid-body Gibson with a 1960s slim neck, milky green tuning pegs, a trapezoidal pick plate and mother-of-pearl fret marker inlays, top-hat knobs and Gibson-issue humbucker pickups, solid color, no sunburst pattern and the kicker to all this — my Rumpelstiltskin-impossible feature — I wanted it to weigh less than eight pounds. There is no such thing as a Gibson that weighs less than eight pounds. I assumed that Peter would now spend the rest of his life trawling guitar stores on my behalf, and I could safely continue paddling about in my duck pond.

Peter phoned me two weeks later to say he had found it. It was at 30th Street Guitars in Manhattan, an old school guitar shop off 8th Avenue run by Matt Brewster. I dropped everything to visit this dusty cave of a store, frequented by a few men with long ZZ Top–style flowing grey beards, sunglasses and knowledgeable running commentary about any guitar on the wall, to the point where it was impossible to tell who worked there and who was merely keeping his opinions to himself. Near the guitar repair table, a languid pet iguana watched it all.

My first impulse was to summarily execute Peter for the crime of finding exactly what I wanted, but then I had to accept with resignation that it was entirely my fault for conjuring it, for having been so thorough in describing my perfect electric guitar. It was a chocolate brown '90s-era Gibson with worn gold-tone hardware and covered humbucker pickups as well as everything else I had spewed out off the top of my head, right down to the weight being under eight pounds. It was one of 150 Gibsons manufactured in Nashville as a batch intended for shipment to Japan, and so the body had been entirely hollowed out to accommodate a smaller player. The left-hand action flew with impossible ease and the tone sounded like angels singing through six strings.

The price tag, however, sent me searching for some other, more reasonable option. Peter and I headed up to 48th Street to scour Sam Ash's selection of back-breaking eleven-pound '70s-era Gibsons. I was torn, yearning for that special sound a Fender makes and recalling Dick Dale's passionate tale of working with Leo Fender to make that sound right. Yet Les Paul's voice came back, too, as I recalled his desire to make a guitar as beautiful as a violin, with the same graceful surface curves. We also visited Rudy's Guitar Stop at the end of the block. I picked and plucked my way through their used electric guitar selection upstairs like Goldilocks sticking my fingers into various bowls of porridge. I liked the feel of an ancient sky blue Hagström with a filthy-looking waffle grille that looked as if movie popcorn butter had petrified on the pick guard. Though it was more affordable, the Hagström was not, by any means, in the same class as my eight-pound chocolate Gibson.

My Gibson. It had felt like my own Excalibur the minute I'd had it in my hands. After years of playing an oar-necked classical, playing an electric felt like I switching to a modern-day keyboard after years of pounding on an old Royal — my fingers flew unimpeded all the way up to the frets in its upper bout with ease.

I was not the only prospective suitor to the chocolate brown Gibson. It had the cool demeanor of a suave pickup artist, changing its voice to suit whoever played it. I endured hearing it crunch out some wailing, gnashing chords in someone else's hands in the back room, with Matt's iguana mirroring my baleful expression. I had no choice, really. I asked the bank teller to count out my life savings in twenties and was prepared to karate chop anyone who looked at me the wrong way as I headed back to the store. Whenever I walk into 30th Street Guitars, Matt still says, "There's the heartbreaker who bought that chocolate Gibson guitar." Five people had been circling my guitar, and Matt had the dirty job of telling them it had been sold.

With my new guitar in hand, I had no more excuses. It was time to figure out if it walked like a duck and quacked like a duck, it might just be a sheep dog.

Kerry Keane

When I was compiling the interviews for this book, I was struck by the pained memories artists had of stolen guitars. Who but the lowest form of humanity steals a guitar? Why? What for? To a thief, stealing a guitar is not about the value of making music as much as how much money they can surreptitiously obtain for a guitar, which can quickly and easily change hands. But what *is* it that makes a guitar valuable? To a musician, a guitar is valued for its playability, craftsmanship and voice. It is a physical and musical extension of the artist, almost magically so, for how it allows this expression. The first guitars discussed in this book are, with rare exception, mostly cheaply made, humble instruments that have achieved pricelessness for being the guitar that launched a career. There is, however, the phenomena of the fabled guitar that sells at auction for a fortune.

Part of the mystique and allure of collecting such an instrument is the idea of proximity and transference—to be able to view up close, each nick, ding, worn fretboard and character incurred by the instrument over the years which hints of a secret life along with the idea that some magical understanding might rub off for being able to hold the instrument that created such memorable music. I knew there was no other person in the world who comprehends this dynamic better than Kerry Keane, the international department head of fine musical instruments at Christies. Keane began his career as an apprentice to master guitar builder Augustino LoPrinzi in 1975 before enrolling in the Violin Making School of America in Salt Lake City. He studied Italian violin-making in Cremona, Italy, and ran his own violin shop in New York from 1985–1994. He joined Christie's in 1999.

Keane invited me to attend their auction named "Trigger," for the star attraction of the collection — Roy Rogers' OM-45 Deluxe Martin, which he used for much of his career. The guitar was expected to sell for $250,000. Other guitars at the auction included an 1864 Antonio de Torres, a 1939 Hermann Hauser Sr.; a 1929 Simplicio and an assortment of Kalamazoo-era Gibson electrics, Fender guitars and basses, Martin guitars and ukuleles. Keane oversaw the Christie's auction of the world's most expensive guitar in 2004 — Eric Clapton's Blackie '56–'57 Stratocaster, which sold for $959,500. Clapton had originally purchased six vintage Stratocasters from a store in Nashville in the early '70s. He gave one Strat to Steve Winwood, one to George Harrison and another to Pete Townshend. With the remaining three Strats, made between the years of 1956 and 1957, Clapton took the best parts of these guitars and cobbled them together to create his Blackie Stratocaster.

The proceeds from this guitar auction benefited the Crossroads Centre in Antigua, an addiction treatment facility Clapton had founded.

"Auctions work because they are theater," Keane told me, "The key is to offer a great property and have the right auctioneer."

The pedestal displaying the Roy Rogers guitar was festooned with a confetti-like array of printed guitar picks from the Christie's–Crossroads Centre auction as a totemic gesture of good luck. Two screens flickered with black-and-white footage reels from Rogers' career. The varnish on the back of the Rogers guitar was worn and flaked, more evidence it belonged to a singing cowboy and his belt buckle. On the soundboard just below the bridge gleamed a silver star-shaped sticker.

What makes the guitar prized is its story: an unknown musician, Leonard Slye, purchased this guitar for $30 during the Depression from a California pawnshop. Slye had no idea it had sold brand new for $225 just two years earlier in 1930. In fact, only fifteen of these guitars were manufactured by the C.F. Martin Guitar Company in Nazareth, Pennsylvania. Slye changed his name to Roy Rogers and went on to become a Hollywood cowboy legend, twice inducted into the Country Music Hall of Fame. He died in 1998 without ever knowing that his guitar was the very first OM-45 Deluxe Martin to roll off the line.

The guitar features a 000-size body shortened so that the neck has fourteen frets clear of the body. Its shape, scale length of 25.4 inches, slimmer neck profile, solid headstock and pick guard glued to the top became the prototype that defined the American steel-string flat top guitar design for decades to come. The OM-45 Deluxe added a pearl inlay bridge and elaborate gold plated tuners with pearl buttons.

The Christie's auction room features two large screens at the front. One displays the item for sale while the other monitors the current bid in various world currencies. Those seated all gripped white plastic paddles with bold three-digit numbers.

Said Keane, "The photograph dates from about 1968 or '69 and I am about fourteen or fifteen years old. The guitar was a Giannini made in Brazil. My parents purchased it for me from a music store in Westfield, New Jersey, called the Bandstand. I took lessons there from a young woman named Gale who was in her twenties, very pretty and wore a beret. Lessons were thirty minutes of classical from the Carcassi method book and thirty more of learning Simon & Garfunkel songs. I had a wild crush on Gale and practiced like a fiend for her." (*Courtesy Kerry Keane*)

My first impression of the bidders in the room is that most of them look more like preppy yacht captains than any real working musicians I knew, for their taste in casual navy blue blazers, pink dress shirts and leather loafers. Two desks coordinated incoming bids through the internet and by telephone. Auctioneer Thomas Lecky called out the figures and bids. The entire auction of nearly 100 instruments took just under 90 exhilarating minutes to complete. The bids on the Rogers guitar turned into a white-knuckled drama as the figure soared beyond anyone's expectations. In a space of a few dizzying minutes, the guitar sold to a private American buyer in a purple velvet jacket for $554,500.

Once the Rogers guitar sold, the hipsters and black t-shirt types cleared out, leaving those in shirt collars and neckties to bid on the classical instruments. The Torres opened at $48,000 and sold for a final price of $86,500. The 1939 Hermann Hauser Sr. guitar opened at $45,000 and sold for a final price of $134,500. The Simplicio's final bid was $15,000.

When it comes to appraising an instrument, Keane says, "Sometimes it is instantaneous and other times, it requires research. There are 12,000 violin-makers, for example, and there is not always a body of work for each maker; even less so for guitars. With lesser-known makers, we look for something comparable that has been sold before. This also helps us formulate a presale estimate to drive bidding and competition. The whole auction model is built on making these estimates."

Keane sold two 1947 Hermann Hauser classical guitars in May 2000 that were unique because both guitars had been made for the same owner. "A doctor in California had ordered these guitars sequentially that year," Keane says. "Each time he communicated with Hermann Hauser Sr., he kept a carbon copy of the letter along with the responses he received in return from Hauser. Because of this, we have an archive, which has enabled us to see how this relationship developed over the years. It reached the point where these two gentlemen started exchanging holiday cards. Hauser had asked $200 for the first guitar but had requested that the doctor not to send money because cash was still useless in post-war Germany. Instead, he had asked for bolts of cloth, needles and thread, penicillin, aspirin and dried milk. He also asked for these items to be sent in five separate boxes to increase his chances of actually receiving the goods instead of having them confiscated by customs. These letters were an eye-opening insight into life in Germany at that time.

"When we looked at the Roy Rogers guitar," Keane says, "That instrument extends into the marketplace on two levels. First of all, it is an extremely important guitar in the pantheon of guitar making. In 1930 it was the most expensive of all Martins made, and it is still a beautiful guitar. Then add to it that it was owned by Rogers throughout his entire career, and it makes for an iconic piece of American memorabilia associated with an iconic figure. These are two important facets that generated the figure on that particular guitar. If Segovia's 1931 Hauser were for sale, there would be the same fan-fare due to the guitar and the man.

"Our instrument buyers tend to be personal collectors who are talented amateurs and have made their careers in other areas. In the classical guitar auction market, I've noticed these buyers are at an age when they want to understand and associate with the type of instrument that music is played upon — so there is much crossover among American guitar collectors with both Spanish and classical guitars."

Keane recalls summers spent in the Pocono Mountains where his mother dragged him and his brother to various local auctions and bought them off with and Coca-Cola. When he was twelve, he bid on and won his first musical instrument: an A-Style mandolin for $30. He adds, "I knew exactly how many lawns I had to mow that summer to earn that money."

Lee Ranaldo

Guitarist Lee Ranaldo is one of the cofounders of the rock band Sonic Youth, an alternative rock band that formed in 1981 in Manhattan. Stylistically, they are known for their scordatura guitar tunings and performing on "prepared" guitars, inspired by John Cage's "prepared" piano, with objects like chopsticks and paper clips that alter the sound quality of the instrument.

I was probably seven or eight years old when I received my first guitar, that is, one that wasn't a tennis racket — it was a pink plastic ukulele with The Beatles' pictures silk-screened on it. When they appeared on *The Ed Sullivan Show* in 1964, I caught that Beatles fever. My dad had brought home their first records. I probably had two or three other pseudo-guitars after that. One of these guitars was also made of plastic, but it was more of a guitar size and a dark burgundy or maroon with speckles in it like metal flake. It was a cool guitar, which I somewhat discounted at the time for its being plastic, but I have wondered recently if it might've been one of those Maccaferri guitars I've read about.

I finally did manage to buy a serious acoustic guitar, a big-bodied Martin D-18 copy made in Japan; it was still a piece of junk even though it was way more real than these other plastic guitars I had as a kid. I owned an old wooden

Stella guitar as well that was cool at the time, but it still wasn't a serious guitar. I remember when we visited my grandmother, who lived in Sheepshead Bay, we went to this new shopping mall there called Kings Plaza and that's where I bought this guitar. It was probably about $75 or $100, which was a lot of money for me to spend on an instrument back then and yet it was still pretty cheap for a playable guitar. This was the guitar I played in high school, learning folk music and Beatles songs, and it's the guitar I played in my first band, Tumbleweed, when we played in our high school talent show — my first "gig."

The first serious acoustic guitar I had — a beautiful guitar, handmade by a luthier who owned the company — was a Favilla. These Favilla guitars did very well for a while. Then, at certain point, the market was not as good so he started farming out the guitars for manufacturing in Japan and finished them in the U.S., where he put his name on them. His claim to fame at the time was that Paul Simon was playing Favilla guitars — this would have been during the early '70s, when I was in high school.

When I started playing guitar, it was performers like Crosby, Stills & Nash, Neil Young and James Taylor that were important to me. A girlfriend in high school taught me the chords for some of the acoustic songs off *The White Album*, "Rocky Raccoon" and "I Will" and "Julia" and "Blackbird." I started trying to play fingerpick style. Then, a year or two later, an older cousin of mine who is still a pretty decent guitarist showed me a couple songs in open tunings. These were songs off the first Crosby, Stills & Nash record in open E tuning, like "Suite: Judy Blue Eyes," and stuff off Neil Young's *After the Gold Rush* album in drop-D tuning.

These tunings struck me because they sounded beautiful and it was easy to play something in an open tuning and have it sound nice right away. You didn't have to be that proficient a player, actually — yet it gave me a whole new way of thinking about the guitar and new approaches to playing the guitar. I continued along this path of exploring alternate tunings until Sonic Youth started. Shortly before the band began, I was playing with a guy named Glenn Branca who was making orchestral music for oddly tuned electric guitars and Sonic Youth stepped into this as well. We were tuning guitars in odd ways. From those Crosby, Stills & Nash songs I discovered David Crosby's tunings and Joni Mitchell's and from there I fell into older music like Reverend Gary Davis and people like that who were playing slide or fingerstyle guitar.

By the time I entered high school, I was getting more into electric rock music, especially the San Francisco scene, stepping off from *Sgt. Pepper* and

Lee Ranaldo in his high school band, the Tumbleweeds, at age eighteen.
(*Courtesy Lee Ranaldo*)

the wilder Beatles experiments to The Grateful Dead and Jefferson Airplane. Around that time, I bought my first electric guitar — a Hagström II, a Swedish brand. This electric guitar is the first one I started playing rock songs on and using in the first band I played in, but I was actually mostly just the singer in that band. I was playing with a bunch of guys who were really good players at the time, and they wouldn't always let me play!

The Hagström II had been stripped of its paint, and I repainted it a glossy black. A couple years later, when I was about to graduate from high school, I bought a Fender Telecaster off a friend of mine — a cream white Telecaster like the kind George Harrison played at the Bangladesh concerts. It was a Fender — a *real* guitar. I owned that guitar for several years until I traded it in for another Telecaster, a Tele Deluxe, at about the same time I started my first band in Binghamton, New York, which was called The Fluks.

The guitar became an obsession. I remember getting, along with that Hagström II, a little Sears & Roebuck amplifier. My room was on the second floor of our house so I remember just closing the door and turning this little amp up to 10 and going crazy with the guitar, trying to get all kinds of wild feedback after seeing Hendrix and The Who in the Woodstock movie, and trying to figure out what more aggressive type of stuff the guitar could do. My mother was musical so she was always happy that there was music in the house. My parents didn't really understand '60s music as it moved along, but they were always encouraging of the fact that what I was doing was musical, so I was always playing my guitar. I also sang in vocal groups throughout high school. I think my parents were surprised that it turned out I did something professionally with music and was making this really *crazy* music, as they perceived Sonic Youth to be, and that people were paying money to come and see this!

When I first went to a university, I had a roommate who was into that kind of music, so I moved from '60s folk and rock music to a little further back in time and was learning how to play some of that real fingerstyle stuff, often in open tunings as well. Joni Mitchell songs and some by Jorma Kaukonen in Jefferson Airplane, he had beautiful acoustic guitar songs in open tunings that I figured out how to play. At this point in time, I rarely touch a guitar with a normal tuning. Two other artists whose music influenced me a lot are Leo Kottke and John Fahey. What they were doing with acoustic guitars in strange tunings really knocked me out. I came to Leo's records first, that first record called *6- and 12-String Guitar* that had been released by Fahey on Fahey's label, Tacoma, and I came to Fahey's records through that. I still hold that stuff near and dear. I managed to get to know Fahey during the last decade of his life, and we did a little tour together. He never failed to be inspiring in his approach to the instrument.

My kids just recently wanted to start learning how to play guitar so I tuned up a guitar in normal tuning for them — and I recently wrote a couple songs on it for just picking it up. I approached it the way I do with my other non-standard tuning guitars, that is, not by playing a G chord or A chord, but just putting my fingers down to see what happens and that was kind of cool. Normally if I pick up a standard-tuned guitar I revert back to the songs I learned how to play in high school, because that's really the last time I spent much time playing in normal tuning. But now I picked it up as though it was one of the other alt-tuned guitars I have lying around and just forgot that it was tuned standard!

I love the history and tradition of the guitar, and I found the history of stringed instruments particularly fascinating, especially as I moved further into playing in various open tunings. Stringed instruments have a long history with opening tunings. The piano is a stringed instrument. I think that's where my heart lies. Over time, as I've been playing guitar, I've experimented with lap steel, autoharps and zithers and recently with 4-string tenor guitars — maybe I'm getting back to that little plastic stringed ukulele I once had! I'm back to looking around for 4-stringed guitars. I love that it's a portable concert instrument, whether it's acoustic or electric.

An electric guitar has a whole other set of connotations in terms of what you can do with the power of the volume and sound and what it does to sound in terms of overtones and all these things that happen when you plug a guitar into an amplifier. All that beautiful stuff is there in an acoustic instrument but it is just magnified in different ways in an electric guitar in a way that seems so modern. I love to pick up any instrument and fool around with it, and it's probably the reason I have many instruments because each one has its own particular character that I find interesting.

Even the crappiest guitar, you can pick up and find something inspiring in it. In the early days of Sonic Youth, all we had were crappy guitars, so we were looking to do what we could with these guitars that would prove them useful. We were not going to tune them normally to try to get G chords or C chords because in five minutes they would go out of tune and sound terrible, but you could tune them all to one note or in different ways and obtain wobbly choruses of notes or insert sticks under the strings and turn them into percussion instruments or whatnot. We gravitated toward better guitars over time but never lost the idea that you could pick up any instrument and prove it to be useful.

Playing an F-chord and a B-flat chord, also the A-barre and E-barre were definitely the two biggest challenges I faced when learning the guitar. They were *so* difficult at first! I also remember starting to play on steel strings and how difficult that was on the fingers. I'm working on a solo record at the moment, and I've been playing an awful lot more than I normally play and the steel strings still kick my ass sometimes. They really dig into your fingers and these days, I like to use the absolute heaviest strings possible so it's even more intense of a workout. Definitely getting all the regular chords down was the hardest thing to accomplish early on with the guitar, along with figuring out fingerpicking, and keeping the bass moving with the thumb. I still hate the B-flat chord and will avoid it if I can. The early days were the hardest. After that, it's kind of like you're on a discovery mission, especially when the open tunings came in. You can walk into a shop and pick up a guitar that hasn't been tuned in five years and obviously it is in some tuning and start finding interesting things. It's not that difficult. You could pick up a box made out of wood with some strings on it and an amp and make some sound come out it.

I definitely have photos from my first public performance showing me with my cheap $70 Brooklyn guitar. I can't find any with the Beatles ukulele, but that photograph of my performance in the Brooklyn guitar shows that pre-Favilla halfway-nice acoustic. It was at my high school auditorium, I was in eleventh grade with two other guys playing and we called ourselves Tumbleweed. We all wore flannel shirts with really long hair. We played one original piece and a Stephen Stills song and a Chuck Berry song with a piano player and another guy singing. So it was a trio of guitar players, and then these two other guys.

Sonic Youth had all of our gear stolen at a show in California in 1999 — an entire truckload of stuff. I told you that I'd gotten the Hagström II followed by the George Harrison white Telecaster, which I later traded for an even better Tele, which is a guitar that is super significant in my whole playing history. It was a Fender Tele Deluxe, with a dark wood grain, made in the early '70s, with a white pick guard and an f-hole on one side, so it was kind of semi-hollow as a lot of the Tele Deluxes were. It had these pickups in it called wide range humbuckers, which Fender manufactured at the time. Most Telecasters had single-coil pickups at the time but the Deluxes came with humbucker pickups.

At a certain point, this became my favorite guitar. It was the guitar I played all through my first band, The Fluks. And it was the first official guitar that I brought to Sonic Youth. Thurston had a Harmony guitar and I had this f-hole Tele Deluxe, which was by far the best guitar in the band at the time because we had all these other cheapie ones that I was telling you about. So that guitar continued to be played throughout Sonic Youth's career and can be heard on a lot of those early records, and those pickups, to jump around a little bit, became my favorite. I really liked the warm sound of those pickups, so we started buying more of those guitars. Now I've got four of those Fender Tele Deluxes from the early '70s and they all look identical — that boring brown wood grain. These guitars did not come in an array of fancy colors.

At a certain point, I gravitated toward playing Fender Jazzmasters, and at one point, between myself and one of our crew guys, we got the idea that since I liked the wide range humbucker pickups and I also liked the Jazzmasters that we ought to put these humbucking pickups into the Jazzmaster guitars. We tried making one and dubbed it the "Jazzblaster," we took out the single coil pickups that Thurston loves and put in these wide range Fender humbucker pickups. Doing this launched an entire odyssey. I really loved it — I loved the shape of those Jazzmasters and the sound of those pickups. And at this point, I have about seven or eight of these Jazzblasters.

We'd started calling every guitar store we knew when we were on tour, asking if they had any of the Fender humbucker pickups that came out of Tele Deluxes, and we started to stockpile them. At a certain point, these pickups started to catch on again in favor the same way the Gibson P-90, say, has become famous. Now we're connected to this whole network of younger pickup modifiers and winders who are searching for the "Holy Grail" sound of those pickups. Fender has tried to replicate them in recent years, and these replications have generally fallen far short of the originals. The pickups look the same but they don't sound the same.

There are guys who have dug deeply into this subject who we have managed to become connected with and — this story has a few prongs — a couple years ago, Fender invited Thurston and me to do signature Jazzmaster model guitars with them. They found out I was playing these Jazzblasters, and they wanted to make those and replicate them down to every detail. The first prototype they sent had the new-issue Fender humbucker pickups, and they did not sound so good at all — nothing like the vintage ones we had been buying up at top dollar. So Fender worked with us to get the pickups to sound better and actually went through a couple of iterations of their recent pickup for my guitar to make it sound better. For what they were capable of doing, they did get a pretty nice-sounding pickup out of it, though still not as nice sounding as the old ones. These young guys, these "pickup specialists," take these modern guitar pickups and retrofit them to make them sound more like the old pickups. I've been working closely with a bunch of these guys, which has been interesting because the process takes you down these little rivulets of guitar history and guitar lore.

To get back to that original Tele Deluxe, when we had our gear stolen in '99, that guitar was in the van full of gear — so this guitar that had been with me since probably '80–'81, from the time I was in Binghamton with The Fluks to the early days of Sonic Youth, went missing. An entire truck full of stuff went missing. All of our drums, amps, twenty-five to thirty guitars and basses, all of our pedals, just gone — gear that we had spent the ten years prior, all through the '90s basically, just fine tuning to our purposes, so that we could step onstage feeling assured this gear represented as good as we could sound.

We really had it pretty perfected at that point, for what we were trying to do and the sounds we were looking for. And actually, the original Jazzblaster, this beautiful tobacco-sunburst Fender Jazzmaster — it breaks my heart — that guitar went missing and never came back.

The short story is, none of that gear ever surfaced again, to this day, except for four guitars that slowly filtered their way back to us over time, and for some strange reason, they were all my guitars — none of them were Thurston's guitars. A couple years after the theft, we were in L.A. playing a show and these two young, sort of freaky kids came up to us — they must have been about eighteen to twenty years old — and they told us they had information on the theft. The story was, one of these kids' uncles was involved in the theft. I think the theft had been stealing the van — I don't think they knew what was in it. It was just like, "There's a van full of stuff. Let's steal it." The van was found in East L.A. a few days later with nothing in it, doors hanging open. So this was kind of interesting.

We didn't really know whether to believe these guys or not. They told us their folks had kicked them out of their houses and they were living out of a car and they kind of looked like it. But, subsequently, through intermediaries, we gave them email contacts and they sent us a bunch of photographs that showed our gear that was readily identifiable by little pieces of tape, notes our techs had written on various pieces of the gear. Without showing any people's faces, you could see our gear and close-up shots of a couple effects pedals with someone's sneaker on one. It looked as if they were in a basement somewhere. These guys told us, "We know where some of the gear is."

The theft happened in Southern California, so for some reason I always assumed that much of it probably went into Mexico. Subsequently, through these two guys, we got two guitars back. It was weird because at the time our gear was stolen, there were a number of other artists who'd had their gear stolen. I know that Jon Spencer Blues Explosion had their gear stolen shortly after, along with a couple of other bands. That hadn't happened to anyone in our circle at that time. This was the early days of the internet, and I remember sending out a big missive about the theft online, which someone told me the other day is still floating around out there in cyberspace.

Shortly afterwards, our crew guys, who were very organized at that time, partly because they had these carnets for when you go in and out of countries, where you are required to list all your gear — they were able to post all the guitars with their serial numbers, and all these geeky guitar guys in music stores (and actually friends of ours because they often helped us out) got hold of these lists. And every once in a while, over the years, someone will send us an email saying, "You should check out this eBay auction — this might be one of your guitars." Sometimes it is and sometimes it's not and sometimes it is kind of a copycat, where people will have put those Fender wide-range pickups onto a Jazzmaster or whatever, but twice it turned out to be one of our guitars. So we've found a couple more of the stolen guitars over time.

One of these guitars we tracked down was that original f-hole Telecaster Deluxe, which is back in my lineup now. It came back to us! There were two guitars at the time — I was going to talk about this other kind of guitar called Travis Bean, who made these all-aluminum-necked guitars for a brief period of time during the '70s. They had these pickups that looked very much like the Fender pickups and sounded very much like the Fender pickups, so that's another guitar brand that I've really loved, with similar big shiny silver pickups from that period are the kind I like, for one reason or another.

The Travis Beans were supposedly great for sustain because the guitar was one solid piece of aluminum from the bridge all the way up to the neck, and then they put a wooden body around it to make it look normal. Jerry Garcia played them in the early '70s. Two of the four guitars we got back were the Travis Bean and that Tele Deluxe. The Tele Deluxe had been spray-painted metal flake blue, very poorly. When we got them back they were in bad shape with the electronics falling off, so we had to pay to buy them back and then pay to have our guys fix them up! The blue Tele gets played onstage with Sonic Youth to this day and still has this crappy blue metal flake paint job, which I've left be because I'd always thought that original dark wood grain finish was kind of boring, and I have three more of these guitars that look just like that. In a way, it was kind of cool to get it back painted metal flake blue.

The Travis Bean guitar I'd played a lot onstage, and it was kind of candy apple red and had a target sticker on it like The Who's target sticker. It came back with all the electronics falling off or missing, and it kind of looked like it had been left in a campfire for an hour or two because it was all burned and blackened and disgusting. I probably would have left it that way, but before I could say anything, the crew guys assumed I'd want it to look like it always did so it was actually refinished and it looks shiny and red again and is also back in our lineup. There are pictures of both of those guitars on our site, in "before and after" condition. We have a really extensive website and you can find images of those guitars in the section that's all about our gear and guitars.

So I still have my second real serious electric guitar — the George Harrison cream Telecaster was the first — but this is the first one I ever really seriously played out with in bands, and it was certainly the first guitar I'd ever played in Sonic Youth.

Paul Reed Smith

Paul Reed Smith is a luthier and the founder and owner of the Maryland-based company PRS Guitars.

My first acoustic nylon-string guitar was one I had bought for my mother, and it was called a Hilo. The second guitar I had was a Japanese bass that had sticky wallpaper on it. And the third guitar was a Japanese copy of the Höfner Beatle bass. I was fourteen years old at the time. In shop class, I took the neck off this guitar and made a bass out of it. My first real guitar was a Rickenbacker 6-string and then a three-quarter-sized Melodymaker. My first real, real guitar that I owned was a 1953 Les Paul. It's not about the first guitar. For me it's about the journey to the real guitar. Each guitar is a learning experience.

I loved The Beatles, Jimi Hendrix, Peter Frampton, The Allman Brothers, Jeff Beck, Carlos Santana, John McLaughlin, Al Di Meola and Bill Frisell. My family reacted to my interest in the guitar really well and really poorly — really well because it was music, yet poorly because my father thought I was going to starve and end up being a guitar maker in a one-room shop and never learn how to deal with people. Under any normal circumstances, this would have become true, but my journey ended up not being normal. He and I completely came to terms with this a long time ago and had a beautiful relationship. A parent wants their kid to be intellectually, emotionally and spiritually safe, right? He was worried about the security part because if you do not learn how to deal with people, then spiritually, you are not going to be okay. I had avoided being a lone guitar maker in a room because I had formed a team of family, friends, skilled assistants, engineers, lawyers, top salesmen, machinists and friends, and we decided to form a company.

The guitar is the most intimate instrument after the voice. There is so much you can do with a guitar — you can play rhythm, harmony and melody. The guitar is very cool and expansive. A guitar is a harpsichord where you can change the length of the strings with your fingers. The guitar presents a never-ending learning curve and it is highly competitive. If you walk into a store to buy a toaster, you are likely to find about a dozen brands of toasters in the store, maybe six. If you go into a music store, there are probably 2,500 different brands of amps. It's probably the most competitive market in the world. There are so many people vying for your attention. The guitar world is highly competitive and skill oriented. People who make it know what they're doing. The reason women were screaming when The Beatles came out is because they were that good. They knew they were watching something extraordinary. They were merely reacting to the electricity of the moment.

I was not that good of a guitar player but discovered guitar making very early in my life. I knew I was going to be a guitar maker — and not a guitar *player* — from a very young age. When you go into a store and play a guitar and discover that everyone runs away but you open the case to a guitar you've made and everybody draws a crowd, you'd better listen to the feedback!

Vernon Reid

English-born American guitarist Vernon Reid is best down for being the founder and lead guitarist of the funk metal band Living Colour.

I was fifteen years old when I got my first guitar, a Gibson Dixie Hummingbird that was given to me as a gift by a cousin. My cousin and I had shared a long talk about music and he came to know that I was really into music and fascinated by it. He was very kind, telling me, "Hey, man, I have this guitar and do not play it anymore so you can have it." The Hummingbird is a folk guitar and this one had super-high action. I had tried to play it for a few months and it was so difficult that I stopped, thinking, "Okay, I am on to the next hobby." The guitar sat there and I realized that I still loved music. I thought, "Am I going to let this beat me?" So I started to play it again and realized what I had really wanted all along was an electric guitar.

Wanting an electric guitar became the motivation for me to work because my parents were not going to buy me a guitar. They felt the guitar was going to be another hobby of mine and if I wanted to go further with it, they felt that was up to me. That was actually great, and I did not resent it but accepted it — and it made me find my first job at a local supermarket in Brooklyn.

This job was hell on earth. I was a stock boy at Bernstein Brothers, a locally owned supermarket before all the chains took over. I worked the soda aisle, which is the worst job you can possibly have in the summertime — terrible — because the soda aisle never ends. People are always buying Coca-Cola in the hot weather, and the whole thing about supermarkets is that they are never supposed to look as if they have ever run out of anything. So when you walk into your Pathmark or Kroger or whatever, and you see the shelves magically lined up with stuff, this is because there are imp-like minions running around to give you the illusion that nothing ever changes. To maintain that illusion, the minions are to move faster and ever faster so that the shelves appear to be perpetually filled and neatly aligned, as if nothing has ever been taken. So that was a horrible job.

But it got me my first electric guitar, a Univox Mosrite copy, made in Japan. I wish I still had it. I traded it eventually for another guitar because I did not know at that time that I was going to become a professional guitarist. It wasn't until I had my third guitar that I said to myself, "Okay, I guess I am doing this."

Santana was definitely a musical influence. He was an icon for me since I was a child, and he is still a giant to me now. His guitar on "Black Magic Woman" — that *sound* was *it* for me. As it turns out, I've recently completed a project with his new bride, Cindy Blackman. She plays drums and I started a project called Spectrum Road, which is music inspired by the music of jazz drummer Tony Williams. The band consists of me, Cindy Blackman, Jack Bruce and John Medeski. We did a bunch of shows in Oakland, and Santana sat in, which was great.

My family was concerned, of course, about my interest in the guitar. Basically, I was a straight-edged guy and they had a horrible idea of how a career like this could possibly turn out. When they saw I was still kind of normal, at least fitting the definition for how Vernon Reid might be normal — "He's no weirder than he usually is!" — then they accepted it.

What I love about the guitar is that playing allows me to say and do things that I normally cannot, as verbose as I may be. There is so much more that I cannot really put into words and, for me, the guitar is a conduit to an understanding of the human condition through music. Music is one of the best things that we, as a species, do.

Guitars interact with you in a very personal way and that's the thing: a guitar that is *the* guitar for you is one that allows you to be expressive and to make music in a way that is seamless. So nearly every guitarist is on a quest for the guitar that can do that. However, with some musicians, it doesn't matter what guitar they play because they play their style — and that is a particular type of musician.

I love the shape of the guitar. There's just something about it I find appealing. Also, as much as has been done already on the fretboard grid, I consider it limitless. It engages me intellectually and also engages me on a soul-deep level. It's an instrument that invites techniques. And in order to be as good as one can be, frustration must be acknowledged, yet there are moments when I'm not in the way, not thinking about it, not judging it but am just in the flow. Playing the guitar is an instinct that allows me to experience a different way of living, loving and of being. That's what is great about the guitar.

The challenge of the guitar is not to become ambivalent or frustrated with it because it never ends. For some musicians, they arrive at a level and they're happy, but for me, it never ends in terms of trying to be better, to play, to execute these different elements and to engage the mind and ear. It is a challenge. I'm *always* going to be learning how to play the guitar. I have been fortunate and make no claims about what level of proficiency I happen to be at. It's always curious to me when people claim mastery. That is a state that I do not know if I will ever experience, and I am okay with that. Nobody plays *everything* and certainly not me. The challenge for me is to get out of my own way. My own monkey mind needs to get out of the way and just be with the instrument and stop judging. One needs to be bad on the instrument in order to get better. And that is one beautiful thing about the guitar — that the ugly bit is also the beautiful bit.

I will never forget my first performance. My back was turned to the curtain and I was shouting at the drummer, Kenny, "What's the first tune?!" And the curtains had opened right at that moment. This was at my high school, Brooklyn Tech, and I was playing for a junior assembly that had to be a couple thousand because it is an enormous school. Of all my educational experience, Brooklyn Tech was my favorite without question — it changed my life. After all these many years, it is a great school.

Once I played with Ronald Shannon Jackson's Decoding Society. He is a jazz drummer who plays with Ornette Coleman, and we had this post-fusion band based on Ornette's ideas. We were chosen to play the Montreux Jazz Festival in 1983 in Switzerland and the official artist for the festival was Keith Haring, a very famous New York artist known for his glowing baby drawing. I loved that drawing. The first time I ever saw the glowing baby, I was in love with it. I also loved that Keith Haring was doing his art at the same time as Jean-Michel Basquiat, very minimalist. At that time, Basquiat was going by the moniker of SAMO but Keith became the official artist of the Montreux Jazz Festival and he did all the posters.

He came to our show and said, "Man, that was GREAT!" I asked if he would do a drawing on my guitar and he said, "Yeah, come to my hotel room!" I took my guitar, my Frankenstrat, to his hotel, where he painted two figures on this instrument. He asked if I would like him to sign it, and I said yes. He signed the pick guard. So I have this guitar, which I have stopped playing because I am terrified of what could happen to it. But it is the only one of its kind that I know of. The drawing he made shows two figures. One figure is dancing with a snake for a head and other one is dancing beside this figure with the snakehead. I rubbed off part of one figure because I actually used to play this guitar. Then it dawned on me I was rubbing it off and stopped playing it.

If I had to name my most prized guitars, this guitar would be it, along with the guitar I had used in "Cult of Personality" — the ESP multi-colored guitar. I used the Keith Haring guitar on the first Public Enemy record and the first Living Colour record, and I also used it for recording with Ronald Shannon Jackson. I have a huge amount of affection for that guitar and someday, it will belong to my daughter.

Marty Friedman

Marty Friedman is recognized for being the lead/rhythm guitarist for the thrash metal band Megadeth. He is a resident of Tokyo, Japan, and hosts his own television programs, *Rock Fujiyama* and *Jukebox English*.

I was seven years old when I received a really cheap acoustic guitar from a company called Harmony. It was not a great guitar but I played it for about three years, studying guitar books and taking private lessons. After three years, however, I realized that I did not like anything I was doing because the stupid stuff in those guitar books had been along the lines of "Mary Had a Little Lamb." No matter how good I became, it was still the same content and I went through three of these books, thinking, "This is not sounding *anything* like what I hear on the radio for guitar, so maybe I am doing something wrong." I gave up. In fact, I gave up the guitar for a long time for this reason.

I could play a few chords on the piano and make synthesizers work, but I found I could never really play other musical instruments properly. When I was fourteen years old, it dawned on me the reason why I did not like what I was doing earlier on the guitar was that my guitar was an acoustic and all the guitars on the radio are . . . electric. If someone had just told me, "Dude, get an electric!" I would have saved all that time. I probably would have progressed much further within that amount of time.

When I was fourteen, I saw KISS play and a buddy of mine, who was a KISS fan as well, happened to play guitar. I thought if my friend played guitar, possibly I could play it, too. He was able to play the guitar in a way that sounded exactly like the music we were listening to, so I realized all I had to do was what *he* was doing on the guitar. What my friend did was make playing the guitar look possible. The first electric guitar I owned was a Les Paul copy from a brand called Rythmline, which I've not heard of before or since, and it cost about $100. I wish I had a picture of it, but I gave it away. It wasn't that bad for a beginner's electric guitar.

I loved punk rock, hard rock, heavy rock. Anything with a lot of energy appealed to me because I felt I could do it and the music came naturally. I took lessons with the electric for maybe six months and, though my teacher was good, I was not open to learning the proper way of playing the guitar. Because I wanted to rock right away, I stopped taking lessons and taught myself by ear, by playing along with every album I owned until I started to sound like what I had been envisioning. As a result, I built up a lot of playing stamina at a very early age.

Some guitarists can understand the logic and technical information in instructional books, but I chose to concentrate on exactly what it was I wanted to do. If it did not interest me, I would not pursue learning it. I saved all my energy for exactly the kind of music I wanted to play. For this reason, I became very proficient at what I wanted to do, and, if I did not do something, it was because I did not *want* to do it. I did not want to waste any energy on aspects of playing that are normally taught, such as theory and proper technique, how to stand and hold a guitar, etc. As a result, I would most likely not be a proper teacher for someone who wanted to learn the "most proper" way of playing.

I was not obsessed with playing guitar. I just knew this was what I was going to do with my life. I loved sports but I was too skinny and did not have the body to play football, and I was not tall enough to play basketball. So when I saw rock bands playing, I *knew* I could definitely do that. But I never really felt obsessed, like I was living and breathing guitar — never, to this day even. I stand firm on telling people that one really has to have a life outside of playing their instrument, whether this means listening to other music or doing some

The young Marty Friedman with his Harmony acoustic guitar.
(*Courtesy Marty Friedman*)

other activity entirely unrelated to music. It is very important to have other real-life experiences to draw from when you are creating your own music. You have to experience happiness and heartbreak and sadness and toughness, otherwise you'll have no real emotion to bring into the music you create.

My family was supportive about my playing the guitar and I did not want to let them down because they had bought me my guitar and amp. Later, I used my college fund to buy another amp, so I felt that I was putting them at a risk and I did not want to let them down. I felt responsible about keeping up my goals.

I know I could be speaking for any musician when I say that the guitar allows you to express yourself in a way that a non-musician would not be able to experience. Some of us are not so eloquent with words at the right time in the right situation but, with your instrument, you can express yourself. Perhaps you do not necessarily get your point across, but at least you get it out in a way that, sadly, non-musicians will never be able to experience. I think that is the coolest thing about playing the guitar.

You can always sit down with your instrument and play something and get emotions out of you that would be harder to get out of you with actual words, simply by emoting a phrase on the guitar or playing hard or soft, fast or slow or the way you pause and linger over a chord. There are so many nuances to how phrasing can be shaped. If only we could have those weapons available to us in our verbal language it would be so beautiful. When you play music for a long time, you become good at shaping notes exactly the way you want to get them out and it becomes a natural extension of you. With the guitar, it is possible to utter the perfect sentence and that is what I love about it.

I always wanted playing the guitar to be a challenge or else I would be bored. And of course, some challenges with the guitar are bigger than others. For example, I just played with the Tokyo Philharmonic recently. I was playing the piano part of the Rachmaninoff Concerto No. 2, Op. 18 on guitar. I had to arrange the piece for my own playing yet I could not alter the piece much because I was playing with a seventy-piece orchestra. I had to create an arrangement they could follow. I love challenges like that. Every day I try not to repeat myself too much in music. So trying to come up with something new and interesting all the time, especially when it comes to phrasing and playing melodies, that is a challenge but it's one that makes me want to play.

My first paid performance was for a party at a neighbor's house. It was official because we were paid for it! I had a four-piece band and we received $80, which was $20 a head. At the time, I must have been fifteen and my first thought was "Oh my god, I'm getting paid money to do this! I cannot believe it!" That probably clinched it for me because just making money at all for playing my guitar was great. That being said, we did work very hard and we had to play music we hated because the neighbors wanted to hear certain songs. They had made a list full of these lame songs, and we played enough of their songs, which enabled us to squeeze in songs we liked. You have to bite the bullet a little on the stuff you do not like but, at the end of the day, we were playing our instruments and making actual money.

I've never been one of those guys who develops an emotional attachment to their instruments. If my guitar broke, I would be upset that something happened to my guitar, but in terms of having any emotional attachment to a guitar, really, it is a tool to me, no different from a knife or a fork. I do not have any one big attraction to any of my guitars but I can tell you a funny story about one of them. When I was endorsing Jackson Guitars, I was playing a big concert at the end of a tour and I had the brilliant idea to smash my guitar. It is an exciting moment in any concert — KISS did it every night. You just get caught up in things, the show is going crazy and you want to smash your guitar because it looks cool. So I tried to smash this guitar. And I discovered that Jacksons are made like a brick house. It was a very strong, solid piece of equipment. I kept smashing and smashing it on the drum rack. And the guitar was not breaking.

So there I am waving this thing like a baseball bat, banging and banging it against the rack, and there must have been about 15,000 people watching this. I thought, "God, what a weakling when you cannot even break this guitar!" I banged it about ten or fifteen times and it finally broke, but oh my god, I felt so lame and so embarrassed and I made the vow right there and then that I was never going to break a real guitar again.

Joey Santiago

Filipino-American guitarist and composer Joey Santiago is the lead guitarist for rock band The Pixies, which formed in Boston in 1986. They're known for extreme dynamics and stop-start rhythms, and their album *Surfer Rosa* has been cited by Kurt Cobain as a considerable musical influence. Their fans include U2 and David Bowie.

It's kind of blurry to me how old I was — I think I was in junior high, like about thirteen or fourteen years old, when I got my first guitar. My older brother had this guitar hanging up on his bedroom wall like it was a piece of art, and one day I was bored and thought to myself, "Hey, I think that's a real guitar." I learned how to tune it. We had an organ in the house, and I picked up a Mel Bay book to figure out how to tune the guitar at the organ, figuring out which string was the E. My brother didn't mind at all that I had taken over his guitar.

I had five brothers and my dad had us learn how to play this organ. We all had to wait to take turns and we would have contests to see who could learn the most from the books. My dad could only play about two songs, which were Filipino standards.

One day — I might have been in high school — I came home really drunk and out of frustration, my dad blistered my guitar. He just trashed it right in front of me. I was like, "WHAT ARE YOU DOING?" This sobered me up real quick. I was totally obsessed with the guitar and with music.

My brother had a turntable with Van Morrison, the album with "Blue Money" on it and variations of the blue scales — G-C-D, whatever variations of that shape. I also loved The Velvet Underground song "Rock 'n' Roll." The whole album is so playful and childlike, the way they strummed. Hendrix was another favorite. I read somewhere that Robin Trower was his English equivalent.

After my dad trashed my guitar, I saved up for an electric Les Paul copy because I figured it would be harder for him to break. I bought it out of this guy's house and felt frustrated with it because it didn't play the same way the acoustic had. My mom surprised me. Somehow she had a belief in my playing and wanted to keep me busy, so she bought me an Ovation Viper, which was an expensive thing to give a kid. It was nice and small and played very well — the action was great. I had a little amp and would play this thing loudly and annoy my family. I lost this guitar. I have a feeling what happened was I'd broken up with a girlfriend a little too early and I left my guitar at her apartment. Needless to say, I think it ended up in the Dumpster. [Pixies bandmate] Charles [Thompson IV, a.k.a. Frank Black] bought me a new Viper four years ago.

What I love about the guitar is that it's portable. With five kids in the house, I could take this thing into the basement and have my privacy there rather than wait in line to play the behemoth organ stuck in the living room. I would also take my guitar to parties and jam along. In high school, I yearned to play with cover bands, but the person who really challenged me to become original was my little brother. He played drums and my parents wouldn't allow a drum set in the house. He was amazing on the drum pad. I showed him what I knew on the guitar and he soon surpassed me. He learned Van Halen's "Eruption" and that entire album, just from listening to it. So I had to find another way to play in order to impress him.

I did have a guitar teacher briefly — a guy who taught me how to do barre chords. But then once I learned them I said thank you and sent him on his way. Most of what I learn is by ear.

I broke a Les Paul on purpose during a concert, right in front of the audience. I was playing a Pixies crazy solo and had run out of ideas and thought, "Hey, I'll just break this thing." I will never do that again. I felt shitty afterward.

It was so embarrassing. My guitar tech came up to take away the pieces and had this really sad look on his face. You know, it took someone longer to make that guitar than it did for me to break it. I think if I ever saw someone do that at a concert, I would walk out. I just couldn't watch it.

Benjamin Verdery

Classical guitarist and composer Benjamin Verdery heads the guitar department at Yale University and is the Artistic Director of the Art of the Guitar concert series at the 92nd Street Y in New York City. The Assad Duo premiered his work, *What He Said*, dedicated to the late luthier Thomas Humphrey. His other works include "Now and Ever," recorded by David Russell on Telarc and "Peace, Love and Guitars," written for guitarists John Williams and John Etheridge.

My first guitar was a gift from my parents — an Emenee, a little plastic guitar with cowboys on it. I don't know what happened to it, but I most likely learned an E chord on it. It was like a Maccaferri imitation, a plastic yet very playable guitar. My brother once held it out the window, threatening to drop it if I didn't do something he wanted me to do at the time. (I forget what it was he wanted me to do. All I remember was my guitar was hanging out the window.) The funny thing is my brother is now my manager. Later on in life I picked up a similar model of that little Emenee at a shop in Maine for about $50, well over what my parents first paid for it.

My second guitar met with a tragic end. It was a no-label little steel-string, plywood guitar — reddish purple and maroon with white purfling. The action on it was so high you could do chin-ups on it. On this guitar, I learned to play a D chord, an A chord and possibly "Day Tripper." My friend John Marshall, who is the percussionist for my band Ufonia, and I were about thirteen years old at the time we saw The Who perform on TV. We were very impressed with how they smashed their instruments at the end of the song!

I was now playing a Gibson hollow body single pickup with a sunburst design — my first really great guitar — with a small pickup amp. John had also gotten some new drums. We got together and played "Louie, Louie." When we were done, we grabbed our old instruments and trashed them. I'll tell you, after looking at all that wood splintered all over the place, I just felt horrible and sad! It was not at all satisfying. Let the moral here be that just because you see other people do things that look cool, you should not try to imitate. I would give anything to have that guitar back again.

My first classical guitar I picked up in Danbury, Connecticut, at The Music Guild, where I studied with Russ Mumo. It was $100, which seemed like a lot at the time, but I'd saved up for it. The label inside said Hauser but I didn't know what that meant. When I went to audition at the Hart School of Music, I was told my guitar was *not* a Hauser and I was like, "Yeah, okay, whatever," because but I didn't know what that meant anyway. When I first started teaching, I loaned it to an adult student and she took it with her when she moved. Strangely enough, I still have an affinity for Hauser guitars though that one was apparently never a Hauser.

My huge thrill was the second electric guitar I got, which was the same guitar that John Lennon played in his early days — a Gibson J-160E from my friend Dave Achelis. On my website I used to have a photo of me at age fifteen holding this guitar with my hair in my face. It was an acoustic electric guitar, and I believe The Everly Brothers played the same make.

As a kid, I was guitar crazed. I constantly looked for someone who knew something I didn't know and then I learned it. I also lived for new record releases — I remember walking five miles into town in the middle of winter to buy a copy of The Beatles' *White Album*, and I paid for part of it in pennies.

I'm an all-around John Lennon freak, and I've even done an arrangement of "Happy Xmas." Lennon had the greatest voice, and his song "Imagine" is his equivalent of Samuel Barber's *Adagio*. I also love Jimi Hendrix and Jeff Beck. To this day, I would love to meet Beck — my heart just leaps when I hear him play. I heard Hendrix play the national anthem at Woodstock, and it was the most powerful thing I'd heard, given the time of the Vietnam War. It was an extraordinary statement.

My father was a minister, and from an early age I was lucky enough to hear a lot of Bach organ music in church. Even though I was immersed in rock, Bach's music was creeping into my musical psyche, particularly as an early teenager. It is probably why I always include a Bach work in my programs. For classical guitar music, my mother had bought me a Julian Bream album — classic Julian Bream where he is playing Giuliani and Aguado. Segovia was not really in the picture for me. I was really very lucky to meet and study with Leo Brouwer in 1974–1975 at a master class when I went to Arles, France. This was back before anyone had really heard of Brouwer. He's an incredibly dynamic teacher, and John Williams and Abel Carlevaro and Alirio Díaz also came there to play. As far as teachers go, I studied at SUNY Purchase with Phillip de Fremery and then Frederic Hand, both of who have become dear friends.

I have two stories about how my family dealt with my increasing guitar obsession. One is that I was intent on practicing for an audition to college — I started relatively late in the game at eighteen — but here I was playing Sor's "Study No. 12," which is all thirds up the fretboard. I was nervous about making a mistake whenever I reached the 10th fret and inevitably I would lose it at right about this point and start screaming obscenities. It was as if it was written into the music — "dum-dee-dum, dee-dum, goddammit!" This was all that my mother heard from upstairs, the same étude and me bursting into a fit of shrieking of obscenities. At one point I became so upset I kicked over my music stand and sent it flying. That's when my mother said, "Benjamin, come here right now. If you don't stop it, I will take that guitar away from you, and you will not see it for a week." Now, this was a bit ridiculous because I was already eighteen but, still, the thought of not being able to play for a week struck me as such a startling and awful concept, it just stopped me in my tracks to consider it.

My other story is that I used to live with my grandmother during the summer in Cape Cod. I had an electric guitar — a white SG with a black pickup, the most ferocious, rocked out guitar I've ever owned. I used to practice this thing so loudly that my friends told me they could hear me playing from a mile away as they rode their bikes in. My grandmother never complained. In fact, when my mother asked her how she could possibly stand it, my grandmother's response was calm and placid: "Well, he has to practice." Looking back, I honestly don't know how she put up with me playing the same four licks over and over all day long for weeks on end, making everything rattle in this old house.

I reluctantly sold that SG guitar when I became interested in jazz. It just wasn't a hip guitar for playing jazz. Three or four years ago, I stepped into Rudy's Guitar Stop in New York City and noticed he had a locked up case of vintage guitars, and I saw my old SG in there. I said, "Rudy, you've got to let me play it, that's my guitar!" It was not another SG model but my same exact guitar — it had the dings and marks I'd put on it back when I was fifteen years old! The asking price was $2,000. I went home, told my family this incredible story and my son insisted I should go back there and get it. I was hesitant because $2,000 is a lot of money. I went back to Rudy's two weeks later, but by then the guitar was gone.

Benjamin Verdery with a replica of his first guitar, an Emenee. (*Courtesy Benjamin Verdery*)

This is the thing about guitars: they're somewhat human if you play them, and memories of a particular time in your life come flooding right back.

The guitar is not the easiest instrument to play, but it has always been a joy for me as well as a mystery. I don't have a particularly analytical mind so my first reaction is just, wow! I see the fretboard as an endless source of possibilities, and I will come up with different left-hand fingerings for the majority of what I play. Different fingerings can create both a subtle difference and a huge difference.

Just watch a baby or child reach out to pluck a string and see how their eyes light up. You can see how the act of them reaching out to pluck a string has struck something in their heart right away. And the guitar is not so big or intimidating they'll be afraid of it. It's really magical.

The other thing I find incredible is even though there is a standard tuning for the guitar, you don't have to stick with that. Take slack-key guitar, which relies on other open string chord tunings. The resonance and different voicings it creates is wonderful. There is such universality with the guitar, too. Every country and culture has a guitar piece or some similar instrument, like the ukulele, or the pipa from China. I love the wee folk of the guitar family! Playing the guitar is an endless journey of joy and discovery.

David Leisner

Classical guitarist and composer David Leisner won top prizes in the 1975 Toronto and 1981 Geneva International Guitar competitions. Disabled by focal dystonia, a condition that interrupted his career for twelve years until he recovered, devising his own methods of physical therapy. He is co-chair of the guitar department at the Manhattan School of Music.

I was ten years old when I got my first guitar. I had failed miserably at violin lessons for six months and, after screeching and scraping away at "Mary Had a Little Lamb," I realized it wasn't for me. I gravitated toward the guitar, mostly out of practicality, because it was portable and inexpensive. In fact, I rented my first guitar from a local music store. Since that time I've thought of so many other instruments I could have played, such as piano or cello. I also could have been a singer or a conductor and would have been pretty good at any one of these things. However, I think I gravitated toward the right instrument, because now I can't imagine any other instrument being as right for me as the guitar. It was an intuitive decision, a subconscious one.

I joined a Jewish community center class to learn how to play folk guitar and after that, I found my first real guitar teacher, Mildred Brown. She was very important to me because she instilled in me lots of good, basic ideas about music and life. A lot of the things she taught me are still with me, and we are still in contact. She introduced me to classical guitar when I was thirteen years old, and after six months, she told me, "I've given you everything I can teach." I studied with a flamenco guitarist and then after that, I did not study much at all. Basically, I am a self-taught classical guitarist. I did study with John Duarte for nine months and with David Starobin for six weeks. Violist Karen Tuttle gave me some incredible advice when I played her the Bach chaconne. It turned me around 180 degrees in just one lesson. That's my style — intense lessons for a short time. I get a tremendous amount out of them and then just run with it.

My mother was the kind of person who wanted exactly the opposite of whatever it was I was doing. When I traded the violin for the guitar, she'd say she wished I had stayed with the violin. Recently she wished I could have been a singer. But in the end, she was thrilled that I ended up doing this and that I have been successful. My dad was a great music lover and was thrilled as well. Both of my parents were puzzled by my seriousness and accomplishment, since our family was not musical. They did, however, give me the gift of listening. When I was four, I was listening intently to records of Mozart and Beethoven, Count Basie and Duke Ellington. They were astonished and intrigued by the intensity I gave to listening. They didn't quite know what to make of it and we were not economically privileged, so I had to find my own path.

I've always seen myself as a musician first and a guitarist second. I've been a singer in choral groups from the age of thirteen onward, and I knew since then that I was going to be a musician. I didn't know what form it would take. Guitar or choral music? Between the ages of thirteen and seventeen, I divided my musical interests on guitar with folk, pop and classical with little performances around Los Angeles. I liked to sing international folk songs in many different languages. Joni Mitchell and James Taylor were my idols. Laura Nyro was important to me, too.

My teacher Mildred ended up giving me her Goya guitar, which is a Swedish, factory-made guitar. It was made of spruce and had a fairly wide body. Later, when I visited New York for the first time, I went to the Wolf guitar store where Beverly Maher (now of the famed Greenwich Village Guitar Salon) worked as an assistant, and I bought a 1970 Ramírez with the initials MT inside (for maker Manuel Torres). It had a cedar lining to it that gave it a great sound but also shortened its effective playing life. I played this guitar for ten years before I sold it.

David Leisner with guitar, ten years old. Los Angeles, California.
(*Courtesy David Leisner*)

I'd have to say there is just something about the plucked sound of the guitar that moves me. When I was a teenager living in Los Angeles, I used to listen every week to a classical guitar show on the radio and the sound was very pure and calming. This is my earliest memory of being fascinated by it. Also, physically, I felt very natural with the instrument. Maybe this has to do with the old troubadour tradition of singing and playing at the same time.

When I was twenty-nine, I came down with a condition known as focal dystonia. What happens is the fingers start to curl inward toward the palm without control or pain. This completely stopped my career. I have learned in the meantime that there are hundreds, if not thousands of people, who develop this condition, and yet it is still a mystery as to why it develops and how to cure it. I visited many specialists over a period of years, and no one was able to help me. In the end I stopped seeing the specialists and followed my own intuition. In the process, I did some pioneering work on the use of the large muscles, which ultimately cured me. It was twelve years from the beginning of this condition to its end, but I now play better than I ever did before. Also, I am helping to cure people around the world who have this disorder.

One interesting guitar experience I had was when I entered the 1981 guitar competition in Geneva, Switzerland, where we were all required to prepare an unbelievably demanding program of the Ginastera *Sonata*, Britten's *Nocturnal*, two Villa-Lobos études, Giuliani's "Sonata Eroica," the Villa-Lobos concerto and a Giuliani concerto. We had three months to prepare, and out of sixty applicants, only fourteen of them showed up. The Ginastera, which was hot off the press at the time, probably scared everyone off. I was one of the three finalists, but I didn't play my best and received the silver medal, while Marco de Santi won the top prize. The finalists were all pissed off when we found out that they gave us our choice of concerto rather than choosing for us, so we could have learned one less concerto!

Afterward, I got the chance to meet with the composer Alberto Ginastera. He lived in Geneva and invited me to his house for a coaching on his sonata. The piece has a passage that opens with a triple forte, and he was trying to get me to play it louder. I was playing as loudly as I could, practically starting to sweat, when he finally said to me, in a raspy voice, "Brrrreaaaak the gui-taaaaarr!" I'll never forget him saying that. "Brrrreaaaak the guitaaaaarr!" Ginastera unfortunately passed away two years later, in 1983. He was sixty-seven years old.

Tom Morello

Tom Morello is a Harvard graduate and Grammy-winning guitarist from the rock bands Rage Against the Machine and Audioslave. He also plays solo acoustic as The Nightwatchman and his newest group is the Street Sweeper Social Club.

I was thirteen years old when I got my first guitar, a Kay guitar, which was basically a red copy of a Les Paul sg, for $50. It met my criteria as being the cheapest guitar with the most knobs. I'd started off playing the French horn, but I was so bad at it that it nearly made me swear off music forever — I was the fourth chair out of four chairs in third grade, when I attempted this.

I loved listening to heavy metal like KISS, Led Zeppelin, Aerosmith and Alice Cooper. I had two guitar lessons at thirteen, which had been so discouraging that I put the guitar down for four years. The reason is the guy showed me how to tune the guitar and then he taught me the c Major scale. BORING! I wanted to play "Black Dog" by Led Zeppelin and "Detroit Rock City" by KISS, so I felt frustrated.

Punk music like The Sex Pistols is what got me to rock. With punk rock, anything's possible. You don't have to have any technical expertise. You just have to have the desire to do it. Within forty-eight hours of this revelation, I put together a band with some of my friends. My mom was supportive and allowed this horrendously noisy band to practice at our house.

What first drew me to the guitar was, in part, that it really was a replacement for social interaction. Before I played guitar, I saw myself as an artist, writer and political activist. But with the guitar, I sort of sunk into it like a compulsion that borders on a disorder and poured myself into it to avoid the discomfort I felt with social relationships. Plus the guitar is predictable — it won't suddenly want to break up with you. Fate is in your own hands with the guitar.

Initially, I practiced the guitar for an hour a day. Then later, I practiced up to eight hours a day. Playing the guitar provided a kind of magical experience and expression that I didn't have anywhere else. I am pretty articulate and I did well in school, yet the guitar is visceral. The guitar allows me to tap into a world where intellect and academics don't matter. I started playing late, at age seventeen. None of my guitar heroes started out playing late, so I felt way behind and just practiced for hours on end. Every inch of my ability is something that I've fought for, and I can say that ten years later, I finally broke the wall down and was able to enter a world where I could express myself on the instrument and find a unique artistic voice, which was in Rage Against the Machine.

My first gig was in high school with my band, The Electric Sheep (with bassist Adam Jones who plays now with the band Tool). I went to Libertyville High School in Illinois and was part of the Drama Club. At the end of the school year, they had an award ceremony and with little talent but lots of vivid imagination, we had our band rush out onto the stage and break through a banner that had our Electric Sheep moniker on it. We played abysmally, choking on every note. We were absolutely terrified. But the seed was planted.

Six months after our first gig, we were asked to play Steppenwolf's "Born to Be Wild." Up to this point, we had to write all our own music because we didn't have the ability to play cover songs. So we lied to the director and said, "Oh, no problem! We can play 'Born to be Wild.'" We did our best in front of a crowd of about 800 people. All I remember was this roar coming from the crowd. We felt like a real rock band. They were cheering.

I was standing on a little platform and jumped off, thinking, "Awright, rock 'n' roll!" The place just went crazy. So, I figured as far as this line of work goes, I had some potential.

An older friend of my mom's helped me pick out my first guitar. I had $50 to spend, and the Kay guitar I'd chosen had very poor action, especially in the upper register of the fretboard. I recall the salesman telling my friend, "If this is the guitar he wants, I guess he can't play very extensive leads, then, ha!"

I remember this really got to me. It pissed me off, like "What exactly do you mean? How dare you say that? I'll show you, you S.O.B.!"

That Kay guitar is sitting in the closet now at my mom's, surrounded by some of my platinum records.

Daron Malakian

Daron Vartan Malakian is the guitarist and songwriter for the metal band System of a Down as well as the lead vocalist, lead guitarist and songwriter of the alt-rock band Scars on Broadway.

I was twelve years old when I received my first guitar as a birthday gift from my parents, though I had always dreamed of being a drummer. We had lived in a very small apartment and, when my parents finally saved up to be able to buy a house, at last I had my own bedroom and we also had a garage. I asked for a drum set. But my parents decided that, in spite of all this new space, drum sets cannot be "turned off," so they bought me a guitar instead — a black Arbor.

The only other person I knew who played an Arbor, though it was not the reason I received one, was the bass player of Slaughter. He might have played an Arbor bass. My Arbor guitar looked like a black Strat, but it did not have Strat headstock. If I remember correctly, it might have had more of a pointy headstock. I did not have this guitar for a very long time. Before speaking with you, I'd called home and learned only two minutes ago the *real* story of what happened to this guitar. I'd had the Arbor for a couple of years and learned to play some on it before I bought a Carvin guitar with winnings from a horse track bet. At that time, Carvins were considered a step up from an Arbor. I gave the Arbor guitar to my cousin, who lived in Northern California, and I never saw that guitar again.

For years, after System of a Down landed a record deal and I became a professional musician, I kept asking my cousin whatever happened to that guitar? He would always seem guilty because he would say to me, "Bro, I think it got lost when we moved." These things will happen. I was not even tripping on it but he always struck me as having a big time guilt trip about it. I called him right before this interview and told him that I was about to talk about my first guitar and I said, "You might come up." I don't think he liked that very much. He said, "Let me tell you what really happened then." He told me he was screwed up as a teenager and sold it for about $80 or $90 to go party with his friends. I'm not angry or upset about it at all because I know that he is truly sorry.

I played the drums in addition to the guitar and, to be honest, I am more of a natural drummer than I am a guitarist. When I first started playing the guitar, I had to actually learn the instrument. However, the first time I ever sat at a drum set, I immediately could keep a beat. I was flying and found it easy to keep up. I always felt like percussion and vocals were my main musical interests when I was young.

I started a record collection when I was five years old and much of it was KISS and music that had been popular during the late '70s and mid-'80s. I used to drag my mom to records stores and she would buy me all the Mötley Crüe, Twisted Sister, Judas Priest — whatever was really popular at that time. This evolved into heavier stuff as I grew older. Nobody ever pushed music with me, and in a way I kind of wish they had. It's weird because both of my parents are artists — my mom has an art degree and my dad was a dance choreographer. He's done the album art for System of a Down records like *Hypnotize* and *Mesmerize*. But my parents never pushed me into art. I always wanted music, but our apartment was so small that I think they were afraid of making noise. I never had music lessons, nor did I want music lessons. Music is just something I had wanted so much that I do not think anyone *had* to push it. Music was something I gravitated toward at a young age, and I always knew it was what I wanted to do when I became older, even before I had learned to play an instrument.

I practiced my guitar because I wanted to practice. I'd easily spend eleven hours a day in my room just playing, and my cousins who would come over and just sit in the living room, often not seeing me at all, just hearing me. The hours would go by like nothing and I would not even notice. That's how I was as a teenager. I never had a practice regimen, I never had a lesson and I never had a teacher standing over me and saying, "You need to learn this or that." I learned by watching other guys play and I picked up music by ear. I do not think music or anything should ever be something that is a struggle. If you struggle with something, then maybe it is not coming naturally to you. I've never been the kind of guy who has tried to play fastest or do something to try to impress another musician. I've always tried to play for a song.

Every guitar that I grew up playing — including the guitars I played in the club years and with System of a Down on Sunset Strip — I do not have anymore. The Carvin was stolen out of my dad's truck. I was eating at a Denny's and came out and found the window shattered and the guitar missing. The next guitar I'd bought after the Carvin I bought directly from the L.A. Guns guitar player Tracii Guns. I was only about seventeen years old at the time. He saw me playing at a guitar store and he said to me, "Hey, are you going to buy that thing?" And I said, "Yeah." He said, "You should come to my house because I've got a couple of them and I will sell you one." I'd seen Guns on MTV, and there I was going to his house. My cousin drove me there and I bought a Washburn Nuno Bettencourt N4 off none other than Tracii Guns. I was in a dreamland, asking him all sorts of questions on how to make it big. You know what? That is the only guitar I still have! After that, all the guitars I played in the club years were stolen. We were on tour with Fear Factory and all of our equipment got stolen. I think they found those guitars burnt in a warehouse.

I was in the eighth grade at a school assembly when I played my first official performance. We played the Sam Kinison version of "Wild Thing." It was just me and a couple other guys who played guitar and who were into rock music. I was having a blast. I always wanted to be onstage — it's not just about the guitar. It's also about being in front of an audience and performing. I get off on that and that particular experience was my first. Up until then, I had been in front of my mirror, just pretending. Whether it was a school audience or any audience, I didn't care! I was up there headbanging and going crazy. That's always how it has been for me. Any time, if you put me with a guitar on a stage, something comes out of me that would never come out of me just sitting in my room playing. You would never catch me dancing at a club or a wedding. I'm not the guy who does that, but when I get up onstage with the guitar, I turn into a dancing fool. It always feels right at the time.

It worked out great that I started playing the guitar, whether I'd wanted to or not, because my love in life is songwriting. I love to write music and vocals, and the cool thing about it is I feel that being in love with the drums makes me a stronger guitar player. I see many guitarists who really do not know much about the drums and often their music is about a solo or lead. I personally see the guitar as a tool I can use to create what I want the drums to do, what I want the vocals to do, what I want the bass to do — while I am playing the guitar, I hear all these parts inside my head. Whether it's System of a Down or Scars on Broadway or anything I've ever done, I've always written the music on the guitar with the big picture playing inside my head. The guitar is a medium for this. Another person sitting in the same room would just hear me playing the guitar, but what I'm hearing in my head is the drums, the vocals, the bass and everything else. Until I explain it or put my music onto a record, people are not likely to see my vision. I am very happy that I wound up learning how to play the guitar because that's my favorite thing to do in life. That's what I live for.

Tracii Guns

Tracii Guns is the guitarist who founded the glam metal band L.A. Guns with singer Axl Rose and later, the bands Brides of Destruction and Contraband. He was also the guitarist in the first lineup of Guns N' Roses.

I was six years old and I actually owned my first guitar, a Harmony solid-body electric that my uncle owned and gave to me. It looked a bit like a Fender Mustang, and I think they were made in Japan during the mid-1960s. As soon as the guitar spoke to me, that was it. I had played piano and drums, but the guitar always felt like the perfect shield to protect me from the rest of the world. The first song I learned to play on that Harmony guitar was "Pinball Wizard" by The Who. My uncle showed me how to play it. Then I heard "Whole Lotta Love" on the radio and *that* was the end of my life as I knew it at the time. It was like, "Oh my god: Led Zeppelin, Led Zeppelin, Led Zeppelin!" Really, that's all I cared about — Led Zeppelin and then maybe some Black Sabbath. In my early teens, it was Ted Nugent, Van Halen and Randy Rhodes. It was all really hard-hitting music that I'd liked at first because my mom was playing country music at the time on pedal steel guitar so I couldn't get far away enough from it.

Of course, when I was little, everyone was excited by my interest in the guitar. As I became a teenager, playing the guitar was all that I did. Basically, by the time I was fifteen all I did was surf and play guitar. Everybody was supportive of my playing, but then eventually it got to the point of them asking, "Hey. Um, so what else are you going to do?" My response was "What do you *mean*, what else am I going to do?" Thank god I got signed and had a record deal by the time I was twenty and it all made sense, so there was not a lot of resistance after that.

From an emotional standpoint, the guitar meant much to me, especially as an only child. My cousin, who was more like a brother to me, died when I was seventeen, so playing the guitar gave me a completely new sense of reality. It never fails to bring me somewhere else. It is easy to be alone when you play guitar. A guitar can get you through a lot of challenging moments and music in general taps into people's emotions. To be able to express and create music in your own way and gain an emotional release is what is great about the guitar. Oddly, I might seem unemotional on the outside and come across to some people as being distant, but the guitar has always been healthy for me.

The one thing that's been a bit of a stumbling block for me, which in truth helped me create my own musical style, is that I've had a really difficult time picking out other people's music by ear alone. I can remember being obsessed by Led Zeppelin's *The Song Remains the Same*. I played along with that record relentlessly for years, and I could never pick out exactly what it was that Page was doing by ear alone — which kind of had me playing things my own way. Over the years this has become less of an issue. With the help of YouTube, if I need to learn stuff, there is always some fourteen- or fifteen-year-old kid who knows a song note-for-note. You just put a little bit of feeling into it and then everything is okay!

My first official performance was at summer camp when I was twelve. I had just received my first Les Paul and my buddies and I put together a little band. We played three songs total — "Mongoloid" by Devo, "Rock 'n' Roll" by Led Zeppelin and "Stranglehold" by Ted Nugent.

My very first signature model guitar was a B.C. Rich Gunslinger. When the L.A. Guns were in Japan, performing the last show of an eighteen-month tour for our first record, I decided I'd smash the last guitar of the tour. I had four or five guitars and the one guitar I happened to be playing, of course, at the very end of this set, was the prototype. I just trashed it into pieces, into ashes almost. Afterward, I thought, "Ohhhh nooooo, what did I do?!"

My guitar tech at the time, Kent Holmes, actually gathered up every last bit of wood and kind of Frankensteined it back together with big metal plates and screws. He did all this surgery on it and it ended up hanging from the ceiling of the Lip Service store on Melrose for years. I guess the owner still has that guitar. The first prototypes of a few signature model guitars I've had are important and dear to me. Yet I must say most guitars, honestly, are just tools for me because I really do not clean them or take care of them, and they eventually all disintegrate from sweat, salt, weather and travel.

Incredibly, I have not managed to own a single guitar for the past twenty-five years that really held up long enough for me to be able to say, "That's my guitar!" I have new guitars that I've owned for a couple years that I have taken care of because I do not want anything to happen to them — these are signature model guitars that look a bit like a Telecaster and they have only a black satin finish on them so they're already susceptible to wear and tear. These guitars are almost vintage at this point, and after two years of playing them, they're as vintage as any of my '50s guitars, so I want to be able to use them for the next twenty to thirty years.

I remember when Daron Malakian bought my Washburn Nunobettencourt N4. I think he was $200 to 300 short and he just walked up to me and said, "Hey, aren't you with Washburn?" and I said, "Yeah!" He told me he really wanted an N4 and that they were expensive and he only had this much money. I said, "Why don't you come over to my house later and I'll sell you mine?" I think I sold him one for $300. It's so cool to know he still has that guitar!

Let me tell you something — I've owned close to a thousand guitars in the last thirty years, and I've given about ninety percent of them away to friends and fans, and Daron Malakian from System of a Down is the only person I know who ever really appreciated it and did not sell it or do something weird with the guitar. I swear every other guitar I can track on eBay from year to year. Someone is always selling one of my guitars and I'm like, "Awwww, man!" Now I do not give guitars away for this reason.

Joscho Stephan

Joscho Stephan is a German jazz guitarist known for his virtuosic technique for playing in the gypsy jazz style.

I received my first guitar when I was about three or four years old — an old red Höfner, which looked a bit like a 335 model. Because I was so young, I accidentally stepped on the guitar and broke the neck. My first guitar that I truly remember is one that I received as a Christmas gift when I was about five or six years old — a Seiwa Powersonic. To be honest, the first "real guitar," which I still have at home, was a Gibson Les Paul red sunburst '68 reissue. I did not play any other instrument, though I did wish to become a drummer. My parents felt that drums were too loud, I started to play guitar instead. I am very glad for this decision today, though I do play a little bit of electric bass these days.

When I started playing guitar, I was an absolute Beatles fan. Later, when I learned that I would never be a singer, I focused more on the guitar itself and listened mostly to rock guitarists like Carlos Santana, Gary Moore, Joe Satriani, etc. After this spell, I started playing jazz. Some guitar players say they listened to saxophone or piano players for their influences, but I've always preferred looking toward other guitarists for inspiration. One of the first jazz guitarists I heard and saw playing in concert was the legendary Hungarian jazz guitarist Attila Zoller, who was very famous in Germany, but I would have to say I am more influenced by artists like George Benson, Wes Montgomery and of course Django Reinhardt.

I chose jazz, or let's say, "improvised music," because I discovered I have the talent to improvise. I found that I was always more nervous if I had to play classical music because there is no space to cut loose. When I played rock music, I felt more comfortable. Because I do not sing, however, I still felt the need to search for another suitable playing style because it seemed as if even rock guitarists like Carlos Santana and Jimi Hendrix always worked with vocals. I wanted to find a style where my instrument would serve as a voice. Gypsy Swing proved to be perfect. Everything that I love is in that style of music — rhythm, melody and virtuosity.

My family arranged guitar lessons for me when they noticed my talent for playing. I am very glad about this because I think that so many children have no chance at all to learn a musical instrument. I was fortunate because my father also played guitar, and he recognized that I had talent and potential.

Initially, I faced many technical challenges of playing the guitar, but I was always ambitious. I have always looked up to the best guitar players in the world. I never just wanted to play as well as my neighbor — I wanted to play like Carlos Santana, Django Reinhardt, George Benson, among others. If one aspires to reach that level of mastery and proficiency on the guitar, this of course requires talent but also it requires discipline. I practiced for hours between the ages of fourteen and seventeen, and I continue to spend hours practicing today. No one ever forced me to practice; it was always my own wish to master the guitar.

My first official performance was probably between the ages of seven and eight. It was classical guitar, but I really cannot remember what piece I played. What I do remember is building my first musical group with my father and double bass player when I was sixteen. Since that time I've performed probably more than five hundred concerts. What I love most about playing the guitar is performing and making people laugh and cry at the same time for playing funny fast songs or slow and sad ballads.

One funny story I have is from when I had won the Youth Jazz division of the Jugend Jazz competition in Dortmund, Germany, when I was fifteen. At that time I was playing my Gibson Les Paul. As the winner, I was invited to return to Dortmund as a student for a workshop with professional jazz musicians. I was incredibly overwhelmed and proud of this honor. Unfortunately, when we left home, I forgot to bring my guitar with me and did not notice it was missing until it was far too late and I had to borrow a guitar. This never happened to me again.

My father, Günter Stephan, plays now a Hoyer 3063 model guitar, which I first played. We bought it for a very cheap price in a music shop in Düren, Germany, near the town of Aachen. A man by the name of Hajo Hintzen who organized concerts in Aachen saw that I enjoyed playing the Hoyer 3063 model guitar and kindly arranged a contact between myself and the Hoyer Company, which, for a couple of years, had built a Joscho Stephan model guitar until company ownership changed. I played this instrument until I discovered the guitar love of my life: the Jürgen Volkert D-hole Maccaferri. I have been playing this guitar since 2003.

I also have a new O-hole version, which I use especially for recordings. The D-hole model I have played so much that its maker, Jürgen Volkert, had to refinish the guitar two years ago. Many people wanted to buy a guitar that had that same great, vintage look, but Jürgen and I had to tell them that he is not able to built a guitar like that — they first must play the guitar five years straight, like I did.

Johnny Hiland

Guitarist Johnny Hiland, who is legally blind, began his career as a bluegrass player and has developed his own hybrid sound of country, rock, blues and swing.

My first guitar belonged to my grandfather. He passed on when my dad was six months old. I'm his namesake, in fact. He was John William Hiland and I'm John Edward Hiland — I have my dad's middle name. Back in the day Gramps used to play on his guitar, which was a 1939 J-45 Gibson that was left to my aunt. She had it up in her attic for a long, long time and it was supposed to be passed onto my dad. Of course my dad played drums back in the '60s and he never really picked up guitar. So it got passed on to me when I was three or four years old.

Before that, I had a toy guitar and I'd jump all over the living room with it, listening to Bee Gees records. When I was given my grandfather's guitar, it was really my first good guitar that I knew was going to stick with me forever. I wouldn't part with that guitar for a million dollars. It has so many playing hours on it from Gramps and then more from me. The guitar was a little bigger than me, of course, but I just wanted to be with it all the time.

The guitar has always been my best friend. I was born legally blind with an eye disease called Nystagmus, which really hindered me from playing kickball with all my other friends, so I sat in my room playing my guitar instead. Basically, as a kid with a visual impairment, I went through kids teasing, calling me names and stuff, so instead of sharing these details with my parents, I chose to share it through my guitar. And later on, being a sixteen-year-old kid who can never drive a car while all my friends were out taking their first spin just drove me closer to the guitar. It was a great emotional release. That's why I consider it my best friend.

I'd yearn for it after being in school all day. I just wanted to run home, grab it and play. For me, the guitar became a strong love. I did my first TV show, *Stacey's Country Jamboree*, in Bangor, Maine, with that guitar, playing Willie Nelson's "On the Road Again." My dad tuned the guitar to an open E chord and I used my thumb to walk the bass line as I played it flat on my lap. It was so funny because the steel guitar player kept looking over my shoulder, wondering if I was playing lap steel. Back home, I used to take it onto the school bus and sing "On the Road Again" to the bus driver.

I later took my guitar to Dana Bourgeois to refurbish it so it's like a brand new Gibson. Dana builds the most beautiful flat tops these days and makes the Ricky Skaggs model and builds for Nickel Creek and a lot of the contemporary acoustic bands. He left in Gramps' traits, like a thumb nick in the neck where Gramps used to rest his thumb, and then of course, where his arm rested, there is still a blemish there, which is kind of neat.

Ricky Skaggs is one of my biggest heroes. My mom and dad took me to see Ricky when I was ten years old at the Bangor Auditorium, and from then on, I decided the Telecaster is what I wanted to play instead of playing acoustic. Then again, Ricky had a huge bluegrass element in his show. Waylon Jennings, Willie Nelson, Don Williams, Merle Haggard. My granddad on my mom's side had all the old Faron Young records, and I'd listen to them for hours and hours on end. Early country music was my big thing.

I had two main teachers in my life. The first was Phil Gallup, a jazz player in Hartford, Connecticut, who is now playing in a band called Men in the White Coats. He's a phenomenal jazz player. He taught me my first seven chords when I was ten years old, and seven chords can get you through a show, I guess. I was about thirteen or fourteen when I studied in Bangor, Maine, with a guy named Billy Pierce who taught me theory and the chalkboard stuff.

I think my mom and dad thought the guitar would be a hobby, but later on it tended to take up all of my time. They wanted me to go on to college and have something else to fall back on if music didn't work for me. But being visually impaired and having to learn from books on cassette really just didn't work with me. I basically spent my college years cramming guitar for eight to twelve hours a day. My junior year of college, I decided Nashville was where I wanted to be, and guitar was what I planned to do for the rest of my life. Since then, my mom and dad have seen me get a standing ovation at the Grand Ole Opry, which is the mother church of country music. And whenever I showed up on a new record, I'd send it home. Of course, my own first record is coming out now on Favored Nations, which is a huge dream come true for me.

I live, eat, sleep and breathe the guitar, even now. It's such a wonderful instrument that I want to have it in my hands all the time. I kept telling people all the time, even when I was seven years old, "Someday, I'm going to play at the Grand Ole Opry." They'd give me a look like, "Okay, kid. Keep dreaming." I ignored all that and said this was where my heart was. I knew that, with help from the right people, the industry was not out of the question. It was a matter of finding those people. Of course, when you go to Nashville, you're on Broadway playing honkytonks and the typical barroom bootcamp kind of thing, so you're like, "Oh man, here I am in a nightclub again with a bunch of drinkers. Is this really where it is? Is this really where I am?" For a while there in Nashville, I wondered if I was going to be a club player for the rest of my life. But when the TNN shows started happening, I knew Nashville was the place to be, because I sure wasn't going to get discovered in Woodland, Maine, two hours outside of Bangor! I knew that music was going to be the focus of my life. So as many dreams as I kept shouting at people, I didn't care what it was going to take, figuring as long as I kept reaching out to find someone who could help me reach the next level. Believe me, I did have moments where I second-guessed myself, thinking maybe I should have gone to college and gotten a degree. But really, I think it's like anything — if you put your heart and your mind to it, stick with it and don't ever let it rest, you're bound to create some kind of a buzz somehow. When you love something so much, you just can't help but keep at it.

I've got a funny story for you about one of my guitars. Historically, whenever an artist signed on with Fender to have a custom guitar model made, Fender has never let anyone watch their guitar get built. But I was their very first. I was standing there in front of a big pane of glass and Jim DeCola, the gentleman who built my guitar at Fender, was in the paint booth. I'm watching through this big window and he's got this big apron on, goggles, the whole works. He's got the guitar body on a stick and he's spraying the living daylights out of the thing with sparkles and gold paint flying everywhere. I looked over at my manager, Mac Wilson, and Bruce Bouton Sr., the vice president at Fender, and I said, "Wouldn't you just doggone know it but they let a blind guy come in to watch his guitar being built?"

I didn't really even think about it when I said it, but the place just lit up. My mom and dad actually have the stick that the guitar was hanging from when Jim painted the guitar. Jim wrote something on it, like, "Here's to the birth of Johnny's new baby," and he dated it. Mom said to me, "You get a beautiful, high-dollar guitar and we get a stick."

Andy McKee

Self-taught fingerstyle guitarist Andy McKee is a YouTube phenom from Topeka, Kansas, with his song "Drifting" garnering over 40 million views. He is known for his Michael Hedges–style fretboard tapping.

For my thirteenth birthday, my dad bought me my first guitar — a used, nylon-string Aria guitar, which had cost about $50. I had really wanted an electric guitar because I had been into hard rock at the time, but I wound up with this classical guitar instead.

My parents had me take about a year-and-a-half of private guitar lessons, where I learned chords and basic scales. We had a piano in the house, but I did not really know how to play it. Sometimes I just messed around on it. The main reason I'd wanted a guitar is because, when I was twelve years old, I had heard Eric Johnson playing on the radio. He was playing an instrumental song called "Cliffs of Dover," a really big hit at the time, and I had never really listened to much instrumental music before, especially guitar music. I thought his playing was awesome and amazing and that was why I wanted a guitar. Hearing him play is what started my fascination with instrumental guitar music. I was also into Metallica and hard rock bands at the time.

The young Andy McKee. (*Courtesy Andy McKee*)

Since I had an acoustic guitar, I did try learning some acoustic guitar songs like "Dust in the Wind" by Kansas and a couple of acoustic songs from Led Zeppelin, like "Stairway to Heaven," and "Babe I'm Gonna Leave You." My family was encouraging, and my brother started playing the guitar at the same time as well. He was deeply into playing Jimi Hendrix and Stevie Ray Vaughan while I was into Eric Johnson and harder rock music. And every now and then, we were both into trying to one-up each other.

I actually have fairly small hands, so I learned how to play chords that were specifically difficult for my left hand. I wanted to stretch my fingers and make it possible to fret these types of chords. Later on, I expanded into using different tunings and exploring how to make different sounds on the guitar as well. I like to explore different chord voicings that make it possible to play a certain melody over a certain chord progression that might be impossible or very difficult otherwise.

I was fourteen years old when I had first performed in a talent show at my middle school. I had a band with a few of my friends, and we played a version of "Enter Sandman" by Metallica. Because we had all just hit puberty, none of us had a voice that was deep enough to actually sing the song so we just did this instrumental version instead — it was kind of funny. Everyone else seemed to think it was cool, so we had fun.

My first actual steel-string acoustic guitar that I owned was a 12-string Takamine, but I took off six of the strings. That is what I primarily play now these days. It's similar to the nylon-string guitar for having a wider fret board, sometimes even two inches up at the nut, so it was not too bad getting used to playing on the wider fretboard. I bought my first electric guitar and an amp from a cousin of mine who played, but he's about the only other musical guy in my family. I check my guitars and take three guitars with me when I tour — my standard pitch guitar, my baritone acoustic guitar and my harp guitar. I usually travel with all three guitars, so it is impossible to bring them all on board but I have some really good Calton flight cases.

Playing the guitar is a way to express oneself, and I am not too creative in any other way, so I like to experiment with the guitar and find new ways of expressing emotions I have and turning them into music. That is the best part. It's also great when people connect with you for the music and you discover a connection with others that you might not have had otherwise. We might have different lifestyles and philosophies but music can bring people together in a special way.

Fabio Zanon

Brazilian classical guitarist Fabio Zanon studied guitar at the Royal Academy of Music in London and is the first instrumental performer to be presented with the Santista Prize in Brazil for his contributions to Brazilian music.

My first guitar was my father's guitar because he was the person in our family who played. My sister, who is five years older than I am, started to have lessons when she was seven years old, so for me, from the age of two onward, there was always a guitar present within our house. My sister had a quarter-sized guitar so that was the very first one that I picked up. It was called Fiesta and it was a terrible guitar, very poorly made. My sister still has this guitar. My father's guitar was a full-sized Di Giorgio and very hard to play.

This was a big deterrent when I started to play because I had asked him to teach me when I was seven, and he would always say, "No, the guitar is too large for you." Of course, I tried and found that I could not even reach the F. It was very hard and I could not get any sound out of it. It was difficult because my father was trying to teach me to play chords. To even make a G Major chord was impossible and I went away from the guitar for about two or three years.

He started to teach me again when I was nine. I still have my father's guitar. The Di Giorgio is like a fat lady, very thick. It's kind of dyed orange in color and flashy.

My first desire was always to play the piano. I chose music, but the guitar chose me. I asked my father if I could play piano, but he urged me to read music using the guitar, and I became happy with that. I did not ever come back to the piano. It was very expensive; it would have taken a few years before my family could buy one. By the time they managed to save up enough, I was already fairly proficient on the guitar and did not care for the piano anymore.

My father taught me to read music. When it came to multi-voiced music, I taught myself along with knowledge of music theory, which I learned from basic Brazilian books. We still had solfège, too, in school. Bach's Brandenburg Concerto, Handel's *Water Music*, Hadyn's Symphony No. 30, Mozart's Symphony No. 4. I remember the order, and I can sing *La Traviata* to you from beginning to end, if you wish — and this is because we had these records at home. So there was not much guitar beyond Baden Powell, who played on television at the time. I bought Dilermando Reis' records from a record shop and these were the exposure I had to professional solo guitar. I heard Segovia on the radio once, playing a very brief piece.

My next influence was my guitar teacher when I was thirteen. I was very lucky because he used to work in a car factory and taught only on Saturdays. But he was just a brilliant guitarist, absolutely unbelievable, with the best tremolo I have ever heard. *La Catedral* by Barrios? Perfect. And he was a very uncultured guy, which was funny. This was my very first teacher, who had studied with Abel Carlevaro just by chance in his youth. I started to borrow his records, and the first I listened to were the Abreu brothers. That spoiled my enjoyment of the guitar for the rest of my life because everything comes in second after hearing them play. Segovia did not impress me much at the time. Then I heard Julian Bream, which was great and I was lucky. Segovia and the Presti-Lagoya duo recordings I have only started to enjoy in the past fifteen years. The technique of the Abreu brothers is unsurpassable. Even the very best guitarists of today are just as good. I've never seen anything beyond that.

My first ambition was to become a composer with the guitar and I did do that for a while, but then I realized that becoming a mediocre composer is a lot of work. I attended the University of São Paulo for composing and conducting because there was no guitar course at the time. Only in my last year was an official guitar department created, and I graduated with a degree in guitar. I lived off conducting for two years. I had wanted to learn more about music and the best way to do that is to learn composition.

My father pretty much told me I should pursue other interests and a sport as well. My father came from a very deprived background and managed to study, I'm not sure how, because he was working full time from the age of twelve. He loved music and the fact that I was doing it was a bit of self-realization for him. He was fulfilling his dreams through me and quite happy with that. He felt even if you love music more than anything else, it is important to lead a balanced life.

The guitar is a microcosm of life. It is the horse to the Arab. It's like a boat for the sailor. The guitar is my very life and is something so close to me and at the same time is so uncontrollable because the guitar does not do exactly what you want. You have to create a partnership with it if you are to produce anything worthwhile. I would never put the guitar away because the self-expression one has with the guitar is so direct. The way you put your fingers on the guitar is a direct contact with sound that I cannot get from anything else.

I'm not naturally a fast player. I do not naturally have a good sound. Many people file their nails for the first time and achieve a sound that is already quite acceptable. Mine was not. I've spent many years working on that, but this is part of the enjoyment. I can tell what is my forte and musicianship, being part of my background, is what comes easily to me. If I have any difficulty with the rhythm of a piece or a formal understanding of the piece, that is something I can solve in a very intuitive way.

I thought perhaps I might be a writer and had some poetry published when I was twelve years old. We had literary circles in my hometown of São Paulo with teenagers who read their poetry for each other. One of these meetings was at a music school, and for some reason, someone asked one of the guitar students at this school to come and play a few pieces. The guy played Villa-Lobos "Prelude No. 3" and when someone asked if anyone else in the gathering played guitar, I said that I played a little. So I played *Lagrima*, the first movement of Beethoven's *Moonlight Sonata* — but my hand was shaking one inch away from the guitar. I was so, so scared. I managed to get to the end of playing, and it was not so bad because I did know those pieces inside out. But then I started to realize the inadequacy of my preparation. That is when I started to have lessons with the man who taught at this music school. That had been my first performing experience, and six months later I gave a proper half-recital of Carcassi studies, Villa-Lobos' "Choros No. 1" and Visée's "Suite in D Minor," Bach's "Gavotte en Rondeau." I was nearly fourteen at the time. I would still get nervous and shaky but not to the extent that it prevented me from playing properly. My teacher was very thorough. Normally I learned a piece and performed it. What he had me do is practice a piece for three weeks. Then I'd put it away and learn something else. After a month, I would return to the first piece, pick it up again, work on it for another three weeks. Then I would put it away again and let six months pass until my teacher asked me to play that piece. You learned to play a piece anytime, anywhere.

I remember playing a concert in Saudi Arabia, and the strings snapped in both concerts. I had to change the strings in concert and this is something I learned early, to always carry new strings. For me, forgetting the strings is like forgetting the footstool or the nail file. I am currently playing a Dale Perry guitar from Winnipeg, Canada. I had a chance to meet him at the St. Louis '96 Guitar Foundation of America competitions, and then I had a chance to tour in Winnipeg and bought the guitar there. I've always played, though, on Abreu guitars from Brazil because among Brazilian guitar makers of international standing, Abreu was the first. I also have a Paul Galbraith guitar made by David Rubio's son. I have two Roberto Gomez guitars. You can only have one wife but of guitars, you can have many.

Jonny Lang

Grammy award-winning blues guitarist and singer Jonny Lang has toured with the Rolling Stones, Buddy Guy, Aerosmith, B.B. King, Jeff Beck and Sting. He has also performed at Eric Clapton's Crossroads Guitar Festival to raise money for the Crossroads Centre Antigua.

It was my thirteenth birthday when my dad gave me a guitar, a Stratocaster. Prior to this, maybe a month earlier, I had seen a blues band play in my hometown of Fargo, North Dakota, called the Bad Medicine Blues band, who were friends of my dad. And after hearing them play, I just fell in love with the guitar. My dad arranged to have me take guitar lessons from their guitarist, Ted Larsen. I ended up joining their band a little while later on as their singer and also played guitar a little. That is how I got started.

I played saxophone when I was in school and played a little bit of viola, too. I liked the sax but was not all that great at it. I was more passionate about guitar and that is what I wanted to focus on. I've loved music ever since I could remember because I wanted to be a singer. I grew up listening to Motown mostly. Michael Jackson and Stevie Wonder were my favorites. When I'd started playing the guitar, I was really into Nirvana, Pearl Jam, Stone Temple

Pilots and Jane's Addiction. I wanted to learn how to play grunge rock guitar, and when I showed up at Ted's place saying I wanted to learn how to play like Kurt Cobain, he'd told me that he could not really teach me that stuff, but he gave me an Albert King record to take home. When I listened to it, I became hooked and started obsessing over blues guitar players after that.

My parents were happy to see me focusing that hard on something because school was just a loss for me, sadly. I was a lazy, disobedient student with horrible grades and I'm not sure how I advanced from grade to grade after sixth grade, really. I'd made it halfway through ninth grade and promised I would get my GED but never did. Fortunately, music worked out for me. I'm lucky.

One day when I was onstage early on, playing the guitar gave me the same feeling as the day my dad had taken the training wheels off my bicycle and given me that push that allowed me to experience riding on two wheels for the first time all by myself. I just felt like all of a sudden I could see my options in front of me and that I could do whatever I wanted. It feels like a breakthrough and it's the same feeling I keep chasing with the guitar — unanchored, untethered — this entire feeling of the whole world open in front of me and that I have control over the direction I want to take. I had never realized this feeling was possible so I've become addicted to it. Places that I can go and the energy that is available at some points while playing, when I'm just being reckless and free — all that goes back to this place of raw emotion. The only way I can achieve this feeling is from playing and singing. That is what I love most about the guitar.

The biggest issue I had with the guitar was learning to play vibrato. My Strat had a whammy bar on it and, with those types of guitars, you can shake the bridge with your hand and create a fake tremolo. I did that for a long time, and it was a crutch for me before I started to learn how to play tremolo. It was Ted Larsen from Bad Medicine Blues Band who made me stop doing that. Ted put all five springs on that bridge piece so that the tension was too great for me to slip back into that old habit. He told me, "You're not doing that anymore. You're going to learn how to play vibrato." Thankfully he did that, because it was the biggest hump for me to get over. I'd actually almost stopped playing the guitar because it made me so frustrated. But I got it, one day.

I knew I would be a musician for the rest of my life even before I had started playing. I just knew that there was no other route for me and this is what was I wanted to be doing. I never wavered. My very first gig was at a very big festival in Fargo called Riverfront Days, and we had rehearsed for weeks.

Performing was nothing at all what I'd thought it would be, in terms of my preconceptions. Even from rehearsing, performing is about coming from a place of focus in a way I was not accustomed to. It was really challenging and hard for a while to get used to that feeling. Performing was not a fairytale, like imagining all these slow-motion moments of great choreography and sweat flying off your hair while you do some cool move. It was just this stark sensation of "Oh man, everybody's looking at me and I'd better not mess up."

I had this Telecaster that I bought when I was sixteen, after I had started falling in love with Telecasters. After I discovered Albert Collins, who is the master of the Telecaster, I was hooked on the idea of playing the Telecaster. I bought this 1976 Tele Custom and it wound up getting stolen with all the other band gear in Detroit one year. It was just heartbreaking. There was another guitar that I loved equally and the same thing happened, where gear had been stolen from the "security-guarded" parking lot of a hotel. It seemed like an inside job, though this really couldn't be proved. Then a fan who used to attend our shows a lot with his son phoned and informed me he was an FBI agent. He'd heard what had happened with our stolen band gear and offered to help. He wound up getting us much of that gear back, including one of my guitars. It was like seeing your long lost love again.

During the "Lie to Me" video shoots, which were shot at the Black Market Music in San Francisco, there was a '57 Fender Esquire, basically a Telecaster, hanging from the ceiling and that's the one I used in the video. I just fell in love with this guitar. But it cost $6,500. I did not have that kind of money. The president of our label, Al Cafaro, heard that I loved this guitar and got it for me as a birthday present. That is a very, very special guitar for me because the whole experience I had early on with A&M and Al Cafaro and other people had been incredible. They were so kind and just great people. That is very hard to come by, especially these days in the music industry.

Frank Vignola

New York–born Frank Vignola is an American jazz guitarist who has worked as a sideman with artists such as Madonna, Leon Redbone, Wynton Marsalis, Les Paul and Ringo Starr. Known for his incredible technique, he has written eighteen instructional guitar books and recorded multiple instructional CD-ROMs. His record *Vignola Plays Gershwin* (Mel Bay Records) ranked #2 in National Public Radio airplay charts.

I started playing when I was six years old. My step-grandmother's first husband, who was a guitarist, had a 1958 D'Angelico New Yorker guitar. That is the guitar I started to play. It had an eighteen-inch body with a blond spruce top, so the guitar was basically bigger than me. I don't know if you're familiar with a 1958 D'Angelico New Yorker, but they're considered the Stradivarius of guitars, worth about $80,000.

I did not play any other instruments until I was about thirteen years old. I learned to play the tenor banjo. My father played it and I played a few chords, but I did this because I started to land opportunities to play in Dixieland bands. Once I learned a bit more, I started playing gigs with four to five Dixieland bands per week. My father had jam sessions with guitars and banjos, so the dynamic at first was that everybody in the house seemed to play an instrument. I knew I wanted to learn to play something, and I probably realized that it was wiser for me to learn how to play the guitar first rather than choose a novelty instrument, like the tenor banjo, at least as a start. My fascination came from desire to play guitar with these older guys. After a couple of guitar lessons, I remember specifically thinking, "This is what I want to do!" I knew from the age of seven that I was going to be a professional guitar player. I know that sounds crazy, but I never thought about anything else. I had no other interest besides the guitar. I just knew I was going to be a guitar player. I've always believed that either you're a musician or you're not. If you want to play the horn, you're going to do every possible thing you can to play that horn, even starve, if your passion is there to do it. It is a gift to want to play. People who have another job on the side and play only semi-professionally — they're not really musicians. Musicians are born with the desire to do that and nothing but that.

My father was supportive of my interest in playing and used to take me on his gigs with him. My mother was a little freaked out because at age sixteen I had started playing at a club with my dad's friends and did not come home until the sun was coming up. We played until two thirty a.m., and then I went out to have breakfast with my dad's friends, who were nearly my grandfather's age, and then I came home. My mom told me that I had to get a summer job. I became a counselor at a camp that summer but then would take at least two days off each week to go play some gig. After that summer, I think she saw that I was making more playing two gigs than I was weekly as a camp counselor. She finally gave in at that point.

There is nothing more fun than being able to make music with people. That is the real joy in playing. It was a social outlet for me, too. I couldn't stand school. I did well but I felt I was learning more for being able to practice along with Joe Pass! Socially, playing the guitar was great for me because it allowed me to meet other people who were interested in the same things I was.

When I was just supporting myself, playing the guitar professionally was relatively easy. I was fortunate because I always had about eight to ten gigs weekly ever since high school. Sometimes it was Dixieland gigs. Sometimes it was dressed as Santa playing guitar and strolling around a Macy's department store. And sometimes I played music that I really enjoyed playing at a jazz club. When you have a family, it makes you look at all this again and ask if you'll be able to get along by just playing the guitar.

Every college brochure I looked at for studying music said that you could not work professionally during the first year of study. My thought was "What? I have to give up a living in order to study?" I found a place to live in Manhattan and started playing professionally. I was very lucky, but I had worked very hard, too. I auditioned and played for people. You go knock on doors. My first break, so to speak, came about this way. I was playing society parties at the time, wearing a tuxedo and playing with a big band. After about a year of this, I started feeling down about it all. I felt it was not working. I was not happy. So I remember walking straight into Michael's Club, which was a big cabaret in New York — I was still wearing my tuxedo — and Michael, the owner, had a reputation for being a little odd. But I walked in there anyway and asked him if he would consider hiring a Django Reinhardt tribute band. He said to me rather gruffly, "I want to hear a tape! Send me a tape!" The next night, I went into the studio at about three a.m., had a little faith and handed a tape to him the next night. He called back a few days later to tell me he had a spot open for two weeks. I did not even have a band and this was a three-week-long engagement in New York City in one of its top clubs! I got a band together and put a show together.

When I walked out onstage, the entire front row was filled with music critics from the *New York Times*, *Newsday*, *New York Post* and *Variety* magazine. They loved the show. It turned into a feature story. This just proved to me that you've *got* to knock on doors, whether it's the top club or a little storefront. You've got to knock on doors to get work because no one else is going to do it for you. They do not teach you how to do this in college.

I taught at Arizona State University for two years. I started a jazz guitar program there. I had all my students out there working, playing. I would help them hook up with little church cafés and the Starbucks. Once they started making a little extra cash, they couldn't stop. The other wonderful thing is that my students set themselves to learning fifteen songs they could play within an hour instead of simply choosing to learn two. That is how anyone learns to play. I remember that the head of the Jazz Department called me into his office and said, "Listen, I understand you have the guys out there working but you're taking away the teachers' work and the lesson plans that you should be using." I thought, "You know what? Back to New York I go." That was it for me. What are these guys going to do when they get out of school? So what if they have a degree they've paid some $80,000 for? They're not going to know how to get a gig, so how are they going to be able to pay off their student loans? Not only did my plan for them work in the sense of encouraging and teaching them how to go get work — it taught them how to play. With gigs comes rehearsal and that is *what we do* as musicians, whether you are in school or not. You rehearse and try to get gigs. It never stops.

A Cup of Coffee with Jimmy Page

Five minutes before my appointed time with Mr. Page, I moved away from the bus stop, repositioning myself just outside the London coffee shop. I was wearing a long brown silk scarf with red poppies, easily identifiable, especially as the ends floated upward like the tail of a kite twisting in the breeze. Not to mention, I was the only one standing outside this place like a doofus. From halfway down the block, I heard his voice: "Juuuulllllliiaaaaaaa!"

Jimmy Page was walking toward me, smiling, with tousled black hair and a sportsman's jacket thrown on over a gray wool cable sweater. I'd expected him to be taller and larger for some reason, possibly because every time I have seen him, he fills the entire length and width of any magazine cover. He surprised me with a bear hug that swooped me off my feet.

"Nice weather, no?" he remarked.

"The Cuban composer Leo Brouwer has a piece that would describe it — 'Un Dia de Noviembre.'"

"What do you make of the sky? It's unusual, isn't it?" he asked, scanning the enormous grey-bellied cumulus clouds hung low and luminous against the winter sun. They were unlike anything I'd seen back home.

"Silvery," he said.

"Pewter. It's a pewter sky," I offered.

Jimmy's eyes widened a little. "I like that!" He nodded toward the door of the café.

He ordered two cappuccinos for us and winked at the flustered girl behind the counter who, along with other patrons in the restaurant, reflected instantly knowing looks and perceptible smiles as the tumblers finally fell into place as to why the Yankee had come in earlier asking mad questions about possible telephone messages left for her at a café. It was vindication mixed with embarrassment all over again. Jimmy stuffed a generous tip inside the jar at the counter and we carried our milk foam–topped cups toward a table in back and settled in. Jimmy removed a small matchbook-sized plastic case from his pocket that neatly dispensed one sugar-free sweetener tablet into his cup and gave me a bit of a self-conscious look because he probably knew I was taking in that detail.

"I have a feeling we know a few people in common," he told me.

I was stumped and surprised. "Oh you must mean Santa Claus? The Tooth Fairy?"

He pointed out I was from Chicago, the home of Chess Records. Let's fast-forward a moment through the pewter sky of this day into the not-too-distant future, when I would complete recording my first CD and meet with my eighty-three-year-old great uncle, great aunt and cousin downtown at a restaurant called The Chicago Pizza and Oven Grinder. The restaurant is housed in a building where Al Capone's lookout counted the men walking into a long gone garage to meet their fate on St. Valentine's Day. And it is located a few blocks away from the Biograph Theater, where John Dillinger saw his last moving picture show. You can't get any more Chicagoan than this collision of old gangster history with Sicilian-style pizza.

I had not seen my uncle (or my aunt) since I was seventeen years old, and my basic recollection of him was as The Uncle Who Gave Us Dreaded Fruitcakes every Christmas, which my grandmother hung out on the back fence with suet for the birds to eat, a favor they'd repay by shitting all over her white Pontiac. Reputedly, he had a hit song from back in the day on his basement jukebox. Whatever it had been, I did not have a clue because, as a ten-year-old, I had been more interested in hitting the jukebox buttons to play Jim Croce's "Bad, Bad Leroy Brown" to hear the word *damn*.

"Is that a Les Paul?" my uncle asked of the guitar I had carried protectively with me inside the restaurant. I unzipped the case to show him. "Have you met Les Paul?" he asked me. "I used to play with him on the WLS *National Barn Dance* show." My jaw fell open. And stayed open as he told me he had been friends with Stan Kenton, Harry James and Nat King Cole, for whom he'd written the song "Pretend," the song he had on his basement jukebox. My uncle, it turns out, had been a producer at Chess Records. One day he received a phone call from his pal Sam Phillips, asking his opinion on some new kid named Elvis who had recorded a demo. "Not my cup of tea, but the kid's got talent. He will be a hit" had been his response.

Elvis later invited him and Aunt Maryon to be on the film set of *Love Me Tender*. Toward the end of his career, my uncle had also managed The Buckinghams — and played the trumpet section in their hit song, "Kind of a Drag." My uncle told me that he does not really play his trumpet or saxophone anymore except on rare occasions, with a few buddies of his at the retirement home where he lives out West.

Let's rewind to the pewter sky now, back to a thin ray of light shining through the coffee shop where I sat with Jimmy Page. Guitars . . . Chess Records . . . of course we had something in common, and I had to come all the way to London to find that out.

"I hear you are a rather mobile young lady," Page said, referring to what he had evidently learned from the office regarding my adventures in London, which included covering a concert at Wigmore Hall. "I've not ever been to Wigmore Hall! What is it like?"

I could scarcely believe I had been to a concert hall in London that Page had not. I explained that my boss Maurice had taken pity on me and proposed that I accompany him to a guitar and flute concert to write a review for Her Worshipful Society of Musicians, an ancient guild of English formality dating back to the Middle Ages that holds itself in service to Her Majesty Queen Elizabeth II.

The following morning after the concert I had spent criss-crossing London in search of guitar shops. Later, I wondered if this had not all been a strange test that I had passed unwittingly, one that revealed my true heart and devotion to the guitar and had allowed me this interview. Jimmy surprised me by wanting to hear the details of where I had gone and what things I saw. "I cannot go inside guitar shops anymore," he said.

He told me of taking classical guitar lessons from Len Williams at the Spanish Guitar Centre on Cranbourn Street in Soho and how distracting it had been when people outside the shop caught sight of him in the window and made him feel like an animal at the zoo. I suggested that if we visited some shops together and played "Stairway to Heaven," it would provide a magical cloak of invisibility.

Jimmy asked if I might have any recommendations for a decent child-sized electric guitar for his son. The perfect child-size electric guitar he envisioned happened to be one he had seen twenty years ago when he was last on tour in Japan and he was now kicking himself for not buying it on the spot, though of course, this had long been before his son arrived. His son was showing interest in playing now, though he was still physically a little small for a full-sized electric.

"He's good! He's talented! And I'm not just saying that because I am his father. He is fearless about trying to get sounds out of the guitar in a way that I had never tried or even thought to try when I was his age." Jimmy told me they had gone outside to the park the other day and his son had brought along his guitar. Not only had a couple of girls stopped to listen, "but he made £8 from busking! That's *good* money!"

Let's linger here and freeze-frame this moment because nothing more really needs to be said. I was no longer talking to a rock star in a café in London. This could have been absolutely anywhere in the world, any parent, speaking with pride and wonder to see their child discovering themselves and finding ways of relating and interacting with the world — all from the simple enjoyment of a guitar.

Jimmy Page

British guitarist Jimmy Page had been a member of The Yardbirds and founded the rock band Led Zeppelin.

The guitar that was my first guitar — it's a bit of a mystery. My parents lived quite near London airport and we moved from there to a house in Epsom, which was, relatively speaking, in the countryside. The guitar was there in this house. I remember seeing it. It was just there in a corner, hanging around. We certainly didn't bring it with us from Feltham. Whose was it then? My guess is maybe the guitar might have been left behind at this house. So it was there.

When I was about eleven or twelve years old, I'd really been seduced by this music that I heard coming out of the speakers from the radio. It drew me in, along with what limited access we had to music through television. At the time, skiffle and rock 'n' roll was tolerated by the authorities, but there soon came a point when it was no longer tolerated and they tried to stamp it underground. And that didn't work. But it became quite a rebellious thing to tune into AFN radio, the American Forces Network in Europe, and listen a Ventures or rock 'n' roll tune, or whatever.

I remember going to school one day and there was one boy who had a guitar. And he was actually playing the songs I'd heard on the radio. This was before I'd even gotten a record player or 78s — we had no money to be buying records at that point. This boy was playing the sort of music I'd heard, and I thought to myself, "I've got one of those at home." It was a Spanish guitar but it was steel-strung. A round-hole guitar. I don't know what make it was. Or where'd it come from. And unfortunately, I don't know where it went. It was there and it was out of tune.

I might have looked at it and might have touched it and played pretty much what my son does now with the guitar, but I did this at twelve years old. I didn't have the confidence to just pick it up and start playing. The reason for that was there wasn't anybody who played guitar and the sort of people that you see playing on the television were already stars. It never crossed my mind at that point that it could be a career, but it was certainly a hobby.

The thing that happened was this boy said, "Why don't you bring it along to school and I'll show you how to tune it." And that's exactly what he did. He showed me how to tune it and he showed me some chords. And that was it. Before I knew where I was I was actually able to do what he was doing, playing the same tunes from the radio. So, the essence of it was, given a sort of helping hand, I was self-taught, and then it came from buying and listening to records.

There weren't many guitarists around. I mean, this boy was a year older, actually two years older, than I was and he and I were the only guitarists that I knew of, nobody else. By then I could actually play reasonably well. I could play some Chuck Berry and all of that sort music from Chess in Chicago, Bo Diddley and the blues, rockabilly and all the music that meant so much to me in my formative years, like Cliff Gallup, Elmore James and James Burton. And all these sorts of people and their identities were so strong. In those days, I had no access to Robert Johnson — it was too rare. Collectors who had that sort of thing kept it to themselves. It didn't come out until a few years later for the rest of us.

I don't know whether the penny dropped at the time, but the fact is each person's character and identity was so firmly stamped within six strings. You could just recognize them from listening to a little part. And that's been a major part of my playing. I always wanted to develop a style so that people would go, "Well, that it *is* Jimmy." In those days there would be two guitarists in the local store where I went to in order to hear of other guitarists. You'd hear of maybe a handful of guitarists in the whole of the county. And what we'd met even out of the county, too. I met Jeff Beck. He was another guitarist. And then there was

Eric Clapton. There was another guitarist called Martin Stone, whom everybody had thought was a messianic player, except nobody had ever heard him. But he was fantastic. He now runs a bookshop in Paris. I'm not even sure I've ever heard him play. But he's one of these where you'd say of another guitarist, "Yeah, he's awright but *Martin Stone* is the guitarist of all guitarists!" Now, even almost twenty years ago, you could almost say that everyone sort of knew someone who had been in a group or who was about to be in a group, playing guitar, if they didn't play themselves.

I took the guitar with me to school to let this older boy tune it. I used to take it to school all the time. For me, the guitar was like — even as a child — having a family relative there at school with me. It was something I could communicate with. Consequently I spent most of my time playing the guitar from the first thing in the morning to the last thing at night. My family wanted me to do more homework, actually. Nothing got in the way of that. That was fair enough. They didn't really know what I was doing. They didn't understand it. I suppose they probably employed the same logic or principles of logic that people would today. That's all right. It must have been awful to witness, though, because I'd spent hours and hours listening to records. They must have thought I was doing something besides training for going mad. I had a voracious appetite for listening to everything. It amazes me what six strings can do with application and imagination.

I never considered myself a natural guitarist. I'd seen other guitarists who seemed to be able to play so easily, but they didn't even make a career out of it. For me, it was always a hobby. Apart from the point time I was doing sessions and studio work and I really had to be responsible in terms of arriving on time and delivering what was required. Even though I really enjoyed studio work, it was really a challenge because I never knew what I was walking into. I knew I might not be walking into a rock session or even, dare I say, a pop session. It could have been a jazz session or folk. It was really kind of an apprenticeship. Again, it never really seemed like hard work, except when I had a muzak session. That's when I'd thought it was hard work. I was so accepted — I was one of the lads, even though I was the youngest. But I thought, "No, I can't do this."

My friends, like Eric Clapton and Jeff Beck, were starting to make statements of their own. So of course I really wanted to get out there and play. I was twenty-two when I took the plunge. I found a sort of fluency of playing and developed my own style even though I didn't have the best technique. Then again, I had to keep developing that technique.

I knew the guitar was going to be part of my life from the first time I was able to play something and put together a sequence of chords. I enjoyed the playing more than the singing. I knew that was my life, whether I wanted it to be or not. I had no choice. That's what it was.

After my first guitar, my dad got me the next guitar — but it was still an f-hole guitar with a pickup. As I was learning, I was getting an instrument that was more appropriate for the job. But I had this Les Paul Custom. It was absolutely gorgeous. And it's the guitar I used all the way through my studio work. It was magnificent. When Led Zeppelin started to do very, very well, I was using it. We were doing these numbers where there were encores, so it was a good backup guitar in case I blew a string. I was going on Les Pauls by then, and a Telecaster had been relegated to staying at home and not going on tour anymore. So anyway I was using this Les Paul Custom. I started to feel so confident about this guitar with me on tour. One time we were going from Boston to Montreal. Whatever happened, the guitar did not return back. In those days, we were flying things on local airlines. I just couldn't believe it. That was really heartbreaking at the time because that was the major guitar from all those formative years.

Is it floating out there somewhere? Yeah, it's floating under somebody's bed. They wouldn't dare show it to too many people, in case word got out.

You know, it's marvelous, the whole thing of the guitar and what it has meant to people. In Victorian times, the equivalent was the piano. The guitar became the piano. It was everyone in the parlor, listening to Artie Moore playing the piano while he sang. That was it. It was just a fantastic movement going on, thanks to America, really, with rock 'n' roll, rockabilly, country and country blues, country western — all these different aspects of guitar playing. It's an application and some fascinating techniques have been developed on the guitar. Coming back to it, it's all still six strings. It never ceases to amaze me. And hopefully it will never cease to amaze me.

Glossary

action A term used to describe the distance between the strings and the surface of the fretboard. The "higher" the action, the more difficult it is to press down the strings. "High action" can indicate a warped guitar neck on an acoustic, though a high action is preferred for the slide guitar technique. Action can be modified on guitars by lowering the bridge or adjusting a truss rod, if the guitar has one.

alegrías A flamenco musical form that means "happiness." It is rhythmically similar to the *soleá* for consisting of 12 beats, stressing the third, sixth, eighth, tenth and twelfth beats.

archtop guitar A 6-string, steel-string acoustic or semi-acoustic guitar with an arched top and an adjustable bridge. This guitar is generally favored by blues and jazz musicians.

autoharp A musical stringed instrument that features chord bars attached to dampers, which mute and prevent selected strings from sounding apart from the intended chord. It is often played with fingers or a plectrum and is used in country western music.

bandurrias A type of Spanish mandolin that is played with a plectrum. They date back to the Middle Ages and have evolved from having three strings to the 12-strings of modern *bandurrias*.

barre chord A chord that requires a single finger pressing down three strings simultaneously within one fret space (known as a half-barre) or else six strings (called a full barre).

Bigsby tremolo A type of tremolo arm developed for use on electric guitars by Paul A. Bigsby that allows musicians to bend the pitch of notes or entire chords with their pick hand.

binding *see "purfling"*

bluegrass American roots music from Appalachia that derives from traditional Irish, English, Welsh and Scottish music. One instrument typically performs the melody and improvises on it as the other instruments perform accompaniment.

bracing The system of wooden struts that support and reinforce the soundboard and back of an acoustic guitar while also enhancing and maintaining the tonal response of the instrument. Many bracing patterns exist and vary according to their own special alchemy developed by individual makers.

bridge The device that supports the strings on a stringed instrument and transports the vibration of those strings to the "nut" on the headstock of a guitar. The bridge, along with the inserted saddle, helps to collect, raise and anchor the strings.

bulería A flamenco style of guitar playing that stems from the *soleá*. It shares the same rhythmical structure, yet it is more up-tempo and often serves as a finale. The *bulería* has many variations in melody and meter and often incorporates hand claps on the off beats and turns made by the dancer.

camber Curvature of a guitar neck, fingerboard or fret.

cavaquinho A small four-stringed instrument from the guitar family that originated in Portugal. The ukulele derives from the *cavaquinho*, which was brought to Hawaii by Portuguese immigrants in the late nineteenth century. The strings of the *cavaquinho* are commonly tuned from lower pitch to higher pitch as D-G-B-D, while ukuleles are often tuned G-C-E-A.

choros* or *chorinho A popular, spirited form of instrumental Brazilian street music marked by a fast, syncopated rhythm.

clavija de madera The Spanish description for old peghead tuning keys on flamenco guitars.

clawhammer style A rhythmic banjo picking style that consists of shaping the hand into a stiff claw-like shape and striking the strings by the motion of the hand at the wrist. The thumb does not pick on the downbeat.

cutaway guitar/double cutaway A construction where the body of the guitar is literally "cut away" either on one side of both sides of the guitar neck in order to allow a player easier access to the upper bout of the fretboard.

dampit A humidifier for classical and acoustic guitars that looks like a perforated piece of rubber tubing with a mildly damp sponge inside. It is inserted between the strings of a guitar and into the sound hole so that one end of the hose dangles inside the guitar. It lessens the chance of the wood cracking during dry winter months.

Dobro guitar (Lurrie Bell, Taj Mahal) A type of resonator guitar constructed by the Dopyera Brothers as competition to the tricone and biscuit designs patented by the National String Instrument Corporation. "Dobro" is a combination of the Dopyera Brothers and is also a pun that translates from their native Slovak to the word "good." John Dopyera originally worked for the National String Instrument Corporation, who failed to recognize his idea to lower the price of the guitar with a cheaper single-cone version. So Dopyera applied for a patent for an alternative design, which inverted the cone set into a spider web framework, providing an early source of amplification and projection for this type of guitar.

Dreadnought guitar A type of acoustic guitar made by C.F. Martin with a large body, which creates a louder tone. This guitar, developed by Martin in 1916 for the Oliver Ditson Company, had been named for the large battleship, the HMS *Dreadnought*, built in 1906. Martin began producing these guitars under their own name in 1931 with the first two models being D-1 and D-2.

falsetas A melody or riff of a few short musical phrases played by flamenco guitarists either between sung verses of flamenco or to accompany dancers.

f-holes A sound hole in the upper soundboard of a stringed musical instrument that has a lowercase letter f shape, often seen in the violin and viol families and in archtop guitars. The f-holes allow the soundboards to vibrate more freely and allow the sound inside the instrument to project outward.

flat top guitar Refers to an acoustic, steel-string guitar with a flat soundboard, as opposed to an archtop guitar.

fret Metal posts on the neck of a guitar, known collectively as the fretboard. Each fret designates a single note when the string is depressed near the fret post. Frets are configured according to a mathematical ratio that results in an equal tempered division of an octave. Often the 3rd, 5th, 7th, 12th, 15th, 17th, 19th, 21st and 24th frets are marked by inlay designs of exotic colored woods, ivory, mother of pearl or, on cheaper guitars, abalone or plastic. The 12th fret is often marked with double-dots or designs to demarcate the octave.

Hawaiian slack key guitar A fingerstyle genre that refers to playing in tunings, often requiring the strings to be loosened or slackened until the six strings form a single chord, often G Major.

Hawaiian steel guitar A basic Spanish style steel-string guitar played on the lap, using a metal bar that slides across the strings.

headstock The top portion of a guitar where the tuning keys or pegheads are located. This portion of the guitar starts at the nut up on through the tuning keys.

heel The point at which the neck and fretboard of a guitar is either bolted or glued to the body of the guitar. Classical guitars often have a "Spanish heel" — a neck and headblock carved from a single piece of wood. Most acoustic steel-string guitars except for Taylor guitars have glued or set necks. Electric guitars are constructed both ways.

inlays Decorative visual details on a guitar, which can be located on the headstock, the rosette of a guitar or the fretboard. Parlor guitars from the late seventeenth and early eighteenth centuries happen to be particularly decorative and showy, with inlay featured on the back of the guitar as well.

Kalamazoo Gibsons The Gibson Guitar manufacturing plant was originally based in Kalamazoo, Michigan, from the late 1890s, when Orville Gibson first made mandolins, to 1984, when the company was sold to new owners and moved to Nashville. Gibsons made during the Kalamazoo era are considered to be collector's items.

kalimba An African thumb piano consisting of pitched tines set against a resonant chamber, such as a carved gourd or piece of wood.

malagueña A traditional style of Andalusian flamenco music influenced by Moorish music from the region of Málaga, Spain.

marker dots *see "inlay"*

National guitar *see "resonator guitar"*

neck The part of the guitar that serves as the base for fretboard and headstock and is attached to the body of the guitar.

neck joint *see "heel"*

nut A slim ivory, steel, brass or plastic bar inserted at the point where the headstock meets the fretboard. It often features grooves, which guide the strings into a consistent position over the fretboard.

pickguard Often a plastic or laminated piece of material that is placed under the strings on the body of a guitar in order to protect its finished from being scratched by a guitar pick.

pickups A transducer that converts vibrations from the guitar strings to an electric signal that is amplified. There are many different makes and brands of pickups, and their placement and configuration on the guitar beneath the strings is both an art and a science. Pickups are generally made of a magnet with a core material such as alnico, wrapped with a coil of enameled copper wire, which react together with magnetized guitar strings to create a current that conveys the sound through the guitar cable into the amp.

piezo pickup system A type of crystal rather than magnetic pickup used on semi-acoustics and acoustic guitars that is fitted at the bridge. They tend not to pick up on any other magnetic fields and are often inlaid into the bridge or affixed onto the top of the soundboard with putty.

purfling The narrow binding inlaid into the edges of the top and bottom of a guitar.

rasqueado A rapid-fire, rhythmically precise strumming technique used in flamenco guitar playing.

resonator guitar A guitar designed to be louder than conventional acoustic guitars by having the sound produced by one or more spun metal cones known as resonators, which replace the traditional wooden soundboard. Blues musicians often favored resonator guitars for being at least three to five times louder than a conventional wooden acoustic guitar. There are three main resonator styles — the "tricone" with three metal cones in the first National resonator guitars; the single cone "biscuit" design of other National guitars that features a wooden biscuit at the cone apex to support the bridge; and the single inverted "spider" resonator cone of the Dobro guitar. The body of a resonator guitar is often either of wood or metal.

rosette The decorative inlaid design circling the sound hole of any guitar.

saddle The raised part of the bridge, often made of plastic or bone on an acoustic guitar and of metal for an electric guitar. It serves as an endpoint to allow the strings to vibrate freely and transfer the vibrations through the bridge into the soundboard and body of the guitar.

scordatura Refers to alternate tunings, apart from the standard E-A-D-G-B-E guitar tuning.

semi-hollow body guitar A type of electric guitar with a hollow or chambered sound box body and one or more electric pickups. It is not an electric acoustic guitar, which is an acoustic guitar with added pickups. The term generally refers to f-hole archtop guitars.

skiffle music A term that originated in the U.S. during the first half of the twentieth century to describe music with a blues, jazz, folk, roots and country influence. The instruments often include washboard, jug, cigar-box fiddle and musical saw, and perhaps a banjo. There was a skiffle revival in the U.K. during the 1950s as part of the post-war British jazz scene.

slide guitar A method of playing the guitar that refers to sliding a glass bottleneck or a metal socket over the strings. This method is traditionally used in blues music.

soleá A style of flamenco music with a rhythm similar to the *alegrías* with its 12-count rhythm. It evolved from the *jaleo* Spanish gypsy dance in the late 18th century. It tends to have a sorrowful tone.

solfège A method of sight-singing, using the syllables *do-re-mi-fa-so-la-ti* to represent notes of the octave. There are two methods of solfège, one called "fixed do," where each syllable corresponds to the name of a note and "moveable do," where each syllable corresponds to a scale degree.

solid-body guitar A guitar build without a sound box but from a solid piece of wood instead, relying on an electronic pickup system to convey the string vibrations.

soundboard The top piece of wood on a guitar, which usually features a sound hole and interior bracing.

sound hole An opening in the sound board of a guitar. They help acoustic guitars project their sound and allow the sound board to vibrate more freely and transmit the sound outside the guitar.

Spanish heel *see "heel"*

string gauge Strings come in varying diameters and tension. Heavier strings with a thicker diameter require more tension for the same pitch. For classical guitar, the bass strings are wound with nickel-plated wire while the treble strings are made of nylon. String diameters are measured by the thousandth of an inch.

trapeze tailpiece A style of a bridge often used on archtop guitars, it was invented to help the guitar's top support the tension sustained by steel-strings.

tremolo bar or arm A bar device on a guitar that is used to add vibrato or a quavery tone to the sound by altering the tension of the strings at the bridge or tailpiece of the guitar. The tremolo or whammy bar, as it is also called, allows a player to quickly and temporarily vary this string tension to alter the pitch and create a bended note or bended chord.

tuning keys The pegheads and winding machinery that adjust the tension of the strings at the headstock of the guitar and create the pitch of sound that the strings produce.

truss rod A metal rod that is imbedded inside the neck of a guitar that can be adjusted in tension to correct changes in the neck's curvatures caused by changes in string tension or changes in the humidity or aging of the wood. Classical guitars do not often feature truss rods because nylon strings exert less tension, creating fewer structural issues.

whammy bar *see "tremolo bar"*

woodshed A jazz term that means to practice one's instrument. It originated as a drumming term and refers to the fact that drumsticks will start to flake off small bits of wood after long hours of practice.

Guitar Makes/Models Mentioned in This Book

This list is intended to be a simple rundown of the types of guitars mentioned in this book and which artist played them.

Antigua Casa Nuñez guitars (Morel)
Arbor guitar (Malakian)
Aria guitars (McKee)
Astro Tone guitar (Lukather)
B.C. Rich Gunslinger (Guns)
Benedetto guitars (Vignola)
Canora guitar (Lifeson)
Carvin guitars (Malakian)
Conde Hermanos flamenco guitar (Juan Martin)
Danelectro guitars (Koster)
David Bailey guitar (Scott Tennant)
D'Angelico guitars (Benson, Vignola)
Decca guitars Vintage guitars manufactured during the '60s.
Di Giorgio guitars (Barbosa-Lima, Zanon)
Echosonic amplifier by Ray Butts (Moore)

Emenee guitar (Verdery)

Epiphone guitars (Landreth, Alvin, Lucas)

Juan Estruch guitar (Koster)

Favilla (Ranaldo)

'57 Fender Esquire (Lang)

Fender Jazzmaster a.k.a "Jazzblaster" (Ranaldo)

Fender Mustang (Tronzo, Alvin)

Fender Stratocaster (Dale, Duncan, Vaughan, Alvin, Lucas, Guest, Lang)

Fender Telecaster (Dale)

Fender Telecaster Deluxe guitars (Ranaldo)

Fleta guitars (Segovia)

Frankenstrat (Reid)

Paul Galbraith guitar (Zanon)

Galiano guitars (Block)

Giannini guitars (Bruné, The Assad Brothers)

Gibson 120T (Thompson)

Gibson Country Western model (Hammond)

Gibson Dixie Hummingbird (Reid)

Double-necked Gibson EDS-1275 (Lifeson)

Gibson ES-140 (Metheny)

Gibson ES-175 (Metheny)

Gibson ES-295 (Moore)

Gibson ES-335 (Bell, Anderson)

Gibson J-45 acoustic (Hiland)

Gibson J-55 acoustic (Lifeson)

Gibson J-100 "The Sailor's Model" (Hammond)

Gibson J-160E (Verdery)

Gibson J-200 (Lee)

Gibson L-4C (Howe)

Gibson L-5 archtop guitar (Moore)

Gibson LG-1 (Guest)

Gibson SG (Frampton)

Gibson Super 400 (Lee)

Roberto Gomez guitar (Zanon)

Goya guitar (Leisner)

Gretsch guitars

Hagström guitar (Satriani, Ranaldo)

Harmony Sovereign (McKean)

Hauser guitar (Segovia, mentioned by Ben Verdery)

Hilo guitars (Paul Reed Smith)

Höfner President archtop (Lee, Tronzo, Taylor)

Hoyer 3063 guitar (Stephan)

Thomas Humphrey Millennium model guitar (Assad Brothers)

Ibanez Pat Metheny guitar (Metheny)

Ibanez Jem guitar (Vai)

Jackson guitar (Friedman)

Kay guitars (Landreth, Marshall, Lukather, Morello)

Kent classic guitar (Lifeson)

Les Paul Gibson Standard (Martino)

Les Paul SG (Frampton)

Les Paul Special (Margolin)

Maccaferri guitars (Ranaldo)

Martin 00-21 (McGuinn)

Martin 5-18 (Martin IV)

Martin D-18 (Ranaldo)

Martin D-28 (Guest)

Martin D-28E with DeArmond pickups (Lee)

Martin D-35 (Anderson)

Martin D-45 (Hammond)

Maton guitars (Emmanuel)

Music Man guitar (McKean)

National Reso-Phonic guitars (Mahal, Lucas)

Old Kraftsman guitar (Vaughan)

Ovation guitar (McKee, Santiago)

Paul Reed Smith guitars (Santana, Smith)

Pikasso guitar (Metheny)

Ramírez guitars (Koster)

Manuel Reyes guitar (Peña, Dearman)

Rickenbacker guitars (Smith, Lanois)

Miguel Rodriguez guitar (Pena, Kanengiser)

Rythmline (Friedman)

Schecter pickups

Sears Silvertone Jupiter 1423L (Duncan)

Seiwa Powersonic (Stephan)

Stella guitars (Ranaldo)
Takamine (McKee)
Taylor Guitars (Taylor)
Teisco del Rey guitar (Vai)
Telegib (Duncan)
Torres guitars
Travis Bean (Ranaldo)
Vega 12-string guitar (McGuinn)
Univox Les Paul (Vai, Lukather)
Univox Mosrite
Washburn Nuno Bettencourt N4 (Guns, Daron Malakian)

Acknowledgments

I have to express the depths of my gratitude to everyone involved in this book, starting with the artists who were so enthusiastic and generous with their time. Profound thanks goes to my literary agent Susan Schulman for her unwavering dedication. Also to Sonia Michelson, the wisest guitar teacher and best friend anyone could ask for; to the Practical Theatre/703 Howard Street & Rockme gang; to Jimmy Page for being one of the first guitarists to believe in this book; to Carlos Santana, Andy Summers, Lee Ranaldo, Graham Parker, John & Marla Hammond; to Gary Lucas and Caroline Sinclair and Gods & Monsters; John Gabrysiak; Joan Hudson and Sue Frankland-Haile.

I am deeply indebted to my editor Jen Hale for recognizing the joy and spirit of this book, and I enjoyed every minute of writing it all the more for sharing a kindred sense of humor. My appreciation goes to the superb work of editor Jennifer Knoch and the entire ECW crew. Heartfelt acknowledgements go to Terrence & Taidgh for their patience and good humor and enduring endless take-out food.

I am also grateful for the friendship and guidance from Richard G. Stern, Maurice J. Summerfield, Peter Van Wagner, Sheri Holman, Tim Brookes, Sherri Phillips, Clarice Assad, Michael Newman & Laura Oltman, Lisa & Alex Hoffman. I acknowledge the kind assistance of Paki Newell, Gina Mendello,

Lisa-Marie Mazzucco, Robbie Mendel, Joan Grossman, Tom McCourt, Harriet Sternberg, Marcel Pariseau, Jean Sievers, Mick Brigden, Cailin McCarthy, David Sholemson, Jennifer Sousa, Amanda Dawes, Helen Martin, Gail Pollock, Sung-Hee Park, Lana Dale, Paul Babin, Nancy Sefton, Camilla McGuinn, Brooke Zoslocki, Michael Jensen, Erin Podbereski, Russ D'Angelo, Brad Hunt, Megan Barra, Gus Canazio, Michele Garzanti, Rick Bates, Mick Houghton, Tim Bernett, Ze Beekeeper, Meghan Symsyk, Kevin Calabro, Greg Classen, Ruta Sepetys, Chalise Zolezzi, Jonathan Forstot, Maricela Juarez, Evan Skopp, Stephanie Gonzalez, Joel Hoffner, Lisa Jenkins, Kathi Whitley, Corey Moore, Robin Vaughan, Adam Fells, Maria Russell, Jason Rothberg, Dan & Maryon Bellack. To my dance sisters at Solstice Studios for their encouraging words and shared love for twirling as Gumby Ghawazis year round, enduring lobster red–faced sweating summer and causing the coat rack to crash down from the weight of winter garb. In closing, I must mention my college roommate, Lisa Eret, in memory, for always believing that I would include her someday in a future book acknowledgment. Last but not least, I give thanks to my mother and to my father.

Julia Crowe is a guitarist and columnist for both *Classical Guitar* (U.K.) and *Gendai Guitar* (Japan). She has written numerous cover stories and features for several guitar magazines internationally. Her music has been featured on National Public Radio and she has written music for the feature film documentary *Drop City*, which saw its "sneak preview" this year at the Denver Museum of Contemporary Art. She lives in New York, New York.

At ECW Press, we want you to enjoy this book in whatever format you like, whenever you like. Leave your print book at home and take the eBook to go! Purchase the print edition and receive the eBook free. Just send an email to ebook@ecwpress.com and include:

Get the eBook free!*
*proof of purchase required

- the book title
- the name of the store where you purchased it
- your receipt number
- your preference of file type: PDF or ePub?

A real person will respond to your email with your eBook attached. And thanks for supporting an independently owned publisher with your purchase!